The North American Porcupine

The North American Porcupine

Uldis Roze

Smithsonian Institution Press   *Washington, D.C.   London*

Designer: Janice Wheeler
Editor: Lorraine Atherton
Production Editor: Leigh Alvarado Benson
Artwork: John Winsch
Cover photo: Uldis Roze

Library of Congress Cataloging-in-Publication Data
Roze, Uldis, 1938–
  The North American porcupine.
  Bibliography: p.
  Includes index.
  1. North American porcupine. I. Title.
QL737.R652R69 1989   599.32'34   89-600055
ISBN 0-87474-786-4 (alk. paper)
British Library Cataloging-in-Publication Data available

Manufactured in the United States of America

10 9 8 7 6 5 4 3 2 1
98 97 96 95 94 93 92 91 90 89

∞ The paper used in this publication meets the minimum requirements of the
American National Standard for Permanence of Paper for Printed Library Materials
Z39.48-1984.

For Steph

Contents

12
Porcupines of the World 205

Preface

A study of the porcupine requires, above everything, time—not only time to follow a population through an annual cycle of energy and mineral acquisition, reproduction, and winter denning but also much longer blocks of time to work out life-history strategies in these long-lived animals: reproductive success, territorial expansion or contraction, dispersal. Those kinds of data are needed to understand social structure and ecological strategies. I have had the luxury of such time, in the form of two sabbatical leaves from Queens College and a liberal teaching schedule that allowed weekly visits to the woods. The study here described began during my sabbatical of 1978–79; the writing of this book, during my sabbatical of 1985–86.

A porcupine study also requires a reliable access to porcupines. My wife and I laid the groundwork for that in 1970, with our purchase of 70 acres of forested Catskills mountainside. We built our own cabin, dug a well, cut firewood. Above us stretched miles of unbroken forest, without human dwellings and with vistas from the mountaintops such as the Indians must have seen. After the hunting season, winter snows showed no human tracks other than my own. But there were other inhabitants in the woods. A black bear behind the house turned over 150-pound rocks searching for grubs. A ruby-throated hummingbird came to feed on trumpet creeper. And one October morning, I discovered a small porcupine in the leafless crown of an apple tree.

My porcupine encounters were rare events in the early years, because I was not seeking out porcupines; the animals, at times, were seeking out me. From 1978, I learned how to find porcupines on my own, by locating them in dens in the winter, at salt sources in the spring, and in apple orchards in the summer. With those techniques alone, I could encounter upwards of 7 animals a day. However, I was not yet marking individual animals. A grant from Queens College in 1981 and subsequent grants from

PSC–City University of New York allowed me to radiocollar animals beginning in 1981. I marked others with eartags and tattoos. I now discovered my study population was well in excess of 7 animals; in 1988 I encountered 39 different animals. An artificial salthouse, as described in Chapter 5, eased my access to animals. Previously, I had sought porcupines at three barns, four assorted outbuildings, and our own cabin on occasion. After building the salthouse, I could conveniently visit a single location.

For capture, I discovered the efficiency of rubberized gloves and a 12-quart plastic ice chest with closable top. I baited my live traps with Red Delicious apples and used aluminum flashing to guide animals into tree traps. My commercial radiocollars were mounted on soft nylon braid and hung around the necks of the animals. From Wendell Dodge, I learned to use ketamine for safe field anesthesia. From Aelita Pinter came the oxytocin technique for establishing lactation status. From Hans Kruuk I borrowed the technique of permanent identification by groin tattoo.

In addition, many people have helped with every aspect of the study, from discussion and ideas to assistance in the field or laboratory: Sheldon Aaronson, David Alsop, Sydney Anderson, Pat Bridges, Helen Cairns, Robert Calhoon, Peter Chabora, Tom Chen, Michael Crooks, Edward Dolensek, Jean Dorst, Robert C. Dowler, Durland Fish, Wayne Graff, Andrew Greller, Max Hecht, Lyndon Hill, Elizabeth Horner, Walter Huggans, Frank A. Iwen, Stuart Landry, Rene Lavocat, Richard Lindroth, David C. Locke, Leslie Marcus, George Mason, Cathy McConnell, Daniel McKinley, Martha Mixon, Milton Nathanson, Dick Pardi, Michael Seidel, Ward B. Stone, George Szilagyi, Donald J. Tipper, Nick Vatakis, and Pam and Judd Weisberg. Wendell Dodge, Roger Powell, and Louise Emmons critically reviewed drafts of chapters 9, 2 and 7, and 10 and 12, respectively. My brother Maris read the entire manuscript, as did two professional mammalogists. John Winsch supplied the drawings and figures. Finally, I thank my wife, Stephanie, for the unfailing support and stimulating atmosphere that made this study possible.

The book that follows has been a pleasure to write. I hope the reader will find it an equal pleasure to read. But many more books on the porcupine remain to be written, because again and again our understanding of these animals, like our understanding of much of the world we live in, ends in a mystery.

The Uses of the Porcupine

It is the summer of 1971, and I am about to meet my first porcupines. My wife and I are sleeping in the cabin we have built on the edge of the woods stretching up a Catskills mountainside. Sometime after midnight, an insistent sound punches through my sleep. I rise up on one elbow and listen. The sound comes again—a deep, resonant rasping from the far corner of the cabin.

I put on my glasses, pick up a flashlight, and go out in the night. The cone of my light reveals two large animals reaching over the foundation and leaning against the wall of the cabin. My rational mind tells me they are porcupines, but they look like creatures out of a dream. They stare back at me with the ragged outlines of the unbelievable, animals more surreal than wild.

Then the rage of the property owner is upon me. It's our new house they are chewing! I pick up a stick, raise it high, and bring it down on the nearest animal. But my aggressiveness leaves me as my glasses fall off in the dark, and I suddenly realize I am both naked and blind. The porcupines escape. Only a scatter of quills on the ground and a patch of damaged plywood on the cabin next morning tell me I was not dreaming.

The porcupines returned, and I am ashamed to say I clubbed several before working out a simple solution: stapling a two-foot belt of chicken wire all around the base of the cabin. The porcupines had been interested only in the plywood walls. With the bait covered, they stopped coming.

My attitudes of the seventies, so embarrassing to me at present, were probably typical among people in the region. Even neighbors who do not believe in hunting deer have told me they kill porcupines because the animals damage trucks, outbuildings, and property in general. In other words, the animals are pests.

Indian-Porcupine Relationships

The porcupine has not always been considered a pest. To the Indian tribes that inhabited North America before the European settlement, the porcupine was a precious resource, treated with reverence by some. Among the woodland tribes, the porcupine held an important place in food-gathering and the economy. That was especially true of the Micmacs of New Brunswick and Nova Scotia and the Montagnais of eastern Quebec, who were collectively known as the Porcupine Indians (Speck and Dexter 1951). These northern woodland Indians subsisted largely on fish, mollusks, and wild plants in the summer and on big game such as moose and woodland caribou in the winter. The big game was hunted by driving the animals in deep snow (Speck and Dexter 1951, Thwaites 1907). Though they gathered wild roots, fruits, and nuts as available, the Indians did not have an agricultural economy as did the Hurons and the Iroquois to the south. The vulnerable period in their hunting-fishing-gathering economy was early winter, when ice restricted fishing but adequate snow cover had not yet accumulated for driving moose and caribou. Then the porcupine became a critical link in the Indians' survival. Along with the beaver, it remained the only animal that could be hunted with relative efficiency.

A fortunate historic accident has left a well-drawn picture of the original lifestyles of the woodland Indians. Almost from the beginnings of the French settlement in present-day Canada, the settlers were accompanied by Jesuit missionaries. Beginning in 1610, these articulate and highly educated men sailed from France to live among the Indians. Although primarily concerned with their Christianizing mission, they recorded in rich detail the techniques of hunting and gathering, social customs, religious beliefs, warfare, commercial relationships, crafts, and much else. Here Father LeJeune, writing in 1633 from Quebec, describes winter hunting of the porcupine:

The porcupine is taken in a trap, or by coursing. The dog having discovered it [, the porcupine] is sure to be killed if it is not very near its abode, which it makes under large rocks; having reached this, it is in a place of safety, for neither men nor dogs can crawl into it. It cannot run upon the snow, and is therefore very soon put to death. . . .

They singe them as we do pigs in France, and after they are scraped, they are boiled or roasted, and are quite edible, although rather tough, especially the old ones, but the young ones are tender and delicate. But in taste they are not equal to either our wild boar or our common pig. [Thwaites 1907]

Every few years the game failed, the Indians starved, and the Jesuits recorded the painful extremities to which they were pushed: the Indians would eat their valuable dogs, their dressed elkskins, and finally their shoes. The weak (usually the children) would begin to die. At such times of famine, the porcupine acquired an almost supernatural significance. Again, Father LeJeune recounts an experience. He and his party of Indians had entered the vast forests of Quebec in November 1633 and had been forced to move camp repeatedly because the thin snow made big-game hunting impossible. The party was starving.

On the 24th of December, the evening before the birth of our Savior, we broke up [camp] for the seventh time. We departed without eating, and journeyed for a long, long time, then worked at house-building; and for our supper Our Lord gave us a Porcupine as large as a suckling pig, and a hare. It was not much for 18 or 20 people, it is true, but the holy Virgin and her glorious Spouse, saint Joseph, were not so well-treated on the same day in the stable at Bethlehem.

Because on many occasions the porcupine saved the Indians' lives, they believed that the animal offered itself to the hunter and must be treated with gratitude and respect. The bones of beavers (whose ecological relationship with the Indians was similar) and porcupines could not be given to the dogs but had to be burned or thrown into the river. Otherwise the animals would make themselves hard to capture in the future. A residue of that belief is retained in the woodlands of Quebec, northern Michigan, and the Maritimes today. Many residents believe that unprovoked killing of a porcupine is a crime, because a porcupine is almost the only animal an unarmed man lost in the woods can capture for food.

Beyond its life-sustaining function, the porcupine played a second important role in the lives of the North American Indians. Its quills, both in the loose state or as elaborate quillwork, came closest to serving as a medium of exchange. Such currency was supplanted during the settlement period by wampum, a European introduction. Porcupine quillwork is an exacting, time-consuming craft. The quills were collected, sorted according to size, dyed with vegetable dyes, and then woven into a ground of deerskin or birch bark. They were held in place by split spruce root or sinew binding, or by forcing them through tiny holes punched in the ground material with a bone awl. The finished article presented a flat, durable, close-grained surface that breathed with subtle natural color (Orchard 1971, Odle 1971). The dyes used for porcupine quills came from a wide range of native trees and wildflowers. Ash and earths were often added as mordants.

Table 1 lists the sources exploited by the Ojibwa of the Great Lakes region. The dyeing process typically required long periods of boiling of quills in the plant extracts. If the color obtained was too pale, the treatment was repeated.

Quillwork found its way into belts, leggings, blouses, boxes and trunks, place mats, bracelets, necklaces, moccasins, purses, medicine bags, and tobacco bags. Though most of the articles were small, the amount of work required was staggering. The finest quillwork was constructed of small, closely spaced quills that modulated complex patterns in the natural pigments of the plant world. Such work often has an unpredictability that is more startling for being set in a convoluted pattern. Perhaps the worker ran out of green-dyed quills and made a small substitution of yellow, or per-

Delaware Indian quillwork: baby carrier ornament (Museum of the American Indian, Heye Foundation).

Nehane Indian quillwork: belt (Museum of the American Indian, Heye Foundation).

haps, like Navaho weavers, the quillworker broke the patterns as a philo-sophical statement. Such work then takes on the qualities of music.

References to porcupine quillwork often find their way into Indian myths and fairy tales. Thus, a Cheyenne myth explains the origin of the Big Dip-per as follows: a beautiful young girl, growing up as an only child, wanted brothers. She fashioned seven buckskin outfits with splendid quillwork and presented them to seven brothers who lived alone in distant woods. De-lighted with the gift, they accepted her as a sister. But a monstrous buffalo heard about the girl, grew jealous, and set out to capture her for himself. Too weak to resist, the girl and her seven brothers used magic to escape into the sky, where they shine in their quillwork outfits as the eight stars of the Big Dipper, the sister being the brightest (Erdoes and Ortiz 1984).

Porcupine quillwork extended well into areas where the porcupine may have been absent or marginal. Tribes such as the Sioux of the Dakotas, Winnebago of Nebraska, Sauk of Iowa, and Potawatomi of Kansas all in-habited territories where the woodland habitat needed by porcupines was scarce or absent. Yet all contained active centers of porcupine quillwork. This required trade with tribes that coexisted with the porcupine: the Mic-mac and Huron in the Northeast, the Ojibwa and Menominee in the Mid-west, the Shoshoni and Nez Percé in the West (Orchard 1971). Thus the porcupine, in centuries before the European settlement, served a cohesive function on the North American continent. Its quills formed the first cur-rency, valuable because it was beautiful and hard to make.

Indians found the porcupine useful in smaller ways as well. One ex-ample is the porcupine combs that the Crow Indians manufactured from the underside of the tail, which is covered not by quills but by firmly anchored, stout bristles used to climb trees. George P. Belden, in an 1872 account, describes the combs: "They are very simple, and consist of a Hedgehog's (i.e., porcupine's) tail, the bristles serving as teeth. When a Hog is killed, the tail is skinned off the bone, and a wooden handle is inserted. When dry, it is ready to use, and is by no means a bad substitute for the bone or horn combs we use. A Hedgehog comb is an indispensable article to every In-dian girl, as it enables her to keep her long black hair in order." Another porcupine application involved the Indian craft of maple sugaring. The Indians, who lacked metal spiles for drawing off the maple sap, used hollowed-out porcupine quills instead (Denys 1908, Speck and Dexter

1951). Clearly, in ways both large and small, the porcupine was a resource to the Indians and therefore an animal to be respected.

Contemporary Porcupine-Human Interactions

With the disappearance of the cultures and economies of the Indians, the status of the porcupine fell. In no state in the U.S. today is the animal protected from hunting at any time. Until recently, many states offered bounties for porcupines killed, and some undertook massive poisoning programs. The justification for eradication campaigns has been economic. There are two main areas of conflict. The first involves the extensive modern use of high-sodium materials, especially plywood in construction and salt for de-icing roads.

Unlike the low-sodium diets available for humans, no low-sodium plywood is available for porcupine-inhabited areas, though such a plywood would be easy to manufacture. Road salt is used on an increasing scale to control winter ice. The salt accumulates on the underbodies of cars and trucks, including tires, hoses, and electrical wiring. When porcupines find these salt morsels in the spring, they can disable a vehicle after a night's chewing.

The porcupine's location of sodium sources is unerring. A neighbor, who runs a camp for young people, observed with some puzzlement that porcupines attacked the wooden outer walls of boys' but not girls' dormitories. I asked him, "Which sex is most likely to urinate against the wall of the dormitory at night?"

The second major human-porcupine conflict involves the timber industry. Porcupines feed on the bark of trees in the winter. Most of their feeding takes place in the crown of the tree, where they may girdle individual branches or the leader of the tree but not the tree itself. The tree that survives many years of porcupine attacks takes on an eerie, witchlike quality. The trunk is shortened, and branches twist in baroque unpredictability. Though often of short stature, the trees may be quite old, like some of the pollarded trees of the European countryside. Such "witch trees" are found in local clusters in the vicinity of porcupine dens and are best seen during their leafless state in winter. From the porcupine's perspective, a grove of witch trees represents good forest management. The short trees are easy to

Porcupine in a linden tree shaped by past feeding.

climb, the thick sprouting of young branches offers food that is easily harvested, and the low, thick crowns provide some shelter from winter wind.

Forest well managed from the porcupine's point of view may not be well managed from the lumberman's point of view. Low trees with twisted crowns produce reduced lumber yields, especially of the long, knot-free timber that lumbermen prefer. For that reason, the porcupine is persecuted wherever it occurs, even when it feeds on trees such as beech and hemlock, which have minimal commercial importance. In many New England states, bounties were formerly offered. Vermont paid out $90,000 in 1952 alone, the last year it had a bounty law. That represents many animals killed at 50 cents per snout. Most bounty laws were repealed during the twenties, though New Hampshire, the last state with a bounty law, ended the practice only in 1979 (Dodge 1982). The bounty system suffered from the energies of private enterprise. William A. Reeks (1942) of New Brunswick mentions problems such as animals brought in from outside the prescribed bounty area and entrepreneurs who have been able to manufacture porcupine snouts out of forepaws and thus multiply each bounty several fold. For three winters beginning in 1957–58, the state of Vermont embarked on a porcupine poisoning program that led to the deaths of 10,800 animals (including 1700 that were shot). The poison used was a sodium arsenite gel injected into apples. In three years, 32,000 poisoned apples were placed in porcupine dens (Faulkner and Dodge 1962). Many states, including California, Idaho, Oregon, Montana, Michigan, Wisconsin, New York, and Vermont, are experimenting with biological control, by the introduction of fisher into areas from which the animal had been previously trapped out (Dodge 1982, Conniff 1986). As described more fully in the following chapter, the fisher appears to be exerting significant control in Michigan. In most states the experiment is proceeding blindly, with no monitoring of the populations involved.

Can these economic conflicts be lessened? Let's consider the conflict over sodium use. Plywood becomes porcupine-proof simply by substituting potassium for sodium as the cation in the resin. The national market for exterior plywood is so large that the porcupine-vulnerable segment may not justify a change for the entire industry. But for a smaller manufacturer, such a product may represent an economic opportunity.

With respect to road salt, the economic arguments are less clear-cut, partly because of the nature of the accounting system used. Road salt is applied by highway departments to clear winter ice. Such an agency has a budget for snow and ice removal and is likely to ask a single question: "What chemical will melt ice at lowest cost?" The answer is rock salt—sodium chloride. But the use of rock salt entails hidden costs. Apart from its porcupine connection, rock salt deteriorates concrete, corrodes underground power lines and steel supports, rusts out car bodies, harms street trees, and pollutes water supplies. Some of those costs came due in the summer of 1988, when New York City had to close the Williamsburg Bridge across East River because of rusted-out steel supports. Engineers blamed rock salt. None of those costs are normally factored into snow-removal budgets. In 1986, rock salt delivered in bulk in New York cost $34 a ton. But if indirect costs are factored in, estimates place the total cost at upwards of $1000 a ton. At that price, alternate de-icing techniques become competitive. None of them—sand, urea, calcium or calcium-magnesium chloride—have the porcupine involvements that sodium chloride does.

Similar economic arguments have ended the state bounty systems and poisoning programs to control timber damage by porcupines. On the one hand, biological control by the introduction of fisher appears to be cheap and effective. On the other hand, heavy damage by porcupines is generally restricted to the vicinity of dens. In mountainous regions dens are located in steep and inaccessible terrain, where lumbering is uneconomical. It has therefore become obvious to the agencies concerned that the damage caused by porcupines is too small to justify the costs of active control.

Where Indians saw in the porcupine a valuable resource, twentieth-century Americans have treated the animal as a pest that destroys property and damages timber, even though part of that economic damage has been self-inflicted. The two attitudes represent opposite sides of a coin; both are based on the economic benefit or cost of the animal.

Study of the Porcupine

A third kind of relationship is possible with porcupines and with the natural world in which they live, one that I will champion in this book: to study them. Ours is a society that encourages inquiry, in part because it can lead to tangible returns. The woods, rivers, mountains, and prairies that surround our cities remain filled with astonishing life stories: insect pupae that spin around inside their cocoons to foil would-be wasp parasitoids; Jack-in-the-pulpit flowers that change sex depending on success during the previous year and that lure fungus gnats to their deaths in female flowers but leave an escape door in males; carrion beetles that carry a platoon of abdominal mites to win the battle against blowfly larvae invading the same carcass. Because the woods are filled with stories, many still undiscovered, careful observation of almost any organism is likely to yield surprise and delight.

The Catskills land we bought in 1970 was part of an abandoned farm. An aerial photo of the area, taken by the U.S. Department of Agriculture in 1959, clearly shows surrounding roads, trails, farmhouses, even individual trees in orchards. Adjacent to Beech Ridge Road lie the remaining fields and pastures of the Decker farm, with the great woods reclaiming the rest. In the pasture, hay-cutting is in progress; a border of white encircles the darker, uncut grass of the center. The camera caught Winnie Decker in one of the last farm chores of his life. He died the following year, and the farm passed into nonfarming hands. But these hillside acres, which supported the Decker family for almost 50 years and the Angle family for 100 years before that, remain productive. The crop they are yielding today, and can continue to yield for centuries to come, is a crop of unfolding knowledge, a crop as nourishing to the human spirit as fresh bread is to the body.

Whether the Indians systematically studied the porcupine we do not know, because they left no written records. Their cultures have been largely swept away, and their knowledge with them. That knowledge must have been considerable, because it was required for survival. Early European travelers and missionaries did leave a written record. Their observations, though sometimes perceptive, tend to be anecdotal; they are seldom presented in quantitative terms, and there are no studies over the long term. The one notable exception is a 1727 study of the North American porcupine, the first to examine the animal with scientific rigor. The author, Michel Sarrazin, was physician to the King at Quebec, correspondent of the Royal Academy of Sciences at Paris, and contemporary of Isaac Newton and DeReaumur (who communicated the article to the academy) (DeReaumur 1727).

Dr. Sarrazin's study of the porcupine set a high standard. He observed that the Canada porcupine belongs to the group of animals that gnaws (the rodents) and that it differs in important ways from the African porcupine. It feeds on the bark of living trees, never dead ones, and prefers above all certain pines and the white cedar. The animal also feeds by grazing. Sarrazin dissected the animal and described its internal anatomy in detail. He described its ability to erect its quills, whose tips he observed under a new instrument, the microscope. He discussed the "great question" of whether the porcupine can throw its quills, and disproved the idea. He explained why porcupine quills travel in only one direction in the body. He examined the popular belief that porcupines mate in the trees with the female suspended head-down from a branch and the male hanging right-side-up from another branch. He dismissed the theory but added modestly that he could not describe the true process in detail. He stated that the animal lives for 12 to 15 years. He correctly observed that porcupines have a gestation period of seven months and bear a single young.

Sarrazin's astonishing paper, inventive in its experimental approach and filled with details of taxonomy, anatomy, and natural history, was correct on every major point it considered. Some of the findings were not confirmed until more than 200 years later. It is therefore unfortunate that Sarrazin's work is seldom remembered today in connection with the porcupine. He is, however, widely commemorated in another context. Named after him are the Sarraceniaceae, the family of carnivorous pitcher plants of sphagnum bogs, whose North American range stretches from Quebec south to Florida and west to the Pacific coast (Gariepy 1961, Rousseau 1957).

Many scientists and naturalists have followed in Sarrazin's footsteps as students of the porcupine. An outstanding figure was Walter Penn Taylor, whose studies were published more than 200 years later, in 1935. His 177-page treatise carries the no-compromise title "Ecology and life history of the porcupine (*Erethizon epixanthum*) as related to the forests of Arizona and the southwestern United States" (Taylor 1935). But from the start, Taylor served notice that he intended to pay attention to more than the peeled bark of trees: "In this study, approached from the standpoint of ecology, an attempt was made to record all facts of possible significance, whether or not they appeared to have definite economic bearing." Taylor's concern was not the discovery of ways to control the porcupine. It was rather "an attempt to determine the actual role of a woods-inhabiting rodent in the ecology of the forest." All aspects of the animal's life came under scrutiny: feeding preferences, annual migrations, navigational abilities, mating behavior, techniques of capture in the field (Taylor recommended climbing after the animal up its tree and tickling its nose with a pine branch to drive it back toward the pursuer). His account remains valuable not only because it is thorough but also because it retains the freshness of the woods and mountains he traveled for so many years.

Large-scale studies of the porcupine that have followed Taylor's include the work of Albert Shadle (reproductive physiology; 1951, 1948), James D. Curtis (porcupine-timber relationships; 1944, 1941), Robert Brander (environmental physiology; 1973, also Clarke and Brander 1973), and Wendell Dodge (ecology and reproduction; 1982, 1967). Each has added fresh insight and shed a bright light on the subject. This book is an attempt to follow in that tradition.

Aims of the Present Study

If naturalists have been studying the porcupine for more than 250 years, the question might be raised whether there is anything left to discover. Indeed there is. The questions a naturalist would like to ask can often not be answered at the time because the technical or conceptual infrastructure is lacking. In natural history, the realm of the possible is continually expanding. Just as the scanning and transmission electron microscopes have revolutionized the study of the cell, so new instruments and new techniques have made a new set of questions possible in natural history.

One of those powerful techniques is radiotelemetry. A small radio transmitter is attached to an animal that is then released in the wild. With a directional antenna and tunable receiver, researchers can locate the animal wherever it wanders. They can then answer questions about food sources, den sites, mating interactions, territoriality, activity budgets, and a mass of other field biology subjects. The study described here represents the longest continuous radiotelemetry study of porcupines reported in the scientific literature. At the time of this writing, the telemetry study has been running for eight years; one old female is entering her seventh year of monitoring.

Three-month-old female with radiocollar.

Such long periods of observation require faith that something new will be discovered every year, that lives will not slip into predictable ruts. That faith has indeed been justified.

Two males, each followed for five years and showing different degrees of success and failure, suddenly emigrated. By doing so, they forced a revision of my understanding of social structure. Another male was found drowned in a river. An autopsy revealed the cause of death. The flesh around the muzzle and lower jaw was reddened from the impact of a fall. The skull was cracked in two places where he had hit projecting boulders in the stream. He had fallen from a hemlock tree leaning over the edge of the stream, where I had seen him the previous week. But why did he fall? The head of the left ilium (hip bone) showed an older fracture, half healed. It may have represented a preceding fall and must have left half his body painful and weakened. In confirmation, the claws of the right front paw were heavily worn; claws of the left side were overgrown because the left arm was being favored. Hence the fatal fall had been brought on by injuries suffered in an earlier accident. The idea of tree-climbing animals falling out of trees sent me to the museums to check porcupine skeletons for healed fractures. More than a third of the specimens showed healed fractures. But if animals fall so often, shouldn't they impale themselves on their own quills? Another surprise: the quills had antibiotic properties.

I remember my surprise and delight when I found my first niptwig under a porcupine feeding tree. A niptwig is a terminal twig, stripped of its leaf blades but with petioles still attached, which the porcupine nips off and discards at the end of its meal. By looking for niptwigs, I could find out not only which trees a porcupine was feeding on but also how intensively the tree was being used. And by realizing how far out on the branches the animals went to feed, I could understand why they risked falls. As the years have gone by, perhaps the most astonishing aspect of this animal has been its ability to astonish—to disprove old assumptions and raise deeper mysteries.

Partly out of a growing understanding of the complexity of their lives, I have refrained from certain kinds of deliberate experiments: those that kill or injure my porcupines. That has closed some avenues of investigation, but it is my belief that only the living, free animal can raise the most inter-

Linden niptwigs on the ground. Petioles and portions of the midrib are left unconsumed.

esting questions, because it holds the power of the unexpected and because I meet it in its own world. A study of dead porcupines would not have told me which animals know each other, how they interact, and how they respond to the changing forest.

It is nevertheless fair to say that a sophisticated understanding of any organism cannot depend entirely on the study of living individuals. The museum skeletons that confirmed my theories about falling out of trees were prepared from dead specimens. The essential digestive role of the caecum was elucidated by a study of sacrificed animals, as was the important role of the accessory corpora lutea in maintaining a long pregnancy, of specially developed muscles used in climbing, of the specialized male accessory sex organs used in hystricomorph reproduction, and so on. The list is long.

A naturalist lives in two worlds: the world of nature and the human world of ideas and shared values. One world is represented by a fallen tree on a mountain ridge, the other by the library, the laboratory, and conversations with fellow scientists. In this study, I have tried to do justice to both. However, I have also tried hard to listen to the porcupine and to observe it free of the constrictions of my own hypotheses. Francis C. Evans (1985), past president of the Ecological Society of America, has perhaps put his finger on the critical role of natural history in ecological thought: "Whatever our chosen frame of reference with respect to observation may be, there is always some larger frame that is possible, and there is always a chance that this larger frame may contain something we did not anticipate, but which is directly relevant to the problem we have chosen to investigate." Time and again the porcupine has forced me to look at the forest, its natural home, in a different perspective. Again and again, the porcupine has been a teacher, a storyteller of the woods, a complexifier and adorner of the world.

2

The Defense Reaction

The legend of Robin Hood, recounting his meeting with Will Scarlet, offers a classic example of deterrent psychology in action.

Robin Hood, attended by Little John and the Tanner, encounters a stranger. The man is walking slowly down the highway, wearing gaudy clothes and a scarlet cap and sniffing a red rose. It is Will Scarlet. Because the stranger looks rich and soft, Robin Hood decides to rob him. He orders the man to hand over his purse and raises his quarterstaff in a threatening manner. But Will Scarlet is not to be intimidated.

"Alas," he says sadly, "I fear very much I must slay you, poor fellow!" and draws his sword.

Robin Hood insists on a fair fight, warning Will that a sword will snap like a straw when hit by Robin's quarterstaff and suggesting that he find a cudgel of his own. Will Scarlet agrees. He puts away his rose, walks over to a clump of oaks, and selects a sapling. Then with a rending and snapping of roots, he pulls it out of the ground. Using his sword as a penknife, he calmly trims the roots and branches and prepares for battle. The would-be robbers are unnerved. Will is asked to join Robin's band.

The Warning of the Porcupine

In my eight years of tracking porcupines in the Catskill Mountains of New York, I have come to feel that the porcupine is something of a Will Scarlet, walking confidently through the forest, working hard to intimidate its enemies, and turning to fight only as a last resort. But when the porcupine does fight, it may so devastate its muggers that they probably regret not heeding the initial warning. Like a patient teacher, the porcupine repeats its warning in three sensory modalities: sight, sound, and smell.

A porcupine carries conspicuous markings of black and white visible from the back, the aspect that it tries to present to its molesters. A black line runs up the middle of the tail and expands along the lower back. The

One-year-old male climbs a sugar maple. The black and white coloration in lower back and top of head serves a warning function.

black area is fringed with white quillshafts that form a chevron on the top and extend as a white border down the sides of the tail. The black-and-white contrast is so strong that it is visible on all but the darkest nights. It is no coincidence that skunks and porcupines use similar warning signals— they can both back up a gentle hint with a devastating follow-through. It is also no coincidence that the warning colors both use are black and white.

They are nocturnal animals, and in the dark that color combination is most easily visible. Animals marked by reds, yellows, and oranges (for example, red efts, coral snakes, monarch butterflies) are diurnally active and address their warnings to daytime predators, typically the birds. The porcupine's most important predators are not birds but other mammals, color-blind and active at night. A baby porcupine lacks the warning coloration of adults and is almost entirely black. Its quills are sharp and fully functional, but they are small and lack a powerful delivery system. Therefore the baby presents little danger to a determined predator. A baby must depend for protection on concealment, not deterrence. As it develops muscle power and quill size, it also develops the warning coloration of the adult. For the first few months of its life, the degree of warning-color development can serve as a rough index of the baby's age. At three months, the warning color is well developed.

The porcupine's second warning comes in the auditory mode: a quiet, ominous clattering of the teeth. A porcupine launches its tooth-clack with a generalized shivering of the body, as though a chill had seized it. Then it closes its jaws, and the clattering ensues. First the incisors vibrate against

All-black baby climbing. Babies a few weeks old lack warning coloration; their best defense is to hide.

each other, then the strike zone shifts to the back, and the cheek teeth come into play. A tooth-clack episode seldom lasts longer than half a minute, but the animal can repeat the performance many times if necessary. A tooth-clack in the dark has an eerie quality. I recall an episode in our woodshed, where porcupines came to chew on a salt spill. On a May night, I picked my way softly over the grass and arrived at the open door of the woodshed, then listened in the dark. Silence. I was about to turn away when a dry, clattering sound rose up out of the back. I almost jumped. My alarmer was a porcupine, a large male, who had heard every step of my approach and had no intention of running or hiding under a log. His clattering teeth were warning me of painful consequences if I came any closer. As it happened, his threat was one I wish I had heeded, but that is a story for later. Porcupines do not tooth-clack unless an encounter is imminent. A porcupine up in a tree will remain silent even though it can see and hear a human visitor below and may even crane its neck to keep it in view. But the same animal will tooth-clack if it wants to come down from a tree under which a human is waiting.

When the visual and auditory warnings have both failed, a porcupine falls back on its third, most immediate signal: odor. Many times, when radiotracking at night, my first indication of a porcupine only a few feet away has come from a wave of smell, pungent and unique to the porcupine. It is not the diffuse, piney-ammoniacal smell associated with den sites and porcupine urine. The warning smell, released only during times of stress, is so invasive that it is impossible to stay in a closed space such as a car or small room with an aroused adult porcupine. One's eyes begin to water and the nose runs. More susceptible persons may wheeze and feel a tingling of the skin. The degree of smell production is proportional to the size of the animal and its degree of arousal. Presumably the odor would serve as effective defense to an animal trapped in the tight confines of a den.

Although both sexes carry a pair of well-developed perineal scent glands, the glands are not involved in the production of the warning smell. The source of the odor appears to be an area of skin above the base of the tail, called the rosette. Quills in this area are relatively short and dark-colored. Most important, the skin below is naked. In other areas of the body, the quills nestle in a layer of insulating hair. But once the quills of the rosette are erected (and the visual signal is lost), skin as hairless as that of a human is presented to view. The rosette is a source of significant heat loss in the winter, as shown by the work of Clarke and Brander (1973). Up to now, the significance of the bare skin in this area has remained elusive. It is my belief that the rosette functions as a skin odor-generating organ. The evidence has been straightforward. I have taken anesthetized porcupines, lifted up the quills in various parts of the body, and smelled the skin below. Although an anesthetized porcupine is not actively generating repellent odor, the strongest smell is emitted from the rosette. Even a baby porcupine's rosette can generate repellent odor, though the smell is much weaker than that produced by an aroused adult. The chemical nature of the odor has not been fully established. All that can be said at the present time is that it smells like a volatile fatty acid, the same class of compounds that give a goat its characteristic odor and that function as sex attractants among certain primates.

The Quill

What if those overlapping warnings are ignored? For its own survival as much as for future credibility, the porcupine now unleashes its ultimate weapon—the quill. Upwards of 30,000 quills cover every part of the body except the underparts, the muzzle, and the ears of the porcupine (Woods 1973, Po-Chedley and Shadle 1955). Quills are modified guard hairs that differ in several ways from more typical hairs. They are much thicker than normal hairs and, at least in the eastern subspecies, are filled with a spongy matrix that makes them lightweight yet stiff. A popular misconception holds that porcupine quills are hollow. One well-known guide to mammals not only repeats this myth but also advises that in case a quill gets embedded in the flesh, the projecting shaft should be cut off to allow air to escape and shrink the quill. That advice could be dangerous. If the projecting shaft is splintered, the quill may be lost in the body. The tips of the quills carry microscopic barbs that make removal difficult once embedded in the flesh. Quill bases are loosely attached, so only a small pull will cause detachment. The porcupine uses its quills in two distinct ways: defensively, as a phalanx of spears, and offensively, as projectiles actively driven into the body of the predator.

Erected quills of the back point in random directions, providing all-quadrant protection.

In defensive terms, the important quills are the long quills of the upper back and neck areas. At rest, they lie in neat alignment and pointing toward the back. A porcupine can groom itself by using its long claws in a front-to-back motion. During arousal, quills spring up to form a random, up-lifted array of spears. Because erected quills are randomly oriented, the porcupine is protected from all directions.[1] The longest quills on a mature porcupine may measure almost four inches (10 cm) long. Their shafts are white, with black tips. When the muzzle of a charging dog or raccoon passes that critical distance, the quills are transferred from porcupine to predator, sharp end out. The predator's own momentum embeds the quills.

On a June night I watched a young raccoon visiting our feeding station after a porcupine encounter. Half a dozen long quill shafts decorated its muzzle like misplaced whiskers. Because the quill tips had come to rest against the upper jawbone, the quills were fixed in place. Over the course of a week, the shafts were reduced to a ragged stubble, and the raccoon survived its ordeal. In more serious cases, a mouthful of quills may prevent feeding and cause the animal to starve to death.

The long quills produce a spectacular effect, but the short black quills on the upper surface of the tail can be far more dangerous. With a flick of the tail almost too fast for the eye to follow, the porcupine can drive the tail quills into a victim. It is probably this split-second tail slap that has given rise to the persistent but false rumor that porcupines throw their quills. Quills driven by a porcupine's tail may penetrate so deeply that they disappear under the skin and become internal projectiles.

I learned that in a painful personal encounter in September 1983 while trying to capture a 17-pound male in a beech tree, the same animal whose tooth-clacking had warned me in the woodshed. I climbed the tree and was met by powerful repellent odor and tooth-clacking. When I pressed closer, the animal's tail began to punish me, driving batteries of quills through my heavy rubber glove. I persisted. Then, with a movement so fast it blurred, the tail whipped up and hit me in an unprotected spot, the inside of my upper arm. I pulled out quills I saw sticking through the shirt, but an intense, deep-lying pain remained. On the ground, I ripped open my shirt to look at the aching spot. To my horror, I saw a large, triangular bulge under the skin. I flexed my arm. The lump, but not the pain, disappeared. The quill had burrowed into my body. I completed a rapid physical examination of the animal, then turned my attention to my arm. I could flex my fingers but could not use the biceps. A deep, paralyzing pain stopped all attempts to lift the arm. I picked my way carefully down the mountain. On the drive home, I had to reach over with my left arm to shift the transmission. At home, the quill caused a sensation, but I firmly rejected my wife's suggestion of surgical excision. Five hours had passed since my encounter with the porcupine, and I had the definite impression that the quill had traveled downward and was now lodged somewhere inside my elbow.

Two days later, there was a strange resolution. When I got up in the morning and flexed my arm, I felt, very sharply, the presence of the quill in my forearm, ten inches down from its point of entry. In the morning light, I saw a tiny cone pushing up from beneath the skin. I flexed my arm again, and the cone disappeared. Later in the morning, I was teaching a lab. As I wrote on the blackboard, a sharp object caught my shirt arm from the inside. My shirt failed to move up and down on my arm as I was writing, then the feeling subsided. Later, in my office, I removed my jacket and rolled up the shirt. A red spot was visible on the forearm, at the point where the quill had bulged out earlier. I felt the arm. There was no pain and no sense of a foreign body inside. The quill had emerged! I flexed and twisted the arm luxuriously. I found the quill inside my jacket arm. It was almost entirely black and looked much smaller than I had imagined it. No part of the quill was missing, but it bent sharply in the middle. It looked beautifully clean, scoured by the body to a glistening freshness. Like some mole of the flesh, it had ratcheted its way past muscles, nerves, and blood vessels to emerge far from the site of entry.

For me, the story had a happy resolution. For many animals in the wild, and for a few unlucky humans, an encounter with a porcupine may lead to permanent injury or death. Drs. H. C. McDade and W. B. Crandell, of White River Junction, Vermont, report an unusual surgical case in a 1958 issue of the *New England Journal of Medicine;* a patient with a small intestine perforated by a porcupine quill. The patient was a 51-year-old woodsman, admitted to the hospital because of severe abdominal pain, fever, and blockage of the bowels. Surgery revealed half a porcupine quill perforating the small intestine. Escaping intestinal bacteria had set up an inflammation inside the abdominal cavity. Following massive doses of penicillin and streptomycin and a three-week hospital stay, the man was discharged in good health. The source of the quill was described as follows: ten days before admission to the hospital, the patient had shot a porcupine while hunting. He handled it with gloves when cutting off the forepart of the head with an ax to collect a bounty. Later, eating his lunch in a truck, he rested his sandwiches on the gloves lying on the seat beside him. It is likely that a fragment of the quill divided by the ax had stuck to the gloves and then was ingested with a sandwich.

The same article describes a less-fortunate patient. The man was admitted to the New London Hospital in New Hampshire in September 1934 with intense abdominal pain. Surgery revealed a quill perforation of the stomach and internal stab wounds from the projecting quill. The description ends, "The course was stormy, and he died on the 8th postoperative day." In 1934, no penicillin was available. Four days before admission to the hospital, the man had eaten a porcupine-meat sandwich.

In wild animals, quill injuries have been described in almost every body location: mouth, eyes, nose, lungs, intestinal tract. Some injuries lead to death or crippling, but a surprising number of the animals recover.

Quills move through the body because their barbed tips pull them forward. The barbs are too fine to be seen by the naked eye, but they can be felt by the fingertip; a quill feels smooth when pushed forward through the fingers, rough when pulled back. The quills on the back of a porcupine's tail show further refinements that adapt them for traveling in the flesh. First, they are notably shorter than quills on the back and sides of the animal and consequently have a much better chance of disappearing under the skin of the victim before they can be pulled out. Second, the tail quills are covered by a visible layer of grease, which lubricates the quills and may allow them to penetrate more deeply into the victim. And the tail houses powerful muscles for driving the quills. The base of the tail in an adult porcupine may be as thick as a man's wrist. The bones and cartilage of the tail vertebrae lie on the top, providing a firm platform for delivery.

For all those reasons, the adult porcupine has few serious enemies in the wild. To most animals of the forest, the porcupine's reputation alone is suf-

Scanning electron microscope view of a quill tip (×200).

ficient to keep it from harm. I got an illustration of that on a bitter winter night in March, when I found one of my porcupines frozen to death. The animal had been lying on crusted snow for about two days. A thin layer of snow had accumulated on top. I could make out, faintly, the tracks of the porcupine as it had moved forward, then lain down and fallen asleep. All around the body I found carnivore tracks, including fox, yet none had dared to touch the dead porcupine. To the little carnivores, the porcupine was inviting food. But it was, even in death, a porcupine, and therefore protected.

Quill Antibiotics

My painful encounter with the large male porcupine, so instructive in terms of quill behavior, led to one more discovery: a porcupine's quills are covered with antibiotics. The quill that had spent two days traveling through my arm left no trace of an infection. A wood splinter traveling the same path would almost certainly have produced a massive inflammation. When I mentioned it to Ward Stone, chief wildlife pathologist for New York State, he asked the logical question: Do porcupine quills have antibiotic properties?

Indeed they do. As mentioned before, the quills of the back and tail have a greasy coating. The grease layer is best developed on animals in good physical condition—that is, during summertime feeding conditions—but it does not entirely disappear even under the difficult conditions of winter. When this grease is extracted with lipid solvents and tested against Gram-positive bacteria in liquid media, the bacteria show growth inhibition. (Gram-negative bacteria are unaffected.) The extract can be fractionated. The fraction responsible for growth inhibition is the fatty acid fraction; the neutral lipids have no effect. David Locke from the Chemistry Department of Queens College has fractionated the fatty acids further into individual components and identified them by the powerful technique of coupled gas chromatography–mass spectroscopy (Roze et al. 1990). Roughly half of the total mixture consists of palmitic acid, a common saturated fatty acid of animal fat. Other major components include palmitoleic, isopalmitic, and oleic acids. In addition, ten minor components account for 5% of the total.

Porcupine quills with grease-coated tips. Surface grease accounts for 8% of a quill's weight and contains fatty acids that have antibiotic properties.

Gas chromatography spectrum of porcupine quill fatty acids. The most abundant component is palmitic acid (peak 4).

None of the fatty acids identified has proved unique to the porcupine; all are known to have bactericidal action (Glassman 1948, Wyss et al. 1945).

The situation is reminiscent of that on human skin, which is also coated by a thin film of lipid consisting of 30% (weight basis) fatty acids (Lindholm et al. 1981, Nicolaides 1974). It has been suggested that human skin surface fatty acids reduce the incidence of bacterial and fungal infections (Sauer 1980).

But the presence of substantial concentrations of fatty acids among the skin lipids is by no means common in the mammalian world. No other mammal is known to share the trait, and it is possible that humans and porcupines may be the only species to do so. Even closely related forms such as gibbons and chimpanzees lack those components (Nicolaides 1974). (Nothing is known of related porcupines.) That raises the question of what the high concentrations of fatty acids are doing in these two species.

Human skin is unique among mammals in being heavily populated with sweat glands, which generate a film of moisture that might provide favorable conditions for bacterial growth. The antibacterial activity of the fatty acids should therefore serve as protection. In mammals other than humans, no film of moisture covers the skin because sweat glands are rare and find primary use as scent glands. Hence there is no need for a defense against superficial skin infections. The following hypothesis suggests a different role for the skin (or quill) fatty acids in porcupines.

In a deciduous forest habitat, porcupines spend a large amount of time in trees. In winter, trees are used for bark-feeding. In summer, the animals rest in trees during the day and feed in the canopies at night. Porcupines are at risk of falling out of trees because they have relatively high body weights, their foods are typically located far out on the branches, and branches of a number of heavily used tree species are brittle. The animals that fall out of trees may suffer a variety of injuries, including impalement on their own quills. Quills that travel through the body should therefore be free of such dangerous Gram-positive organisms as *Clostridium tetani* (the cause of tetanus) and *C. perfringens* (cause of gas gangrene) (Sherris 1984b).

That hypothesis is supported by my personal observations of the arboreal life of radiotelemetered animals, for an aggregate of 39 porcupine-years (Chapters 4, 6, 8). Additional evidence is provided by porcupine anatomy in the form of tree-climbing adaptations (Chapter 3). Also, a number of observers give firsthand accounts of porcupines falling out of trees. Curtis and Kozicky (1944) observed a full-grown porcupine falling from a poplar tree. Marshall (1951) found a porcupine dead in a double-stemmed tamarack. The animal had fallen, wedging itself between the two stems, and had been unable to extricate itself. I have never directly observed a porcupine falling, but the indirect evidence is compelling. At least three times I have found quill masses consistent with falling at the bases of trees. Such quill masses differ from quill masses associated with battles. The latter are dispersed over a wide area, may be found away from trees, and may include tufts of hair mixed with quills. One falling-type quill mass involved the adult male Taylor, another the juvenile female Eft, and a third came from an unknown porcupine. All survived their falls. In Chapter 4 I offer an indirect observation: a large broken branch found below a poplar in which an adult female had been feeding the night before. In this case, the animal appears to have broken its fall, as suggested by the absence of a quill mass below the tree.

The most convincing evidence for porcupine tree-falling comes from observation of injuries. The male found dead of a broken skull, as described in the previous chapter, must have died because of a fall. The adult female Acidie, described in the next chapter, had a crushed pelvis and lower back damage consistent with falling. Even more suggestive is an encounter with the adult male Finder. At the time, Finder had worn a radiocollar for three years, and essentially all of his located positions had been up trees or inside dens. On June 1, 1986, I encountered the animal under a branch tangle. He made no effort to climb the adjacent trees. I captured him, anesthetized him, and made a physical examination. Finder had been gravely injured. He had suffered a blow to the jaw, and pus was oozing from the lower incisors. Two of his footpads were torn, and a laceration of the abdomen, near the left testis, was partly healed. All the injuries were consistent with falling belly-first out of a tree; none were consistent with predator attack. But the clearest suggestion of falling came from the position of the third digit of his left front limb. The digit projected upward at a right angle, a probable consequence of trying to snag a branch as the animal was hurtling down to the ground. Subsequently, I tracked the animal at weekly intervals and repeatedly found him on the ground. It appeared his injuries had left him unable to climb. His weight remained constant at a time when other porcupines were gaining rapidly. Finally, on July 19, I tracked Finder to the heartland of his territory and found him high up a tree. He had resumed normal tree-climbing behavior, but his third left digit remained permanently dislocated.

Wendell Dodge (1967), during autopsies of 200-odd porcupines in western Massachusetts, found healed fractures of legs, hips, and ribs, broken incisors, injured eyes and ears, as well as hernias and miscellaneous soft-tissue injuries. One animal carried an encapsulated four-inch-long pine branch inside its abdominal cavity.

To quantify the incidence of serious injuries in the porcupine, I looked for healed fractures in 37 skeletons from museum collections. I excluded fractures of ribs and phalanges, since they are difficult to classify (Bulstrode et al. 1986). As controls, I examined 45 museum skeletons of the wood-chuck (*Marmota monax*), a rodent of comparable body weight but with little tree-climbing activity. I also examined 39 museum skeletons of the raccoon (*Procyon lotor*). Raccoons climb trees readily but use them primarily for rest and denning, therefore confining their activities to the trunk and large branches. They do not venture out onto the thin, sometimes unpredictable outer branches. The results exceeded my expectations (Roze et al. 1990). Thirteen of the porcupine skeletons (35.1%) showed healed fractures. Only 3 woodchuck and 4 raccoon skeletons showed the same. Statistically, the differences between the three species are highly significant.[2]

A list of the porcupine injuries covers every region of the body, but 9 of the 13 animals show injuries of long bones of the arms and legs; 5 show injuries of the hip region (ilium, ischium, pubis, acetabulum). All but one of the healed fractures in porcupines were found in adults. The exception was a young juvenile with damage to a femur and scapula.

It has been known for many years that large arboreal primates such as gibbons (*Hylobates* spp.) and pygmy chimpanzees (*Pan paniscus*) have a high incidence of healed fractures. The incidence is highest in species that spend the most time in trees (Kano 1984, Schultz 1956). But tree-fall injuries in primates show one interesting difference from porcupines. Bulstrode and coworkers (1986), after analyzing the healed fractures in a sample of 56 gibbons, conclude that all the injuries were suffered during infancy. The reason is obvious: injured infants can recover because their mothers shelter them. Injured adults are dispatched by predators. The opposite condition may hold true in porcupines. Only one of the nine subadults in my sample had healed fractures. The adult-subadult difference in injury rates does not quite achieve statistical significance, however.[3] Juvenile porcupines are poor tree-climbers. They select smaller trees than adults, rest in lower branches, and generally take fewer chances. Their lighter weights put less strain on branches. Should they suffer injury, their mothers might be expected to offer little protection against predators.

Conversely, injured adults are far from defenseless on the ground. Finder was bristling fiercely during his capture. The porcupine's excellent defense system gives it the time needed to knit broken bones before resuming normal life in the trees. Comparable injuries in less-protected mammals would prove fatal.

Assuming accidents serious enough to produce fractures also lead to self-impalement on quills, how effective a defense are quill fatty acids against bacteria? Much of the quill damage would be self-limited since porcupines are skilled in removing embedded foreign quills. However, quill tips may break off and travel beyond reach, as may the small quills of the tail. Under such conditions, the bacteria associated with the quill tip would be in position to start an infection. In humans, the major threats in contaminated puncture wounds are tetanus and gas gangrene, both caused by Gram-positive organisms. By eliminating that group alone, the porcupine quill fatty acids might reduce infection substantially.

Of course, the considerations that make porcupine quills safer for porcupines also make them safer for porcupine predators. Studies by Coulter (1966) in dogs and Maser and Rohweder (1983) in mountain lions show that porcupine quills cause unexpectedly few infections in those predators. But one must not conclude that porcupine quills have little effect against predators. Quills are highly effective, even against skilled predators such as the fisher (Powell 1982, DeVos 1953). But they are effective for strictly physical reasons, not because they cause secondary infections.

Predation

In its complement of quills, the porcupine possesses a formidable weapon. But how secure is a porcupine's life? The answer depends on who is in the woods with it. In the northern Catskill Mountains, a porcupine can feel safe throughout much of the year. In early December 1978, while follow-ing a porcupine track in the snow, I discovered the animal had met a red fox (*Vulpes vulpes*). I found a jumble of tracks where the fox had circled the porcupine and the porcupine kept turning to present its tail to the fox. The evidence signaled a victory for the porcupine. The tracks of the two ani-mals separated again, with the porcupine moving uphill, the fox downhill.

It was probably a typical porcupine–small carnivore interaction. Por-cupine remains have been found in red fox stomachs, but only in low fre-quency, and it is not clear whether the fox had killed a living porcupine or fed on carrion. Other minor porcupine predators on record include the lynx (*Lynx canadensis*), the bobcat *(Lynx rufus)*, the coyote (*Canis latrans*), the wolf (*Canis lupus*), the wolverine (*Gulo luscus*), the great horned owl (*Bubo virginianus*) (Woods 1973, Dodge 1967). None may be called se-rious threats to the porcupine, and they may come out as losers in an at-tack. Ward Stone has documented a coyote that a farmer shot, fearing rabies. The animal had been moving in a circle and acting disoriented. Autopsy revealed a porcupine quill that had entered through the muzzle and traveled backwards to pierce the lower brain (Ward Stone, personal communication).

The porcupine does have a few important predators. The mountain lion (*Felis concolor*) has already been mentioned. Chris Maser's data suggest that this powerful predator feeds regularly on porcupines, making no spe-cial effort to avoid the quills but tolerating the consequences (Maser and Rohweder 1983). Since mountain lions themselves are exceedingly rare throughout most of the range of the porcupine, an encounter must be con-sidered unlikely.

The fisher (*Martes pennanti*), though a much smaller carnivore, appears to be a significant and effective predator. This relative of the weasel makes a profession of hunting porcupines, though snowshoe hares, squirrels, small rodents, and carrion are more important protein sources (Powell 1982). Fishers and porcupines are of comparable size. Adult male fishers generally weigh between 3.5 and 5.5 kilograms; the largest male porcupine I have encountered weighed 8 kg. Though porcupines do not make up a large fraction of a fisher's diet, they are attractive to the predator. Fishers routinely alter their winter movements to inspect active porcupine dens.

Roger Powell of North Carolina State University, who has studied the fisher both in the wild and under captive conditions, observed that the fisher

An adult fisher. This powerful relative of the weasel is one of the few predators able to kill a porcupine (Roger Powell).

is no more immune to porcupine quills than other animals are. The fisher kills porcupines not by tolerating their quills but by avoiding them. It attacks a vital but relatively unprotected region, the face. Powell (1982) describes a fisher's attack inside a fenced enclosure: "An attacking fisher repeatedly circles the porcupine, attempting to bite its face. When it finds a chance, the fisher jumps in, bites the porcupine's face, and jumps back again before the porcupine has a chance to turn and strike the fisher with its tail. Repeated wounds to the face over a period of 30 minutes or more finally kill or bewilder the porcupine so that the fisher can turn it over and begin feeding on its ventral surface. Most attacks to the face are unsuccessful, and a fisher often has to check its attack after it is started because the porcupine is able to move quickly enough to protect itself." Powell believes the fisher's powerful but low-slung body allows it to attack the unprotected face of the porcupine, as opposed to its well-protected neck. In addition, the fisher's agility in trees reduces the protective value of that shelter to the porcupine.

In March 1981 I had a chance to view the results of a fisher-porcupine battle only minutes after the deed. I was visiting Wendell Dodge, the author of a classic study of the porcupine around Quabbin Reservoir, near Amherst, Massachusetts. Wendell took me out for a hike around the reservoir and showed me a cross section of porcupine dens and feeding sites. Most of the dens were empty, and the porcupine population seemed to be greatly diminished. One active den was inside a hollow white oak, about three feet in diameter. Patches of snow still lay on the ground, and Wendell followed a faint feeding trail to a hemlock grove 50 feet away. Under the hemlocks, he knelt down, stared at something on the ground, and called out in his laconic New England way, "Here's something that will interest you." I hurried over. Lying on the ground was a freshly killed porcupine, its body still warm. Our arrival had interrupted the killer, who could be identified from the method of attack: the porcupine's head was missing. This was the attack mode of the fisher. The head had been peeled out of its skin, with tufts of hair, quills, and small patches of skin piled next to the torso. After consuming the soft tissues of the head, the fisher would work into the body. In other fisher kills, the inner tissues are consumed through a hole made in the chest or abdomen. The dead porcupine had been a yearling female. She was not pregnant, and she appeared to be in excellent physical condition, sleek and well fed.

As we continued our hike, we discovered a second porcupine carcass next to a rock den. In this case, the animal had been dead for many months, with only the quills, skin, and bones remaining. The pelvic girdle and lower leg bones were all wonderfully preserved and still linked by cartilage. But once more, the animal's head was missing—another possible fisher kill.

According to Wendell, the fisher is rather common in the area, so much so that local trappers poached on it. (Since the Quabbin Reservoir is part of the Boston city water supply, hunting and trapping are not permitted.)

It is clear that the fisher is an effective predator on porcupines. Two approaches have been used to gauge its importance in controlling porcupine populations. First, porcupine population densities in a given area have been compared before and after the introduction of fisher. That requires serial data spanning several years. The second approach is a parallel comparison: porcupine densities are measured in similar habitats, one with fishers, the other without.

The serial approach was used by Powell and Brander in 1975, with additional data extending the study to 1979 (Powell 1982). Their study site was the Ottawa National Forest in upper Michigan. Before the sixties, the fisher had been extirpated from the area. Between 1961 and 1963, Michigan introduced 61 fishers from Minnesota into the Ottawa National Forest. The release has been successful. It appears that the porcupine population in the national forest has declined severely following fisher introduction (Table 2). The parallel study was carried out by Earle and Kramm (1982) in winter 1976. They compared a 919-ha (3.5-square-mile) area of the Ottawa National Forest with 644 ha (2.5 square miles) in the Hiawatha National Forest. Both sites are in upper Michigan and have a similar tree-species composition and topography. They differed in fisher abundance: the fisher was well established in the Ottawa forest thanks to the 1961–63 releases. Fisher was rare or absent in the Hiawatha forest 120 miles to the east. Porcupine population densities for the two areas were 40 animals per 100 square kilometers in Ottawa and 350 in Hiawatha. Earle and Kramm's figures for Ottawa are much lower than Powell and Brander's 1976 data for the same area. Powell and Brander censused a smaller area (178–283 ha); the difference probably reflects local variation. It is clear that in the fisher-stocked forest, porcupine abundance is significantly reduced. Both data sets should be treated with caution. Porcupine populations undergo natural long-term fluctuations (Spencer 1964). Long-term population studies are necessary to be sure that the observed effect is real.

In my own Catskills study area, where fishers have been introduced but have not become well established, I have found only four sources of porcupine mortality over eight years: disease (2 deaths), winter stress (6), injury (3), and human predation (5). Three animals disappeared for unknown reasons. All four factors appear important.

The body I most hated finding was that of Bus, the 1983 baby of Squirrel. I found her under the melting snows in April 1984, near where her signal had stopped the preceding hunting season. The radio had been cut away. Her paw, perfectly preserved, was stretched in front of her face. She had been alive for six months. Where humans and porcupines coexist, the porcupine's defense system becomes irrelevant, and humans can become more effective predators than any wild carnivore. The category of winter stress includes animals found frozen in their dens. Four of the six had lost more than 30% of their prewinter body weights; one animal's body was too deep inside the den to recover, and another was too decomposed to permit measurement. The two disease victims both died of scabies. As explained in chapters 10 and 11, I believe scabies had a profound effect on local porcupine density. All three injury victims showed damage consistent with falling out of trees. Of the unknowns, two were juveniles that disappeared during their first summers. The third was an adult male who behaved erratically before death. He spent the bulk of his time on the ground and fed on Indian hemp (*Apocynum cannabinum*), a toxic herb. The list of animals dying of unknown causes does not include the much larger number of animals lost because of possible radio failure.

What the list does not include is more important than what it does. (The numbers are too small to make quantitative statements meaningful.) The significant observation is that there were no losses due to predation by local carnivores, whose larger members include bobcat, coyote, and black bear. With the fishers and mountain lions locally absent, the porcupine's defense system is impregnable against every animal except man.

Notes

1. The quill erection mechanism has not been studied. One possibility involves contraction of the sheetlike panniculus carnosus muscle, which extends under the quills and in which the follicles of the quills form depressions. When the muscle is contracted, it may drag the follicular ends posteriorly to erect the quills. An alternate (or simultaneous) possibility involves the contractions of individual piloerector muscles (arrector pili), which are well developed in the porcupine and could generate the observed random orientation of erected quills.
2. $\chi^2 = 11.66$, df $= 2$, $P < 0.005$.
3. $P = 0.063$, Fisher's exact test.

Anatomy

Acidie was a porcupine I knew for only six months, during the summer and fall of 1985. She died on December 27, on the sixth day of winter, but her free life in the woods had ended months earlier.

When I first capture her in June 1985, she is a young mother working to raise her offspring: she is chewing plywood scraps in our woodshed to replace sodium that she is losing in her milk. After radiotagging her and releasing her in the woods, I realize she is behaving differently from my other porcupines. Almost every time I locate her, she is on the ground, not up in a tree. Most often she is hiding under the green tangles of raspberry and blackberry or under the slash left by lumbermen. Sometimes she slithers between thick ground vegetation to find shelter in an available rock den, unusual behavior for a porcupine in the summer. Because I find her so often on the ground, it is easy to capture her and get week-to-week physical data. Again a strange situation reveals itself: Acidie is gaining no weight as the summer progresses, a time when porcupines build up body fat for the winter ahead.

On September 22, I pick up her signal once more. I have spent the day walking through green woods flecked with the first yellows of autumn. Acidie is my last animal of the day; I catch up with her in a mature woods, where the forest canopy closes over bare ground beneath the trees. With no blackberry tangle to hide in, she is attempting a normal escape—climbing a tree. I catch sight of her eight feet off the ground, clinging to a young linden trunk. I stop 30 feet away to study her. Acidie is pressed uncomfortably against the trunk, moving neither up nor down, her limbs spread wide. When I move closer, a gesture that would send an ordinary porcupine scooting up the tree, Acidie attempts to climb but is defeated by a small branch that blocks her path. Standing directly below, I hear a light sound, like raindrops falling. It is her tail bristles slipping as she starts to slide backwards. I grab her.

After anesthetizing her, I learn that her weight is no longer holding constant but has begun to drop precipitously, slipping from 4.0 kg in June to 3.4 kg in September. She should be gaining weight on the year's rich supply of acorns and residual linden leaves, but she is unable to climb trees to reach those important porcupine foods. She has been surviving on ground vegetation, and the quality of that resource is declining. Acidie shows other signs of debilitation: the grease layer on her quills has disappeared, and she is heavily infested with lice. She appears to have poor bladder control. She will die if left alone; I intervene.

In New York City I have Acidie examined at the animal care facility of the Bronx Zoo. My initial diagnosis of a urinary tract infection is ruled out by normal hematology and urine values. There seems to be no reason to take an X-ray, the one procedure that might shed light on her condition. And she is examined under anesthesia, eliminating a second vital clue. Thus the examination only deepens the mystery.

I install Acidie in a cage in our basement and feed her a mixture of apples, rodent chow, and water. She shows excellent appetite but puts on little weight. Over the weeks, the mystery of her condition is gradually unveiled. She lacks all sensation in her tail and hindquarters; I can touch them and get no response. Touching anywhere else produces quill erection, tooth-clacking, and angry screaming. A lower spinal cord injury would explain the numbness and loss of bladder control. She retains some motor control. Her hind legs move in a robot fashion, but gradually that ability diminishes and she drags herself about the cage with her front limbs. Then she somehow gashes the side of her tail. The wound spreads and festers and does not respond to antibiotics. She dies of the infection. An autopsy reveals the underlying cause of her misfortunes. Her pelvis has been crushed in a fall, injuring her spinal cord. The ischial bones have knitted together in an abnormal position; the muscles of her tail and hind legs have atrophied; the bladder is empty.

The wreckage of a once-living body presents a sad picture. Only her front limbs seem to recall some of the music of her existence. The muscles of the forearms, layered thick as a carpenter's, convey a raw power. They alone had pulled her partway up the tree before I captured her, and had propelled her through the underbrush for most of a summer. Even in death, the front limbs retain the beauty of function well executed. The forearm muscles taper down to fine white tendons; a cable of them slips through a deep groove in the wrist, then spreads out in a spiderweb of connections to the fingers. The wrist is ringed by a bracelet of tendons to keep the cables in place. The function of the forelimbs had been to climb trees and to travel long distances on the ground.

General Anatomy

The anatomy of the North American porcupine, *Erethizon dorsatum,* is a composite of general traits shared with all members of its taxonomic group, the hystricomorph rodents, and more specialized (derived) traits that may be shared only with other New World porcupines or may be restricted to *Erethizon* alone.

The porcupine's broadest affinities are with the order Rodentia, and they are broad indeed: some 40% of the roughly 4060 mammal species recognized today are rodents (Vaughan 1978). Rodents possess ever-growing incisors, allowing them to exploit foods that require gnawing. (The German word for rodent, "*Nagetier,*" means "gnawing beast." The English word has a similar root, being derived from the Latin *rodere,* "to gnaw.") They have no canine teeth, which restricts all larger rodents to a herbivorous mode of life. Between the incisors and the cheek teeth lies a toothless space, the diastema, into which the lips can be drawn to facilitate gnawing. The lips can be closed behind the incisors to seal the mouth to unwanted fragments dislodged by the incisors. The cheek teeth often have complex grinding surfaces, an aid in the grinding of plant materials. The grinding motion can be front to back, side to side, or both.

Most rodents also have a free (unfused) radius and ulna (bones of the lower arm). Plantigrade locomotion (walking on the soles of the feet) gives most of them a stable but not particularly speedy travel mode (Macdonald 1984). They are mostly small animals. The largest, the capybara (*Hydrochaeris hydrochaeris*) of Central and South America, may weigh up to 66 kg (146 pounds). The porcupine is close to the high end of the rodent body-weight spectrum. In North America, only the beaver surpasses it. In my study, 15 adult males averaged 6.1 kg, and 29 adult females averaged 5.1 kg. The difference between the sexes is significant ($t = 3.05$, $df = 42$, $P < 0.01$). Porcupines from the Idaho shrub desert appear to reach higher body weights. Craig and Keller (1986) report an average weight of 11.5 kg (25.3 pounds) for 5 adult males.

Within the order Rodentia, the porcupine belongs to the suborder Hystricomorpha ("porcupinelike forms"), which includes not only the New World and Old World porcupines but also such New World families as the guinea pigs, chinchillas, agoutis, and spiny rats and the Old World gundis and mole rats (Macdonald 1984). The hystricomorphs are characterized by a unique positioning of the chewing muscles (the masseter muscles). One arm of the masseter passes through a large opening below the orbit called the infraorbital foramen. That configuration increases the efficiency of chewing. The hystricomorphs are also reproductively specialized (Chapter 12). Females tend to have long gestation periods and produce a small number of young. In males, the penis carries a sacculus urethralis and is normally retracted within the penis sheath. In the words of Stuart Landry (1977), "It is depressing to note how many male hystricomorphs court by urinating on the female and indeed, often on their helpless offspring." In females of most species, a vaginal closure membrane is in place at all times except at estrus and parturition. During pregnancy, the ovaries develop accessory corpora lutea that secrete the large amounts of progesterone needed to support a long pregnancy.

That is the body plan the North American porcupine has modified to fit its own way of life. *Erethizon* feeds largely in trees. Its body is therefore modified for climbing and maneuvering in trees and for feeding on leaves, fruit, and bark. It shares those adaptations with its Central and South American relatives of the genera *Coendou* and *Sphiggurus*. A set of adaptations it does not share with its southern relatives is the ability to survive under conditions of extreme cold. Most porcupines of the world, both Old World and New World forms, are animals of the tropics. *Erethizon* is the only porcupine able to survive up to the tree line in the far north.

Arboreal Adaptations

To get to its food, *Erethizon* must climb. The claws of both front and hind limbs are extremely long, fitting like curved conical hats over the outer segments of each digit. There are four claws in the front, five in the back. A vestigial thumb is visible on the skeleton, and in some individuals a tiny thumb projects to the outside. The claws serve several functions: Most important, they fit into crevices in tree bark, working just like the leg hooks used by telephone linemen. On smooth-barked trees, the progress of a climbing porcupine can be read from residual scratch marks. The claws, which are long enough to reach through the quill layer to the skin below, are also used as a comb in self-grooming. In addition, the front claws can fold in over the palm to manipulate foods such as apples or small branches, and they are used to snag tree branches to bring them into feeding range.

The porcupine's limbs show another tree-climbing adaptation: the palms of the hands and the soles of the feet are naked and have a pebbly texture that suggests crepe rubber. These tuberosities increase friction against the tree trunk. When trunks or branches are too thin to climb with claws, the porcupine can use its palms and soles alone. Its powerful clenching thigh muscles allow it to clasp a small tree trunk by sole-friction, leaving the front limbs free for food-handling or exploration (McEvoy 1982, Woods

Four digits on a porcupine front paw. The naked footpad provides good traction on trunks and branches; the curved claws sink into crevices in tree bark.

A porcupine uses its front claws to grasp an apple.

1972). Footpads also help the animals sense and conform to the branches they traverse on nocturnal feeding expeditions. Footpad size increases with the weight of the animal. Since adult males tend to be larger than females, they generally have larger footpads.

One more important piece of tree-climbing equipment is the tail. The tail of the porcupine is a truly versatile organ—I have already discussed the use of the upper, quill-studded surface in personal defense. The lower surface is unquilled but bears instead stiff, backward-pointing bristles embedded in a deep layer of connective tissue. When this surface is pressed against a tree trunk, the bristles engage the bark and prevent downward sliding. In descent, the tail becomes an exploratory appendage, lifting up and down at each claw-hold and testing the way below.

An observation in the summer of 1983 illustrated how important the tail can be as a tree-climbing aid to the porcupine. In the middle of a July night, I captured a small male that had been sitting immobile for at least an hour in a sweet-apple tree, a great favorite of porcupines. He made no movement as I approached and put up no struggle when I grabbed him. I named him Moribund Porcupine, or MP for short, and held him in a cage overnight to examine him by daylight. I discovered then that his left rear leg was paralyzed, perhaps damaged in some old fall from a tree. He climbed the sides of the cage by using only three legs and walked by throwing out the bad leg like a wooden prosthesis. The leg had been paralyzed for some time; the left footpad was narrower than the right, and its claws were long and sharp, not worn down by climbing. I kept the animal several days for observation, attached a radiocollar, then freed him on a fine summer afternoon. He set off at a brisk but swaying pace, walking on three legs and holding the bad leg off the ground. I followed at a distance. He crossed three stone walls and investigated several trees along the way before choosing one to climb—a tall, medium-sized linden.

How would a three-legged porcupine climb a tree? By using its tail as a fourth leg. Instead of directing his tail vertically, he swung it to the left to oppose the traction of the active right leg and gain an effective four-point purchase. The most difficult maneuvers involved climbing over projecting branches by laborious lifting of the bad leg over the obstacle. But again the tail helped out, becoming a leg substitute. MP did not stop climbing until he reached open sunlight atop the canopy. As I watched through my binoculars, he began to feed slowly, eating leaves directly off the branch he

An adult female climbs a red oak. She presses her tail tightly against the trunk to prevent sliding.

was clinging to, until I could see a row of bristling petioles. He then climbed even higher, for tastier leaves. The branch bent ominously. A small wind picked up, and the top of the once-vertical branch bent to the horizontal before rebounding. As the branch and its clinging porcupine swung in great arcs, MP went on feeding. Happily, I renamed him. No longer would he be MP, the Moribund Porcupine. He was now Imp: Improved Porcupine.

A porcupine's movement up or down a tree is a close-contact experience. The animal spreads its limbs wide and drags its belly along the trunk. There are two interesting consequences to that mode of tree climbing. First, the animals carry no quills along the belly and inner surface of the limbs. Any quills growing there would be scraped off by the intimate contact with tree bark. Second, male porcupines do not carry an external penis. It would suffer continual abrasion as the groin was dragged up and down tree trunks. The penis is normally retracted inside a cloacalike structure, a solution made possible by retractor muscles attached to a tiny bone inside the penis, the baculum. The arrangement is part of the animal's hystricomorph heritage. The female's external reproductive organs are also hidden through most of the year. The vaginal opening is normally covered by a closure membrane. Whatever the original function of the adaptation, it serves to keep bark chips and debris out of the body while the female is crawling up or down tree trunks. There is thus a logical consistency to the body architecture of the porcupine, with all anatomical arrangements contributing to efficient tree climbing.

One final tree-climbing adaptation may not be as satisfactorily resolved; it relates to body weight. As John Eisenberg (1983) has pointed out, there are upper limits to the size of arboreal leaf-eaters, dictated by the mechanical problems of supporting animal bodies among the small branches where the leaves grow. Porcupines may be pushing at that limit, at least when feeding in the more brittle branches of deciduous trees.

Digestive System

Porcupines climb trees primarily to feed on leaves or bark. In this, *Erethizon* has few mammalian competitors, because few other North American mammals (and no widespread species) possess the two traits necessary for that way of life: ability to climb trees and ability to digest leaves or bark. Only a few fellow rodents, wood rats of the genus *Neotoma* and tree voles of the Pacific Northwest, can match those traits, but they are smaller and their distribution is more limited.

Feeding on leaves is a difficult occupation because tree leaves, during most of the growing season, contain only low levels of nutrients such as protein, sugar, or starch. The bulk of the leaf biomass consists of complex molecules not accessible to mammalian digestive enzymes. This is dietary fiber, containing diverse chemical fractions such as celluloses, hemicelluloses, lignin, pectin, cutin, and suberin. Celluloses and hemicelluloses, although resistant to mammalian digestive enzymes, can be digested by enzymes secreted by certain bacteria. The porcupine incorporates such bacteria as essential parts of its digestive system (Balows and Jennison 1949). Because the bacterial enzymes work slowly, the porcupine digestive tract is very long and has a slow passage time. The porcupine's digestive system is a major organ system in its body, making up 26% of total body weight (Table 3). In comparison with man, the porcupine devotes far more of its body resources to digestion and far less to skeletal muscles or to heart and lungs.

Much of the bacterial activity of the digestive system takes place in a large sac, the caecum, at the junction of the small and large intestines. The porcupine caecum is about the same size as its stomach. It is here that a broth of digestive bacteria interacts with finely ground plant materials under anaerobic conditions and for extended periods of time. In the end, much of the plant fiber is fermented to small molecules—acetate, propionate, and butyrate—that are absorbed from the caecum and large intestine and used to supply the animal with energy. Johnson and McBee (1967), who studied the porcupine's caecal fermentation, estimate that on average 16% of the animal's energy requirements are supplied by that process. In some individuals, the figure is as high as 33%. The authors point out that this contribution would be most important during the periods of poorest diet, when snow covers the ground and the only food available is low-quality tree bark.

Unlike rabbits and beavers, who also have large caeca, the porcupine is not coprophagous (it does not reingest feces for a second round of nutrient extraction). That means that the bacteria in the caecum are not themselves used as food sources. The porcupine's relatively long large intestine, which serves to absorb the fermentation products, partially compensates. A number of small arthropods do not overlook that inefficiency and specialize in feeding on porcupine feces.

The digestion of cellulose provides porcupines with an important energy supply, but intestinal bacteria offer a second benefit that is sometimes overlooked: improved protein metabolism. In porcupines, as in all mammals, the nitrogen waste product generated by protein breakdown is urea. Urea in the urine represents an unavoidable nitrogen loss to a mammal; it is why fresh protein must always be present in the diet. But for the digestive bacteria, urea is not a waste product; it is a raw material that can be broken down to ammonia and then resynthesized into protein. That in itself does not help the porcupine, who loses those bacteria in its feces. But by decreasing blood urea levels, the intestinal bacteria take some of the load off kidney function. In effect, they help the animal conserve water (Bauchop 1978, Thornton et al. 1970). As a result, porcupines in the summer can obtain all their water requirements from the leaves they eat. In my study area, most high-mountain water sources such as seeps, pools, and rivulets dry up from mid-July to September, yet my radiotelemetered animals do not migrate to the valleys at that time. I have further documented the absence of drinking by maintaining porcupines on tree leaves alone for five-day periods. They had no interest in water I offered afterward. For that capability, they must give thanks at least in part to their digestive bacteria.

Before the enzymes and bacteria can do their work, the food supplied must be reduced to a fine, almost dust-particle size. Porcupines carry three kinds of teeth well suited to the tasks of scraping, gnawing, and grinding rough foods—4 incisors, 4 premolars, and 12 molars. The teeth are symmetrically placed in each quadrant of the mouth, hence the dental formula reads (I 1/1, C 0/0, P 1/1, M 3/3) × 2 = 20 (I means incisor, C canine, P premolar, M molar). The formula represents the teeth of the upper and lower jaws on one side of the mouth, times 2 for the total for both sides.

Porcupine incisors are the longest teeth in the set. They are faced with a bright orange enamel that contains iron salts, functioning as hardening agents. Because the outer surfaces are harder than the inner ones, they can be sharpened to produce a chisellike occlusal edge on each tooth. The sharpening is done by the reciprocal action of the opposite incisors (Macdonald 1984). The chisel edges are excellent tools for scraping bark and for nipping small twigs (required for leaf-feeding). No amount of scraping or nipping can wear out the incisors because, as in all rodents, they grow continually from deep inside the jaws. Although each incisor loses 100% of its length to wear in a year's chewing, its length always

Skull of a one-year-old porcupine. A diastema separates incisors and cheek teeth. All cheek teeth have erupted, but the deciduous first premolar will be replaced by a larger, permanent premolar at two years of age.

remains the same. The thin layer of enamel reveals a further level of structure when cross-sectioned and studied under a high-powered microscope. The enamel is built up from crystalline prisms. In porcupines as in most other rodents, the enamel contains several layers, with prisms in adjacent layers oriented in different directions. This plywood principle of enamel architecture gives it great resistance against cracking and chipping (Koenigswald 1985).

A porcupine's mouth has two chambers. The incisors sit in the outer chamber, or vestibule. When one examines a porcupine in a tree through binoculars, the animal appears to be grinning, its large orange incisors exposed. In fact, the lips are closed behind the incisors, across the toothless stretch of jaws between incisors and premolars called the diastema. The arrangement allows the animals to rasp off the outer bark of trees in the winter while keeping their inner mouths closed and warm.

Bark or leaves are ground to a fine consistency by the cheek teeth—the premolars and molars inside the inner chamber—which work like millstones. In hystricomorphs (though not in all rodents) the jaw motion is front to back, not sideways as in our own mastication. The cheek teeth have a level, slightly rippled grinding surface, resulting from vertical folds of hard enamel, that is to say, the grinding surfaces have alternating hard and soft domains. Porcupine cheek teeth, unlike the incisors, have fixed roots. Once worn down by a lifetime of chewing, they cannot be replaced. In very old animals, the cheek teeth are ground down close to the gum line and have lost most of their occlusal relief. When the process continues, there may be exposure of the pulp cavity and decay may set in. Porcupines are long-lived animals; the limit on their life expectancy may well be set by erosion of their grinding teeth. In fact, animals over 12 years old are smaller and less well fed than animals of middle age (Earle and Kramm 1980).

As in all mammals, a porcupine's tooth complement changes with age. For the first two years of life, tooth complement alone gives a measure of age (Sutton 1972, Dodge 1967). A porcupine is born with eight teeth: four incisors and four deciduous premolars are fully erupted. During its first summer (by four months of age), its jaw elongates to accommodate additional teeth. It adds a set of first, then second molars. Early next summer, when it has finished its first year of life, it adds the third molars. The adult tooth set is reached a year later, at age 2. At that time, the deciduous premolars are lost and replaced by permanent premolars. Because the permanent premolars are larger than either the deciduous premolars or the molars, they are easily identified in the mouth.

Beyond two years, accurate ages can be obtained by the technique of tooth sectioning (Earle and Kramm 1980). A cheek tooth is extracted from a dead animal and soaked in dilute acid to remove calcium. What remains of the tooth is its collagen matrix, retaining both the original shape and inner structure of the tooth. The matrix can be sectioned and stained to reveal cementum growth rings, one for each year the tooth has been in place. Thus a four-year-old animal will show four growth rings in its first and second molars, three in the third molars (which were added a year later), and two in the premolars (added at age 2). The incisors, growing continuously, show no rings.

Winter Adaptations

During Catskills winters, while bears and woodchucks sleep below the ground, the porcupine remains active in the snow. Its species range extends to the tundra line, and in places porcupines have been reported living on

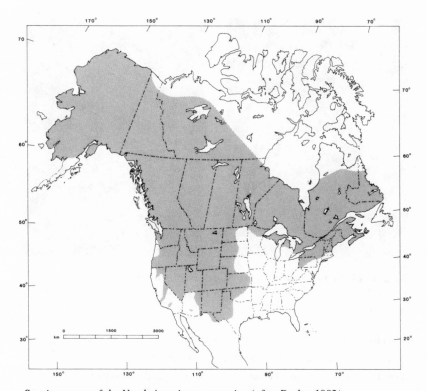

Species range of the North American porcupine (after Dodge 1982).

the tundra itself, a remarkable performance for a South American immigrant. Part of the porcupine's winter adaptation is behavioral. It spends much time in a den (abandoning it after snowmelt); it reduces travel and moves in the snow in its own tracks or under rock overhangs. But for winter survival, porcupines are equally indebted to anatomy. They prepare themselves for the coming winter from midsummer onward. Most important of their preparations is replacement of the underfur they have molted at the beginning of summer.

Porcupines grow five types of hair: the quills, bristles on the undersurface of the tail, vibrissae (whiskers), guard hairs, and fur. The guard hairs, which resemble long, thin, barbless quills, help shed rain and sleet and convey tactile information about the immediate environment (Po-Chedley and Shadle 1955). The fur, however, constitutes the animal's heat shield, helping to maintain a temperature differential from +37°C inside the body

Scanning electron microscope views of quill shaft (left) and guard hair (×200).
The barbs on the quill are responsible for its one-way movement through
the body.

to as low as −35°C outside. The same differential exists between a glass of boiling water and a room-temperature table below it. In the inorganic system, the water soon cools down, the table warms up, and the differential is diminished or lost. But in the porcupine-snowbank system, the temperature differential remains undiminished for weeks, perhaps months of hard winter. Such a performance must begin with good insulation, in this case the porcupine's fur. The fur is renewed each fall, growing back after the spring molt. It is so thick that it hides all but the long rosette quills. Porcupines in the winter have a fluffy, deceptively cuddly appearance. The illusion is enhanced by their tendency to roll up into a ball when resting on a high tree branch. I see them often in the branches, when I walk the mountains on a calm winter day. They are always alone in the tree, lying still and without sound, and symbolizing the dark, banked-down spirits of winter. Fur of the eastern porcupine is typically black, more or less straight, but with a fine undulation that increases the amount of trapped air. When viewed under the scanning electron microscope, the fur shows a groove on one side, which may give rise to its undulating pattern.

As mentioned in Chapter 2, one area of the porcupine's body is sparsely furred even in winter—the rosette. Steven Clarke and Robert Brander

(1973) have made infrared measurements of surface body temperatures of porcupines on winter nights. On the night of February 28, 1969, near Amherst, when outside air temperature measured $-14°C$ and the "sky temperature" was $-32°C$, an adult female in an open field showed the following surface temperatures: back $-13°C$, side $-11°C$, rosette $-7°C$. That is to say, the animal's back was so well insulated that it measured only marginally warmer than air temperature (though still considerably warmer than the heat sink of the sky). The rosette was $6°C$ warmer than the back, indicating increased heat loss. External insulation over the rosette consists mainly of layers of long quills laid horizontally over each other when the animal is at rest. Even though the quills contain internal air cells, they are less effective as insulation than the long underfur. The rosette is also internally insulated by a subcutaneous layer of fat averaging 15 mm thick in early winter. The layer disappears, however, by late winter as the animal taps it for emergency fuel. The reason for the slight warming of the sides is that the fur is shorter there than on the back, especially as it tapers down to the belly.

One reading that Clarke and Brander did not record was thermal emission from the naked and relatively large footpads. How do porcupines avoid heat loss from these potential radiators? The footpads of porcupines in the winter feel cold to the touch, much colder than the belly. Other northern animals with warm bodies but cold feet, such as the snow goose, have a countercurrent heat exchange mechanism. Small arteries, carrying heated blood to the feet, run adjacent to small veins, carrying cold blood back to the body. As the two vessels continue their parallel paths but countercurrent circulations, heat from the arteries radiates out to warm the returning blood in the veins. The process is so efficient that when arterial blood reaches surface capillaries in the feet, almost no heat is dissipated because it has all been returned to the body. It seems possible that porcupines have evolved a similar mechanism.

But porcupines are not perfect thermos flasks—they do lose heat to the environment. At external temperatures variously estimated between $-4°C$ to $-12°C$, resting porcupines cannot maintain body temperature through normal basal metabolism (Clarke 1969, Irving et al. 1955). They increase their metabolic rates, the equivalent of turning on the furnace on a cold winter night. Using the tail when a leg is paralyzed, scraping bark when tree leaves fall, turning up the metabolic rate when insulation fails—these are porcupine responses to adversity. Perhaps it is that flexibility of response, not a perfected body plan, that has allowed the porcupine to expand its species range in a continent it invaded only three million years ago and to hold it almost everywhere the forests grow.

.4.

Spring Foraging

The winter is over. In the second week of April, I spot a drop of lemon yellow on the trail, a round-leaf violet in first bloom. I am sweeping through the valley, tracking Rebecca but not believing my own antenna. Rebecca's radio pulse is coming from the wrong side of the Roarback; I suspect a reflected signal. As I spiral in on her, passing an open Canada anemone and a stand of Carolina spring beauty, I find myself in an unfamiliar part of the valley, a corner of our own woods that I have seldom explored.

Rebecca announces her position from a distance: her dark mass hangs so far out in the small outer branches of a tree that it seems to float in air. The tree is a tall, vigorous sugar maple. As I nail a small plastic identification label to the tree, I notice that Rebecca has begun to move. She is not trying to climb higher—there is nowhere higher left to go. She has begun to feed.

I lie down under the tree to watch. Periodically the dark body elongates and two arms appear, then a branch is gathered in and the body resumes its rounded form. Through the binoculars I see Rebecca has nipped off a good-sized terminal branch and is holding it in her paws. She is nibbling off the maple buds, turning the twig over and over in her paws to check that all buds have been consumed. This is a new mode of feeding. The previous week she was still in her winter feeding mode, concentrating on hemlock and on the bark of sugar maple. The difference is that this week the maple buds have burgeoned large enough to be worth harvesting. As Rebecca turns the twig in her paws, she sometimes abbreviates it by nibbling off a spur. A few twigs have already been processed and thrown away; all remain snagged high up in the canopy. But now she nips off a small piece, which starts its way down, bouncing from branch to branch in the sugar maple yet always managing to break free and struggle lower. Freed of the maple, it hits the top of a second-story beech below it. The twig is almost snagged and hangs, undecided, for a second before plunging its last free fall. I examine it. It has been carefully processed. The smallest twigs have been nipped off in entirety; the large buds along the sides have been excised. Only a few small buds on the inner surfaces of branch forks remain. I silently admire Rebecca's workmanship.

I look again at the trees and sky above me. The vertical masses of tree trunks are holding up the vast lacework of bud-swollen branches. The evenly spaced buds of beech and sugar maple, dark knots against the sky, generate a large-scale rhythmicity. The red maples are in flower, a red smoke rising in the canopy. It is the end of day. The air is absolutely still. High above, I hear the light rasping of the porcupine gathering her spring harvest. For her as for many animals that feed on the forest, the period of greatest abundance is just beginning.

Plant Chemistry

The Catskills forest is deciduous. With few exceptions, the trees shed leaves in the fall and enter six months of winter dormancy. Porcupines who feed on the bark and twigs of the dormant trees are slowly starving. Their weight drops steadily, their fat reserves are depleted, and they reach a low point of existence. Most of the natural deaths in my porcupine population occur during winter. That famine is followed by the richest feast of the year as trees pump nutrients out of deep storage and into swelling buds and unfurling leaves. Major changes are generated in plant tissue chemistry.

The concept of a changing plant tissue composition flies in the face of our deeply ingrained concept of constancy in the body tissues of animals. Regardless of what animals may eat, how much they exercise, or what the time of year may be, there is little change in the balance of major ions and organic molecules in their blood and internal tissues. The same is not true of plants. The cell sap of trees may undergo violent fluctuations in nitrogen, sodium and potassium, hydrogen ion, and a variety of complex organic molecules. Those levels may fluctuate from season to season, from day to night, and from one part of a plant to another. It is the genius of the porcupine to become aware of the changes and to exploit them for its own needs.

We do not know how porcupines learn that the April buds of a sugar maple have suddenly become more nutritious than the maple bark they were gnawing a week before, but it is clear that the porcupines failing to show such discrimination would not survive. It is remarkable not only that porcupines are able to track the changing resources available in the forest but also that they appear to do so almost instantaneously. Springtime changes in sugar maple illustrate some of these principles. While snow still covers the ground and buds are still tiny, the turgor pressure in the sapwood begins to rise on the warm, sunny days that follow cold nights. Catskill farmers know it as the running of maple sap. The sap is collected in buckets, then boiled down in the sugar house to make maple syrup. Porcupines do not appear to share the farmers' excitement. They continue feeding on inner bark, and the tree may bleed along the edges of chewed areas. But the maple tree is changing under the influence of its internal sap flow. At first the roots grope deeper into the ground, searching out nutrients and water. Then buds begin to swell as leaf primordia expand inside. At the same time, the nutritional quality of the buds is rising.

Nitrogen Supply

For porcupines as for most herbivorous animals, the crucial dietary component is nitrogen (Mattson 1980). Nitrogen does not supply metabolic energy in the same sense that carbon does. Instead it is needed to build proteins (muscle, collagen, body enzymes), nucleic acids, and a range of important small molecules. The bulk of our dietary nitrogen comes from meat products, from eating the bodies of other animals. Since porcupines feed on plants exclusively, they depend on them for nitrogen. But plants are generally poor nitrogen sources.

Nitrogen content is typically expressed in terms of crude protein level. The crude protein content of porcupine winter foods (bark, evergreen twigs and needles) ranges from 2% to 6% in the Catskills (as compared with 100% for lean meat). That is not enough to replace normal wear and tear of body tissues, and porcupines lose more nitrogen in urine and feces than they gather in their diet. Their body weights decline.

The swollen buds of sugar maple show nitrogen levels that are, comparatively speaking, stratospheric. The maple buds collected by Rebecca average around 22% crude protein (dry weight basis), more than that of most enriched breads and cereals. The twig tips carrying the buds average only 8.5% crude protein. By excising the buds and throwing away the twigs, Rebecca was showing a fine discrimination in food quality.

Catskills porcupines use other foods with properties similar to sugar maple buds. A food much preferred by Rebecca has been the buds of linden trees. The linden is a rare tree in the mountain forests, hence its contribution to the diet is lower than that of sugar maple. But because the linden is intensively browsed in both spring and summer, the trees often take on a

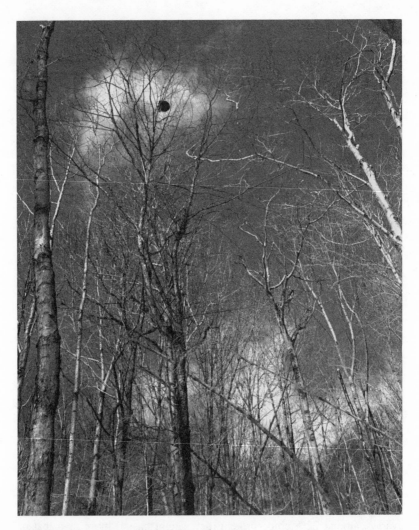

Finder samples sugar maple buds in early spring.

shorn look. I have tracked Rebecca to lindens where the ground below was littered with twigs whose buds had all been surgically excised. Although linden buds show lower crude protein content than sugar maple buds, they are available earlier in the year.

Another spring delicacy is the catkins of quaking aspen. Catkins emerge before the leaves do, and by late April the aspens are hung with fluffy, pen-dulous wind-pollinated flowers that are a promise of brighter green to come. Quaking aspen is a sun-loving tree and is not found in mature forest. The porcupines must therefore travel to find the trees on the edge of forests and in abandoned clearings. They feed as they do in maple and linden, by nipping off terminal twigs, then discarding the twigs. Because aspen branches are brittle, the porcupines nip them closer to the trunk. Aspen niptwigs can be quite large. Again, nitrogen analysis shows a big difference between tree parts harvested and parts rejected. Catkins contain 20% crude protein, the rejected twigs only 7%.

During early spring, some porcupines continue feeding on hemlock twigs and needles, a winter food. The porcupines that do so have left their dens early and are using hemlock habitat for shelter. Edible portions of hemlock average only 8% crude protein. Hemlock drops out of the diet entirely by early May.

Phenolics

Porcupine feeding choices change rapidly during the months of April and May. One week all animals may be feeding on buds of sugar maple. Fourteen days later, not one animal may be found on that diet. The difference is that the forest has turned green with leaves. With bud-break, new opportunities are opened at the same time as old ones are foreclosed. In the case of sugar maple, buds represent food, leaves poison. Once sugar maple leaves are fully open, porcupines climb the trees only to rest, never to feed. The difference between buds and leaves has little to do with crude protein content. Rather, the difference reflects a plant defense against its predators.

In the seventies, Paul Feeny (1976, 1970) of Cornell University showed that young oak leaves defend themselves against winter moth caterpillars by secreting high levels of defensive compounds called tannins, complex molecules composed of phenolic subunits. Their biological effectiveness results from their ability to complex with proteins (Harborne 1988). For example, the reaction of tannins with animal skins converts hides into leather. Feeny classified plant defenses into two categories. Qualitative defenses include all the metabolic poisons such as cyanide of wild cherry, atropine of belladonna, nicotine of tobacco, cucurbitacins of the cucumber. Qualitative defense compounds are often effective in small quantities, requiring little investment from the plant. Their weakness is the relative ease with which herbivores can evolve detoxification pathways. Thus cucumber beetles, far from being deterred by cucurbitacins, have keyed in on the compounds as feeding attractants.

Feeny's second category of plant defenses was quantitative. The tannins produced by oaks, hemlocks, and other trees become increasingly effective as their concentration builds up. Feeny showed that in oak, winter moth larvae feed only on spring leaves with tannin contents below 1%. As tannin levels rise in the leaves, the larvae stop feeding on oak and turn to other food sources. By the end of the summer, oak leaves have accumulated tannin levels of around 6%. Feeny hypothesized that long-lived plants (for example, oak trees) that grow slowly and cannot avoid discovery by their predators should invest in quantitative defenses (see also Bryant et al. 1988). Such defenses are expensive to maintain but relatively sure to be effective. Short-lived plants such as weedy forbs and some wildflowers, which can escape by colonizing fresh locations, should invest in the cheaper qualitative defenses (cyanogens, alkaloids, and the like).

Because sugar maple fits the oak tree model, I wondered if its defense against porcupines might not follow the same strategy. I collected thick spring buds, extracted the tannins in hot methanol-water, and measured total phenol levels (a measure of tannin content). The test tube contents turned a pale blue, indicating tannins were present but in low concentration. Two weeks later, I collected young leaves from the same tree and repeated the measurement. The extract turned as dark as ink. By the first week of May, the phenol levels had risen from less than 2% (wet weight basis) in buds and emergent leaves to 6.5%, a level intolerable to porcupines. That is far more rapid than the rise of tannins in oak leaves.

The maple-porcupine-tannin story has a further twist. The Catskills forest contains four species of maple. The two most abundant species (and the two achieving the most massive sizes) are sugar maple and red maple. My students have trouble distinguishing between them. There are subtle differences in leaf shape and bark texture, but in the summer it takes an experienced eye to tell a red from a sugar. Yet for porcupines, the difference is absolute. In early spring, sugar maple buds form their most important food source. Red maple, either in bud or in the leaf stage, is never touched. The difference, once again, appears to be tannin content. Sugar maple is unde-

Adult male in a budding sugar maple. Once the leaves open, this tree will be abandoned as food.

fended in early spring, but red maple is at all times chemically well armored. Its buds, twigs, and leaves are always heavily laced with phenolics, and porcupines respect the difference.

Beech

With the disappearance of sugar maple from the list of spring foods, my porcupines rapidly move to alternate food sources. I discovered this one mid-May while radio-tracking along a hillside. The sun was setting. Along the ridgetops, the forest was still bare, but here at lower elevations, a fresh green adorned most trees. Ahead of me, Squirrel's signal grew stronger, and then I saw her through the undergrowth. She was up a wrist-diameter beech tree and barely 12 feet off the ground. The tree was kinked at the top, and she rested on an S-shaped twist in the trunk. I stood below my porcupine quarry and looked up. The little beech tree carried young leaves. Canopy-height beech above it were still in the bud stage. In the background, a towering red maple reddened the sky with emerging leaves. Squirrel stared down at me silently. Though she now remained motionless, the evidence of her activities lay under my feet. The ground was littered with fresh niptwigs, their proximal ends cut at an angle and the leaves chewed off except where a twig had fallen out of the animal's grasp. I tasted a few of the leaves. They had a faintly astringent, salad flavor. When I brought the leaves into the lab to measure total phenols, I found a value below 1%, well within the porcupine tolerance.

I reflected on the porcupine's powers of discrimination. It had to realize not only that beech trees are coming into leaf this week but also that the beech trees in leaf are the understory saplings, not the adults in the canopy above. And since most porcupine feeding takes place at night, the distinctions would have to be made in the dark.

Ash

Two or three weeks later, another spring food enters the porcupine menu: the young leaves of white ash. Ash leaves are among the last to emerge in the spring; once they have done so, the forest canopy closes and spring wildflowers melt away. Ash quickly displaces beech as the major porcupine spring food, though beech consumption continues at a lower rate for several weeks. Part of the reason may have to do with the ease of climbing the two trees. The smooth bark of beech places it among the most difficult trees for porcupines to climb. Porcupines almost never climb beech trees to rest. Ash trees, on the contrary, have a finely furrowed bark that offers excellent claw-holds. Ash also have much larger leaves than beech. A single compound ash leaf may weigh three to four grams, a single beech leaf perhaps one tenth that amount. Ash leaves are low in tannin content, below 1% total phenol.

Ash leaves, like all others, are harvested by the niptwigging technique. Ash niptwigs are striking; they look like green-quilled stick-figure porcupines. Each twig is surrounded by a bush of long green petioles (leafstalks). To determine why foraging porcupines reject the petioles, I compared tannin levels and nitrogen content of leaf blade, petiole, and twig. Tannin levels did not differ significantly. But leaf parts collected in June showed marked differences in crude protein levels: leaf blades 16.1%, petioles 5.5%, terminal twigs 7.0%. It is clear that porcupines feed only on the leaf portions richest in protein, a selectivity made possible by the care-

White-ash niptwigs. The small spurs are petioles of leaves whose blades have been consumed.

ful manipulation of individual niptwigs. The rejection of petioles has proved to be a general feature of porcupine tree-feeding; in every case examined, the petioles contain less nitrogen than the leaf blades. Howler monkeys (*Alouatta* spp.), which occupy the leaf-feeding niche in Central and South America, show a similar antipetiole bias in at least some of their feeding.

Ground-feeding

A number of authors report porcupines feeding on ground vegetation during spring and summer months. Wendell Dodge (1967) in western Massachusetts lists grasses, violets, and dandelions as important spring foods. Graham W. Smith (1982), working in a northeast Oregon Douglas fir–juniper forest, found porcupines feeding in the spring on succulent ground vegetation. When the ground cover dried out in July, porcupines returned to their winter diet of tree bark and evergreen needles. One interesting case of ground-feeding comes from the desert country of Colorado and Arizona, as described by Julio Betancourt, Thomas Van Devender, and Martin Rose (1986). Here the porcupines feed on grasses and such flowering herbs as thistle, goosefoot, bindweed, and clover. There is no question the animals do this: the plant remains have been found in their droppings. Desert porcupines probably shelter from daytime heat in caves and emerge at night to harvest available green vegetation.

Ground-feeding represents a geographical variation in feeding behavior. Neither deserts nor evergreen forests present the springtime feeding opportunities available in the mixed hardwood–hemlock forests of the Catskills. The only ground vegetation I have observed my porcupines feeding on consistently has been raspberry leaves. Like all other preferred spring foods, the raspberry is a low-tannin, high-protein food. It makes up a relatively small fraction of the spring food of free-ranging porcupines. However, captive porcupines will eat armfuls of raspberry canes if they are offered. Ion, a giant male and the first porcupine I radiocollared, spent several weeks in our basement until a radiocollar could be shipped. Ion adapted well to a diet of rodent chow and water, but his great love was apples (which he took from my hand) and early-May raspberry canes. Twice a day

I brought in a load from our garden sufficient to crowd his spacious cage. Twice a day I returned to pull out defoliated stems. In the confines of the cage, the porcupine's feeding technique did not show the neatness observed in the wild, but it was clear that he was again avoiding the petioles. Ion ate up so many of our raspberries that our summer crop was significantly reduced.

At least three physiological consequences follow from the rich spring diet of porcupines. First, they put on weight at the most rapid rate seen during the yearly cycle. Second, they molt their winter fur, retaining only guard hairs, quills, and tail bristles. Third, the spring diet leads to sodium loss and hence a sometimes-fatal lust for salt. The last phenomenon is explored in Chapter 5.

Weight Gain

Human beings, accustomed to a relatively constant body weight year-round, may be surprised by the large annual weight swings of wild animals. An adult British hedgehog starts life in spring weighing about 600 g (1.3 pounds). After a summer's feeding, it has ballooned to 900 g, a 50% increase (Morris 1983). Essentially all of that weight will be lost again during winter hibernation. Free-ranging bull elk from Alberta have spring body weights of about 200 kg (440 pounds) and reach 300 kg by late summer (Gates and Hudson 1979). Then they begin to lose weight because of the stress of the breeding season. The loss continues during winter starvation.

Swings in porcupine body weights are less extreme, though still large compared with humans. Adult females gain approximately 25% during the nonwinter feeding period (April 15 to October 15). The weight gain, however, is not evenly distributed over the summer, as illustrated by the 1983 weight data for the porcupine Squirrel (Table 4). From April 30 to June 10, the animal was gaining weight at the spectacular rate of 0.63% per day, corresponding to an annual increase of 230%. Much of the increase was pumped into a growing fetus: Squirrel gave birth on June 12. The weight drop observed on July 10 was caused by the loss on parturition. Despite the drain of lactation, Squirrel continued gaining weight in July and August, almost reaching her weight of June 10. The midsummer weight gain was accomplished at the slower rate of 0.11% per day, corresponding to an annual increase of 40%. The difference is accounted for by lactation drain as well as the lower quality of summer forage.

Molting

Like the spring weight gain, molting is another mammalian phenomenon without a close counterpart in human experience. And like spring weight gain, molting in the porcupine is diet-controlled. Not all mammals go through a synchronized molt. Hedgehogs, the porcupines' spiny look-alikes, molt hair and quills gradually, a few at a time (Morris 1983). Likewise, humans replace their hair gradually, a few strands at a time. Not so the porcupine. It may molt all of its winter fur (but not its quills or guard hairs) in one burst in early spring.

I encountered the male Finder on one such occasion, in early May. The trees were still bare, but maple buds were thick and ready to burst. As Finder's signal pulled me toward the ridgetop, I encountered glades of wildflowers. There were green expanses of wild garlic, its pungent leaves protected against insect and mammal feeders alike. Toothwort was gathered in thick stands, with patches of dark-leaved blue cohosh. Yellow round-leaf violets were in bloom, along with the larger Canada violets, white on top and purple below. But Finder was not wandering among such splendors. He had been feeding on sugar maple buds. Under the tree I found a prodigious amount of niptwigs, most with buds excised but a few still intact, having slipped out of the animal's grasp. I looked up. Pressed vertically against a branch, his body was surrounded by an irregular halo of loosed fur. Every once in a while, a tuft broke loose and floated away on the breeze. A week later, the molt was finished. Finder looked sleek and glistening, clothed now only in quills, guard hairs, and tail bristles.

Other porcupines were molting at the same time. Ten hours after I had watched Finder's fur blowing like a dandelion clock, I captured Eight, a medium-sized male chewing for salt in a woodshed. Great projections of hair gave his body a ragged outline, and in crevices of the woodshed I found tufts of shed fur, lost while the porcupine was squeezing through.

The molt continued through my next encounter six days later. A spring storm had driven Eight into a ground den. In the entrance I found masses of molted fur, plus a dozen quills, presumably loosened by his long claws as he combed himself. Far from the male's ground den, I located my old female Squirrel. She had been sheltering through the storm in a hemlock tree. Under the tree lay a mat of porcupine fur, evidence of ongoing molt.

All three animals were molting in the first and second weeks of May. The snow pack had melted a month before, and rising temperatures would make any winter fur superfluous. But two animals, captured in March of the same year and kept at home, began molting in the last week of that month. Had they done so in the wild, they would have risked freezing to death or exhausting their already depleted body reserves needed to support metabolism. The first animal captured was Cameo, an adult female. On March 10, in deep snow and intense cold, I found her in a moribund state. She allowed me to remove her collar without anesthesia, indicating an alarming decline of the will to live. I decided to gather her in till she rebuilt her strength. A day later I encountered a baby porcupine in a foot-deep open rock crevice. It carried no radiocollar, but an eartag identified it as Topmost, a male born the previous May. Its weight was barely four pounds and its strength so low that I decided to gather it in along with Cameo. The two animals adapted well to captivity and to their diets of apples and rodent chow. Both put on weight. On March 23, twelve days after capture, I found Topmost sitting on top of his food bowl like a teddy bear, all paws folded in front. His appearance was somewhat spoiled by stray tufts of fur emerging from his body. On following mornings the floor of his cage was matted with squashed fur tufts. On March 27 the molt peaked. I had to clean his cage twice a day and collected enough fur to stuff a small pillow. His body had an irregular outline as fuzzy locks raised the contour. He was losing almost no quills or guard hairs. By March 29, his molt was finished. No more hairballs appeared in his cage, and he was looking sleek and well groomed. But now Cameo, sitting in an adjacent cage, began the process. Her hair tufts first appeared on March 28, peaked on April 1, and were substantially finished by April 4. Both animals finished molting within six days, roughly the same time span shown by animals in the wild.

While the animals were captive, I was running Kjeldahl nitrogen analyses of their droppings to get a rough indication of nutritional status. At the time of capture, both sets of droppings were averaging 6% crude protein, typical winter levels in starving animals. Within seven days, crude protein levels in their droppings had jumped to 20%, a value normally reached only during mid-May feeding. The nitrogen status of molting animals in the wild shows the same picture. Droppings collected from molting free-ranging porcupines show crude protein values between 15% and 23%, suggesting that in the wild as well as in captivity, the spring molt of porcupines is induced by a rise in dietary nitrogen. The picture is complicated by an underlying biological clock. Porcupines gathered from the wild and fed high-nitrogen diets in December do not molt.

If a rise in dietary nitrogen induces the spring molt in porcupines, it would constitute an ecologically well-designed trigger. In many mammals, the spring molting trigger appears to be an increase in day length (Ebling and Hale 1970). That might not be a reliable signal for porcupines, who show considerable environmental variability in den-quitting times. A ground-denning animal that is active nocturnally may see little daylight. On the other hand, the high-nitrogen pulse of spring foods represents in itself a climatic as opposed to a calendar signal. The emergence of buds and leaves of spring reflects local growing conditions. For example, sugar maples on top of Vly Mountain (altitude 3530 feet) experience bud-break two weeks later than the same species in the valley below (altitude 1500 feet). The locations differ not in day length but in average temperature and snowfall, the very factors with which the winter fur must cope.

Late Spring Diet

The spring diet of the porcupine continues to evolve. Sugar maple buds, crucial in early spring, drop out of the diet with bud-break. Leaves of beech and ash, which filled the gap left by loss of sugar maple, decline more slowly and are replaced by true summer species. The reasons for the decline of beech and ash remain to be elucidated. For beech, total phenol levels gradually climb to 2% wet weight. Perhaps more important, the succulent young leaves turn tough and papery. Whereas a young beech leaf tastes little different from a tart lettuce, the mature leaf has the quality of parchment. The decline of ash has no such obvious basis. Its leaf tannin content, whether measured as total phenol or as condensed tannin, is among the lowest of all forest trees. It is possible that ash develops other defenses that eliminate it entirely from the porcupine's diet by mid-June.

All trees on the porcupine's spring and summer diet, however, have one potent and unbreachable defense against herbivores. They disrupt the leaf-eater's sodium metabolism, driving porcupines to chew on barns, cabins, and human implements—a topic explored in the following chapter.

.5.

Salt Drive

On a mild May midnight, I am driving north through the Notch, a 3.5-mile stretch of highway with hills rising so steeply on either side that no houses or hunters' cabins punctuate the wilderness. Suddenly I am braking for a small gray shape out of the night. A porcupine, with unhurried dignity, is crossing the road. Down the highway, a less lucky animal lies with quills scattered, hit by a passing car. Driving slowly now, I spot two more porcupines apparently feeding by the road. Then another roadkill, then two more active animals. I am astonished. In 3.5 miles I have encountered five active porcupines. During most of the year, a single porcupine by the road would be noteworthy.

I turn and head back—I want to see if my passage has scattered the animals, and I am curious about their activities. As I reach the first one, I pull off to the side, leave the car's headlights on, and get out for a look. The animal is chewing something, but as I get close, it drops the object and moves back into the shadows. I pick up a small piece of deadwood clearly showing the porcupine's tooth marks. Deadwood contains no food calories for porcupines. The animal has been using the wood for a different purpose: it has been salt-feeding. The Notch is heavily salted by road crews during the winter. The last snows have disappeared a month ago, and spring rains have washed most of the salt out of the soil. But porous deadwood along the roadside has held some salt and attracted the porcupine. I confirm the presence of salt later, by laboratory analysis.

Retracing my path along the Notch, I count not five but six active animals. One is licking a wet spot in the middle of the road; the rest are active along the roadside. At the head of the Notch I pull over to write down my numbers and to recover from the shock of seeing so many porcupines in one night. A car pulls up alongside. A red light begins to flash—the state patrol. An officer leans out and asks, "You have any trouble?"

"No," I answer, and add, "There are a lot of porcupines on this road. Two of them got hit."

The officer looks at me sharply. "You all right?"

I see I have made the wrong impression, but blunder on, "I'm just trying to say to drive carefully."

"Oh, sure," the officer says, and speeds off.

I follow him at a distance and count only four porcupines on my third pass along the road.

69

The Notch remains an excellent place to watch porcupines on spring nights because the surface and shoulders of the road represent the single most concentrated salt source in the region. Farther north, in the old farming country of Lexington and Westkill, more attractive salt sources abound: farm outbuildings, cabins, and human implements. Here the animals are safe from speeding cars but face new dangers from aroused property owners who may resent having their cabin walls or truck undercarriages chewed.

Salt-seeking is not a behavior restricted to porcupines. The urge is observed in all large and medium-sized herbivores living in salt-depleted environments. It has been studied in deer, moose, elephants, woodchucks, fox squirrels, mountain goats, domestic sheep, and cattle, to name only a few. Nor is salt drive restricted to modern herbivores. It was present in sometimes-fatal form in the mastodons and mammoths of the Pleistocene. A spectacular collection of Ice Age elephant remains at Big Bone Lick, near the Kentucky-Ohio border, represents animals trapped in a salt-impregnated quaking bog (Teale 1965). They died ten thousand years ago, attracted by the bog salt and foundering on the unstable bog surface.

The metabolic basis of this ancient and deeply ingrained herbivore habit is tied to the beginnings of life. The first cells are thought to have evolved in a saline solution, and the interior of every cell today remains a salty environment. For animal cells, that is also true of the exterior of every body cell, but the salt components inside are different from the components outside. Salts inside the cells are largely potassium-based, the salts outside largely sodium-based. The opposed ionic gradients across the cell membrane set up an electric potential that is crucial to the function of nerve and muscle cells. During the action potential of nerve or muscle, sodium ions rush into the cell and potassium ions escape, causing a reversal of the electric potential. Without an excess of sodium ions outside the cell and potassium ions inside, a nerve cell cannot send messages and a muscle cell cannot contract. In herbivores, muscle and nervous tissues must maintain a 1:1 ratio of potassium to sodium ions. (Whole-body ratios tend to be closer to 2:1 because intracellular volume is larger than extracellular volume.) But herbivore diets, consisting only of plant tissues, diverge widely from that ratio. Plants contain no nerve or muscle and need only maintain the saline environment inside the cells. The result is that plant tissues contain potassium-to-sodium ratios as high as 500:1 (Weeks and Kirkpatrick

1978, 1976). Herbivores feeding on plant tissues are therefore flooded with unwanted potassium, which must be excreted to maintain internal balance. Because sodium and potassium are closely related chemically, the kidneys may not be able to excrete that volume of potassium without loss of essential sodium as well.

If an animal's potassium-sodium ratio rises significantly above 1, severe consequences may be expected. Perhaps the most dramatic example is the lethal injection used in some criminal executions. The injection is a cocktail consisting of a muscle relaxant, a nervous system depressant, and potassium chloride. The potassium salt stops the heart immediately. For animals in the wild, milder symptoms of a sodium-potassium imbalance appear well before that point. The animal shows apathy and lassitude as nerve and muscle functions decline, followed by weight loss as the body tries to raise its plasma sodium concentration by excreting water. Blood pressure falls, circulatory abnormalities develop (including edema of the brain with associated central nervous disturbances), and death follows.

To forestall such disasters, herbivore bodies tighten up hormonal mechanisms of sodium retention, and the animals actively seek sodium salts. One intensive study of sodium metabolism in a wild animal has focused on the moose of Isle Royale (Belovsky and Jordan 1981). Like the porcupines of the Catskills, the moose of Isle Royale face an environment impoverished in sodium. Terrestrial browse plants in the summer contain only 9 ppm (parts per million) sodium. The concentration in winter browse is even lower. Moose survive by feeding heavily on aquatic vegetation such as bladderwort (*Utricularia*), water lily (*Nuphar*), and the green alga *Spirogyra*, whose average sodium concentration of 2950 ppm approaches physiological levels in animal bodies. One of the surprising findings of the Isle Royale study has been that moose carry a great internal sodium reservoir, their rumen fluid. So much sodium is present in this fermenting stomach that the animals can draw on it during the entire year, whenever external sodium sources may not be available. Presumably a similar mechanism operates in deer, elk, cattle, and other ruminants. No one has studied the possibility that porcupines carry an internal sodium pool comparable to the rumen, but evidence discussed later in this chapter suggests strongly that such a reservoir may exist in the caecal fluid.

The Salthouse

To study salt drive in the porcupine, I built my own version of a Big Bone Lick. The Catskills are a sodium-depleted region, and any salt source will attract herbivorous animals. But what source could I provide that would attract porcupines alone, not white-tailed deer, woodchuck, red and gray squirrels, and other small herbivores? I built a structure I had known only porcupines to attack: a house. And I positioned it along a known porcupine path, a route the animals followed to our orchard and to the old barn beyond. Important details included broad eaves to keep weather off the sides. Finally I applied the attractant, in the form of salt-impregnated two-by-twos arranged as a palisade along the sides of the ten-by-fourteen-foot cabin.

To confirm that sodium was indeed the ion the porcupines were seeking, I interspersed sodium-impregnated sticks with untreated sticks and with sticks impregnated with the salts of other metals (calcium, potassium, iron, magnesium, manganese, copper, aluminum) and the nonmetallic am-

A palisade of salted wood surrounds the salthouse.

monium ion. I was to discover later that summer's end is a poor time to study salt drive. Nevertheless, within one week porcupines began arriving to chew the salt sticks. It was obvious at once that only one ion was being consumed: sodium. No other salts were of interest to the animals.[1]

The next task was to determine whether the porcupines preferred a particular concentration of salt. A feeding-choice experiment by J. C. Bloom and coworkers with captive porcupines in a laboratory setting suggested that they avoid concentrated salt solutions (Bloom et al. 1973). However, the test animals had been maintained for two months on a commercial diet before the tests began; any sodium deficit would have been fully satisfied. To explore the question, I installed sets of wooden pegs impregnated with sodium chloride at three concentrations: 0.15 normal (equivalent to the concentration of sodium in vertebrate blood plasma), 0.3 normal, and 0.45 normal (equivalent to the salinity of seawater). I reversed the pegs at two-week intervals and removed them after 30 days for weighing and replacement with freshly soaked pegs. The attractiveness of each peg was measured as the amount of wood removed per month. Typical results over five months in 1986 are shown in Table 5. For porcupines, the most concentrated salt source (at least up to 0.45 N) is the most attractive source. The data show that as salt concentration rises from 0.15 N to 0.3 N, wood consumption doubles, then levels off at higher concentration. Translated into salt consumption, the difference is larger. The true salt consumption is hard to quantitate because the sodium solutions did not permeate the deeper layers of wood. For that reason the sticks were turned and reimpregnated regularly.

Several nights spent inside the salthouse, listening as animals chewed the walls outside, gave me an insight into how porcupines explore their environment. On a July night, I arrived 15 minutes before midnight, just as a large porcupine, quills maximally erected, skulked off from the west side of the house. I didn't pursue; I expected it to be back later. The night was quiet. Roarback Creek had dried up for the summer, and the late-summer chorus of crickets had not yet tuned up. I had been lying inside the cabin for less than an hour when a loud rasping began from the east wall. A porcupine had arrived. The animal followed a rhythm in its work: five or six rapid scrapes of the wood, then silence for maceration and swallowing. It had been working for only a few minutes when there was a longer silence of about five minutes. When the scraping resumed, it was coming from a new position, a few feet removed from the previous site. After 20 minutes, a second porcupine arrived and started chewing on the middle of the north wall. The first arrival remained at work on the east wall.

I had assumed originally that each porcupine would choose a position and work there till it left. Instead, they were treating the salthouse as a sodium buffet, moving at regular intervals to sample new sticks for shorter or longer periods. At the same time, the two animals maintained a wide spacing between themselves. At 1:25 a.m., the two chewers were grinding on opposite sides of the salthouse, the first animal now on the north side, the second on the south. I felt trapped inside a bass viol as the house vibrated under their powerful teeth. This was porcupine music, the sound of the wood saw. The first animal left at 1:35, one hour and five minutes after it had arrived. The second left ten minutes later. A third animal arrived much later, at 4:15 a.m., and chewed for only a few minutes before departing. At 5:15, in the gray of dawn, there was silence.

At other times when I have emerged from the salthouse to surprise the porcupines at work, I have found them clinging vertically, arms spread out to catch the tops of adjacent salt sticks. They wait silently in the glare of my headlamp, then drop to the ground and depart. But they leave behind an interesting piece of information: the salt stick they have been chewing is wet. That means they lick their targets, monitoring sodium levels continually with their tongues. It also helps explain why no porcupines visited the salthouse on rainy nights. The rain would have leached out surface ions and made all natural salt sources unattractive.

Another question the salthouse helped answer was whether porcupines respond directly to sodium concentration or to the potassium-sodium ratio in the salt source. I impregnated pegs with increasing ratios of potassium to sodium (as the nitrate salts) and followed porcupine response (Table 6). The clear lesson is that porcupines do respond to the ratio of potassium to sodium, not to absolute levels of sodium. That is appropriate behavior because a high potassium-sodium ratio in spring vegetation may be a major cause of their sodium deficit.

Porcupines show a strong seasonality of salt use. Visits to the salthouse stop almost entirely between November and March, only to resume with explosive force in April and May. The salt-feeding rate then declines

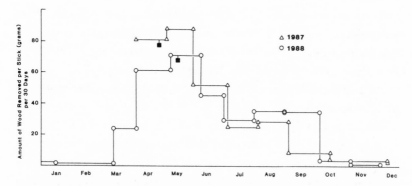

Seasonal demand for salt in 1987 and 1988. In both years, a secondary peak was observed in late summer. The longer secondary peak of 1988 correlated with an extended period of apple feeding. The dark squares in April-May mark bud-break in sugar maple.[2]

through midsummer and rises to a secondary peak in August-September. Any explanation of salt drive in porcupines must address the strong seasonality of salt use. I will return to that point.

Another observation that must be addressed is the strongly skewed sex ratio of salt-chewing porcupines. The porcupines that come to cabins and outbuildings in search of salt are overwhelmingly females. Between 1982 and 1988, I was able to determine the sex of salt-chewing porcupines 131 times; 102 of the animals (78%) were females. Though the sex ratio of my porcupines in the forest is female-biased, the bias is only 65%.[3] A similar female bias in salt drive has been demonstrated in white-tailed deer (*Odocoileus virginianus*) (Wiles and Weeks 1986). Certain females salt-chewed so often that I thought of them as salt junkies. Rebecca salt-chewed 5 times in the summer of 1982, 7 times in 1983, 3 times in 1984. Squirrel did the same 5 times in 1983, Moth 5 times in 1984. In contrast, males were typically found salt-chewing only once a summer. Since salt sources were not monitored every night, all those figures are minimums. For some females, the trips to salt sources represented long journeys (up to one kilometer) over difficult terrain. Rebecca often made the trip in two stages. On the first night, she moved down from her rugged mountain territory and camped out in a tree near the farm outbuildings. On the second night, she moved in to gnaw salted wood, then retreated again before dawn to her normal range up the mountain.

It is intuitively obvious why females should have a stronger salt drive than males: they lose sodium in their milk. Nursing infants don't visit salt sources; their mothers do. Only 3 of my 102 salt-chewing females have been juveniles (less than a year old), and all were accompanied by their mothers. But the intuitive understanding turns out to be an incomplete guide in this instance.

As long ago as 1938, Richter and Barelare showed that pregnant and lactating rats increase their salt intake, reaching a peak during lactation and dropping to normal levels soon after weaning. The phenomenon was explored in depth by D. Denton (1982) and his coworkers in Australia, who studied wild rabbits in a laboratory setting and found a 10-fold increase in salt intake by the end of pregnancy, rising to a 30-fold increase during the peak lactation period. Those spectacular rises in sodium intake cannot be accounted for on the basis of sodium used to build young bodies *in utero* or sodium lost in the milk. Well over 90% of the sodium taken in during pregnancy and lactation was lost in the urine. Clearly, the increased intake did not result from a sodium deficiency. Through a series of careful experiments, Denton showed that the hormones present during pregnancy and lactation, when offered in the appropriate sequence, will by themselves induce sodium drive, even in nonpregnant animals. At least four hormones are involved: estrogen, ACTH, prolactin, and oxytocin. Denton's experiments were carried out on laboratory-confined animals exposed to unlimited amounts of sodium. They could therefore afford to lose 90% of their sodium intake. The same animals in the wild, faced with a much more limited sodium supply, would no doubt have lost little in the urine. The point of the experiment is that hormone-induced sodium hunger in the animal serves a rational need in the wild: the metabolic needs of the fetus and the nursing infant are satisfied. A behavior that is irrational in the laboratory need not be such in the field. The sometimes strange dietary cravings of pregnant humans probably have a similar basis. No comparable experiments have been performed on porcupines, but since the same hormones are present in all pregnant and lactating mammals, there seems little reason to expect a different response.

In the Catskills, baby porcupines are born in May and early June. The broad peak of salt use begins in early April. And although males make up a minority of salt-chewing porcupines, they do visit salt sources on roughly the same schedule as females. Therefore, although hormonal factors may explain the skewed sex ratio of salt-seeking porcupines, they cannot explain the behavior entirely.

Other factors proposed as explanations for the spring salt binge in North American herbivores include changes in dietary potassium-sodium ratios and changes in dietary water content. Weeks and Kirkpatrick (1976), studying the salt-lick behavior of white-tailed deer in Indiana, show that the potassium-sodium ratio goes from 156:1 in winter diets to 485:1 in spring diets. Summer and fall ratios are 348:1 and 368:1 respectively. The authors propose that deer kidneys, which must excrete excess potassium and conserve sodium, cannot cope with the potassium flood and allow enough sodium to pass to drive the animals into a sodium deficit. The theory is an attractive one, but the authors' data on potassium-sodium ratios do not correlate perfectly with salt-lick use by the deer. On the other hand, an unbalanced dietary potassium-sodium ratio may explain the later half of the broad spring peak in porcupine salt drive. The dietary mileposts here are feeding on spring buds and feeding on young leaves. Both food sources have higher potassium-sodium ratios than winter bark, and both follow, rather than precede, the major pulse of spring salt-feeding in porcupines.

Weeks and Kirkpatrick (1976) postulate that one route of sodium loss may involve the spring feces. Many herbivorous animals, including deer and porcupines, produce hard, dry feces for most of the year. But during spring, the feces become soft, almost diarrhetic in nature. The explanation offered is that high dietary intake of potassium leads to high intestinal levels of potassium, which leads to decreased water resorption from the large intestine, which results in increased loss of electrolytes via the feces. I have measured sodium levels in porcupine feces by atomic absorption and found increased losses of potassium, but not sodium, during spring and summer (Table 7). Potassium loss peaked in May, when diarrhetic feces were produced. Fecal sodium loss did not change significantly at that time.

Another difficulty with the fecal loss theory in porcupines is the lack of timing between salt-chewing intensity and the production of diarrhetic feces. In April, when salt drive is near maximal, the porcupines are still feeding on spring buds and occasionally on bark and producing solid droppings. The first soft feces were observed on May 13 in 1986, April 25 in 1987, and May 15 in 1988. In that respect porcupines differ from ruminants such as the white-tailed deer (Weeks and Kirkpatrick 1976) and the mountain goat (Hebert and Cowan 1971), which show increased sodium loss in spring feces. If porcupines do in fact suffer increased sodium loss in the spring, the route would have to be via the kidneys. I have not measured urinary sodium losses in porcupines on an annual basis.

Reproductive hormones, dietary potassium-sodium ratios, and urinary sodium loss may all play a part in the salt drive of the porcupine. One additional hypothesis bears further investigation. The near-absence of winter salt-chewing may not reflect so much a lack of salt hunger as a lack of opportunity for its satisfaction. In the Catskills, the first surge of salt-chewing correlates best with the dates for abandoning winter dens. If the animals build up a sodium deficit through a six-month confinement in winter territory, that would be their earliest opportunity to satisfy it. The hypothesis would be strengthened if the porcupine could be shown to carry an internal sodium pool analogous to the rumen of the ruminants. If such a pool exists, it would most probably be found in the caecal fluid. Fecal sodium loss constitutes indirect evidence for such a pool. Although no annual peak in the process was observed (Table 7), there was a steady, low-level loss throughout the year. Fecal sodium loss would not be possible if gastrointestinal secretions did not contain sodium.

In the fall of 1986, direct evidence for a sodium pool was revealed through an unfortunate incident. An adult porcupine I had kept captive for a feeding-choice experiment suddenly died. (The animal had been kept for three days on an all-apple diet.) I discovered the body while it was still warm and did an immediate autopsy, taking samples of stomach fluid as well as caecal fluid and measuring their sodium and potassium levels by atomic absorption. Both fluids contained low potassium: 9 mM in stomach and 14 mM in caecum. The stomach fluid contained 41 mM sodium, but the caecal fluid had 142 mM sodium. The data show that the caecal fluid is essentially a pool of isotonic saline, similar to plasma or extracellular fluid. Because the volume of the caecum is relatively large, it represents a major sodium store on which the animal can draw over the winter when normal supplies are inaccessible. Those results should be confirmed by examining other porcupines, both through the course of the year and across the species range. I have not felt justified in killing porcupines to pursue this study; one of the challenges of the scientific enterprise is devising experiments to answer questions with greater elegance and smaller injury to the subject.

The hypotheses examined so far have addressed the factors responsible for the spring peak in salt drive. As mentioned earlier, porcupines exhibit a secondary peak in August-September, which coincides with a specific porcupine behavior, the period of apple-feeding (see Chapter 6). As discussed in the following chapter, porcupines consume large numbers of apples in late summer, replacing this food with available mast in the fall. In 1988 the mast crop failed (as it did in 1983 and 1986), and porcupines were forced to extend apple-feeding into early October. Salt drive in 1987 and 1988 paralleled apple use. The same correlation between apple-feeding and increased salt drive was shown in 1985 and 1986 (Table 8).

Apples are an imperfect porcupine food in several respects. One shortcoming is the relatively high acid content. By weight, apples contain several hundred times more organic acid than do alternate summer foods such as linden or aspen leaves. High acid load impairs sodium resorption in the mammalian kidney (Cogan and Rector 1982, Rose 1984), causing animals to lose sodium in their urine. In fact, porcupines showed strong selectivity among apples, avoiding high-acid fruit. To test the impact of apple-feeding on porcupine sodium retention more directly, I captured a number of animals and measured their urinary sodium excretion as a function of apple versus linden-leaf diet. Table 9, displaying the data for the adult male Killer, is illustrative. Sodium loss showed a 36-hour lag in response, increasing steadily for the two days the animal was on an apple diet and rising into the middle of the fourth day, when it plunged and remained very low for the duration of the experiment. The data predict that porcupines who do not feed on apples should not show a secondary peak in sodium drive. As a corollary, porcupines in sodium-rich areas such as seacoasts should show less selectivity in their apple-feeding.

Natural Salt Sources

When I built the salthouse, I designed it as a mineral supply for porcupines. Many other builders of houses and outbuildings near the woods have had no intention of seeing their houses converted to sawdust—porcupines visit them too. Although all large and medium-sized herbivores seek salt in sodium-depleted environments, porcupines alone seem to specialize in human salt artifacts. Yet porcupines have lived in North America incomparably longer than the earliest human inhabitants. How did they satisfy their salt needs before human settlement? A look at current behavior shows that porcupines are surprisingly versatile in locating naturally occurring salt sources.

Naturalists as long ago as the nineteenth century have observed porcupines swimming to reach the yellow water lily (*Nuphar* spp.) and feed on the leaves. the porcupine swims easily, buoyed by its quills, but prefers lily pads it can reach from some solid substrate. The great mammalogist C. Hart Merriam (1884) described the behavior a century ago: "When feeding on lily-pads along the borders of watercourses, they sometimes utter extraordinary noises; and occasionally quarrels arise from the possession of some log which affords them easy access to the coveted plants. At Beaver Lake, in Lewis County, New York, Mr. John Constable once witnessed an encounter during which one of the contestants was tumbled into the water. The animals did not attempt to bite, but growled, and snarled, and pushed."

The data of Jordan, Belovsky, and coworkers show why water lilies are such a prize. The yellow pond lily is the richest sodium source among all plants surveyed (Jordan et al. 1973). Its sodium content is 9375 ppm, as opposed to an average level of 9 ppm in terrestrial vegetation. That is why moose seek the plants, and others below the water's surface. Other high-sodium aquatics consumed by the porcupine include arrowhead leaf (*Sagittaria*) and the aquatic liverworts, as described by Curtis and Kozicky (1944) in Maine: "One animal was observed wading in a shallow pool, with water up to its belly. It kept its tail erect. It was found to be feeding on aquatic liverwort (*Riccia fluitans*), which it devoured with relish and in some quantity before detecting the observers."

Many herbivores obtain sodium from salt-enriched soil. They include white-tailed deer, elephants, colobus monkeys, certain parrots, and many others, along with porcupines. Olaus J. Murie (1926) describes mud-feeding porcupines in Alaska:

Early in June 1921 while hunting bears on the Robertson River, I found porcupines abundant on the river banks and sand bars. Judging by my observations at that time, the porcupines were feeding exclusively on mud. I watched many of them, and almost invariably saw that they were licking or chewing the fine sandy soil of the bars or river bank. At a distance of a few feet one could hear the grating of the sand in the animals' teeth and could plainly see that there was not a vestige of vegetation near. . . .

Parts of the river banks were gnawed and worn, where porcupines, and probably other mammals also, came habitually for a taste of mud.

About a decade after Murie's explorations, Walter P. Taylor (1935) dissected a porcupine in Arizona and found its stomach full of mud. Neither Murie nor Taylor made sodium measurements on their samples, but Taylor suspected the soil was consumed for its salt content.

The Vly Mountain area in the Catskills is poorly supplied with pond vegetation or natural salt licks. In early September 1982, I discovered a porcupine using an alternate salt source. During a round-the-clock monitoring of the female Squirrel, who was resting in an old sugar maple, one of my students encountered a bobcat (*Lynx rufus*). It came down silently from the mountain, stopped 12 feet from the student, and stared at her. After what seemed like a long silence, it turned and moved back up the hill. The student said her heart was pounding. That night, we discovered that the bobcat and the porcupine may have been interacting in a roundabout way. My second student, Cathy, took the dusk-to-midnight shift, when our porcupine should descend from her rest tree and start feeding. Promptly at 9 p.m. Squirrel descended from the rest tree and moved about 40 feet uphill, then began rasping at a hard object with her teeth. She rasped away for 20 minutes until Cathy, overcome by curiosity, finally turned on her light and moved forward to investigate. Squirrel scooted up a nearby ash tree for refuge. Perhaps because she was looking for a tree, Cathy could not find the object Squirrel was gnawing on. The next day we retraced Squirrel's route and found the object almost at once: the front and hind leg bones of a deer. The vertebral column and ribs were a short distance away. The deer-kill was relatively fresh, the bones free of flesh but retaining shreds of tendons, ligaments, and skin. It was clearly what the bobcat had come to pick at. But what a chewing the porcupine had given the remains! Every long bone was scraped as though it were made of soft plastic, exposing the marrow and sometimes leaving only a thin spiral of hard matrix. I studied the surfaces carefully and saw everywhere only the large, powerful groovings of porcupine teeth. There was no evidence of the smaller teeth of mice at work.

The primary mineral constituent of bone is calcium phosphate. Calcium is so abundant in the normal leaf diet of porcupines that it is excreted in high concentration in the urine.[4] Evidence from the salthouse shows that porcupines make no effort to seek that mineral. Fresh bone, however, also contains a significant amount of sodium. Some 25% of an animal's sodium pool is tied up in a poorly exchangeable form in its bones (Robbins 1983). That seemed to explain Squirrel's interest in the deerkill. It also helped explain why I had never observed her chewing on the farm outbuildings in the valley below, where her neighbor Rebecca had been visiting almost weekly and where she herself would visit frequently the following year.

The bobcat and the porcupine may have had an indirect interaction. The deer may well have been killed by the bobcat, though that is a rare event. The porcupine, in turn, may have assisted the bobcat by exposing the marrow cavities of the long bones—several had been eaten out. Years later, Wendell Dodge told me of trying to trap bobcats by using "ripe" meat as bait. The animal found sitting inside was often a porcupine. Walter P. Taylor (1935) also describes a single instance of deliberate scavenging. He quotes M. E. Musgrave, an employee of the Biological Survey, observing a porcupine in open desert near Bonito, Arizona. The animal was gnawing the dry carcass of a cow.

That brings up a related point. Though porcupines are commonly known as strict vegetarians, Taylor, in dissecting many porcupine stomachs in Arizona, notes as a curiosity that three stomachs contained animal matter. One held bits of a beetle plus an ant; two others held ant fragments. Taylor assumes they were ingested accidentally. In collecting fresh linden leaves, I have often found caterpillars clinging to the edge or hidden inside a rolled leaf. Common varieties in the Catskills include the larvae of the fall cankerworm (*Alsophila pometaria*), the fall webworm (*Hyphantria cunea*), the linden looper (*Erannis tiliaria*), and the American daggerwing (*Acronicta americana*). A porcupine feeding in total darkness may inadvertently ingest those tiny packages of sodium. But apparently that source alone cannot satisfy the animal's sodium needs, since the majority, at shorter or longer intervals, continue to seek additional sodium supplies.

Seastedt and Crossley (1981) point out that the outer bark of trees is surprisingly rich in sodium, averaging 546 ppm, probably deposited when stemflow is followed by evaporation of water. Such a source should be most rewarding in dry environments. The ever-observant Walter Taylor

A possible natural sodium supplement: caterpillars of the fall webworm
(Hyphantria cunea) *on linden leaves. Leaf-feeding caterpillars have relatively
low sodium content.*

(1935) notes that porcupine may on occasion feed on outer bark, a behavior
that must be clearly distinguished from winter bark-feeding, when the
inner portion of the bark is consumed.

Porcupines are also able to discover and harvest a novel sodium source in
the forest. The New York State Department of Environmental Conservation maintains a network of trails through the Catskill State Forest. In years
past, circular aluminum trail markers—about 7 cm in diameter and
painted, red, blue, or yellow—identified the different trails. The markers
were nailed to trees along the trail, spaced about 50 feet apart. While
climbing from Devil's Tombstone to the top of Plateau Mountain, I encountered a long string of trail markers with the paint rasped off in a sun-
burst pattern. Bare aluminum gleamed from the markers. The long tracks
of the scrapes identified the worker as a porcupine. The animal (or several
animals) had climbed each trailside tree in turn to reach the marker, then
held on in impossible positions to scrape the paint. None of the trees I ex-

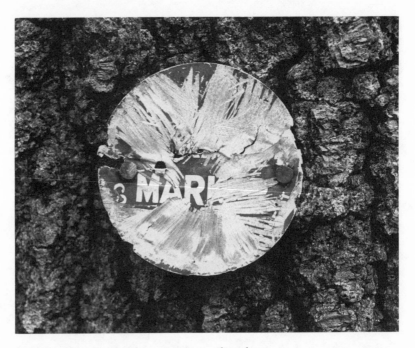

A novel sodium source: blue paint on a trail marker.

amined had been otherwise touched; there were no niptwigs and no signs of bark feeding.

To establish that the animals did not have an unexpected need for aluminum, I nailed 53 clear aluminum markers to one of our own trails. None has been disturbed in five years of observation, despite heavy porcupine traffic along the trail and leaf-feeding in some of the marked trees. The Plateau Mountain animals are therefore hunting the sodium in the blue paint (whose presence I determined by atomic absorption measurement). Their chewing is remarkable because each marker represents only a tiny packet of sodium and because it must be a learned behavior developed in a systematic way. The porcupines know their forests extremely well. New York State, incidentally, has switched to plastic trail markers.

The salt-seeking described here makes the porcupine, like the reindeer, a protodomesticated animal. Salt is a commodity the porcupine needs so badly that it will seek it from human sources. In so doing, it risks death and injury by challenging the most powerful predators in its environment: human beings.

Notes

1. Two-by-two pine lumber (5 cm $\times$ 5 cm $\times$ 39.5 cm) was impregnated with 0.15 N aqueous solutions of the sodium salts NaAc, Na_3 citrate, $Na_2B_4O_7$, Na_2CO_3, NaH_2PO_4, and Na_2SO_4, and with the nonsodium salts $AlCl_3$, $AlNH_4(SO_4)_2$, $Al_2(SO_4)_3$, $CaCl_2$, $FeSO_4$, K_2CO_3, K_3 citrate, KCl, K_2HPO_4, KH_2PO_4, K tartrate, $MgCl_2$, $MnCl_2$, NH_4Cl, $NH_4H_2PO_4$, $(NH_4)_2SO_4$. All salt sticks were prepared in duplicate and mounted randomly among 133 untreated sticks of the same size (ca. 250 g each) and shape. The salthouse was erected July 30, 1984. Between August 18 and September 23 no nonsodium sticks showed signs of chewing; all Na-containing sticks were chewed, with an average weight loss of 8.77 g $\pm$ 8.86 g per stick. Between August 3, 1984, and the end of the summer, five unique porcupines were captured at or near the salthouse.

2. Salt drive was expressed as weight loss per stick per 30 days. Wood was impregnated with 0.3 N NaCl and mounted as described in Note 1 above. Fifteen unique porcupines were captured at the salthouse in 1987, and the same number in 1988. Wood chewed per porcupine, March 13–August 1, was 485 g in 1987 and 471 g in 1988.

3. Salt-chewers between 1982 and 1988 (includes repeat visits): 29 males, 102 females. Unique animals captured over the same period: 33 males, 63 females. $\chi^2 = 4.18$, df $= 1$, $P < 0.05$.

4. Atomic absorption cation values for urine obtained by catheterization of an adult female, on August 21, 1985: Na 0.6 mM, K 106.9 mM, Ca 101.8 mM.

6

Summer and Fall Foraging

The active life of the porcupine, like that of most forest mammals, begins at dusk. Animals that may have spent the whole day in comfortable sleep on a tree branch descend in a darkened forest, travel to a feeding tree, and climb into the canopy for the nightly meal. By staying up the night with a foraging porcupine, one may encounter other forest mammals as well as owls, giant millipedes, and legions of moths, midges, and leaf-feeding caterpillars. And one may discover that the night forest is noisier and more full of life than its daytime counterpart.

A Night in the Woods

On a July night in 1982, I set out to observe Rebecca, a young adult female captured and collared only a week before. Earlier in the day, I tracked her to a linden tree on a steep hillside. As I move after nightfall, her radio signal pulls me back in the same direction. I am laden with gear: a miner's headlamp, radio receiver and directional antenna, rolled foam mattress with groundsheet, rucksack with extra jacket and poncho, altimeter, a small tape recorder, and gear for capturing porcupines. I reach the animal at 10:15. At first I don't recognize the surroundings in the dark. Then, 15 feet from Rebecca's feeding site, the aroma of porcupine urine envelops me. The ground downhill from the tree is saturated with it, but when I reach the main trunk, I smell nothing. Though porcupines seldom sleep by day in the same trees they feed in at night, Rebecca is up the same large linden tree I left her in that afternoon. She is too high to see, and the antenna does not discriminate with pinpoint accuracy. But proof comes at 10:21, with the sound of a large branch falling. That is followed by a porcupine dropping rattling down at 10:25, then more at 10:30, 10:36, and 10:42. The fallen branch is a classic niptwig, about 18 inches long, with the base cut cleanly at a 30-degree angle and leaves consumed down to the petioles. It carries some immature linden fruit—rejected along with the petioles. Rebecca is feeding highly selectively in total darkness.

On a level spot about 12 feet uphill from the trunk, I unroll my mattress and groundsheet and lie down to listen in the dark. A distant bird cries out sleepily.

The porcupine rustles in the canopy overhead. A fine patter of caterpillar frass is falling—caterpillars, like porcupines, feed mostly at night, and seem especially active in this part of the forest. The quiet sounds are punctuated by the thumps of porcupine droppings hitting the dry leaf litter, falling at the rate of approximately 15 per hour, sometimes in barrages of 5 or 6 at a time. The droppings are the size of deer pellets, with a gently crescent shape. At this time of year they are almost dry.

Deer mice keep up long bouts of squeaking, so high-pitched they border on the inaudible. Periodically some beetle buzzes against the dry leaves to get airborne. Most surprising is the heavy foot traffic along a small lumber road, perhaps 50 feet downhill, out of range of my flashlight. All night long I hear animals heading uphill and down. Some come close, catch my scent, and retreat. Others complete the passage and grow inaudible in the distance. Many are probably deer, but some may be porcupines, and I wonder whether Rebecca followed the same path to her present feeding site. Not all the passages are innocent. At midnight, I hear a small death scream in the distance. At 1:15 a.m. there comes the heart-stopping, choking-man cry of a black bear.

Despite the traffic below me, Rebecca dominates the night. In addition to the irregular bombardment of droppings, I hear large-scale movements, as though a branch is being shaken. Sometimes there is a grunting cough. At 1 a.m. a shower of urine splatters down; all of it seems to be caught by the understory of striped maple above me. A second shower comes at 4:25, as the sky begins to lighten. Above all, I hear the insistent tearing and crunching of linden leaves as Rebecca feeds in almost a frenzy in the early part of the night, to about 1 a.m. According to my tape recorder, the feeding tapers off in the small hours of the morning, but I doze off several times in the cocoon of my poncho.

At 6:15, a deep orange sun hangs in the green undercanopy, making it glow. The birds have been singing a loud morning chorus for an hour already, drowning out the subtle rustlings of the porcupine above. A wood thrush sings close to my position while remaining hidden from view. I stand up. A moment later, a small-headed fawn comes bounding down the hillside. Its legs seem to belong to some larger animal; its trunk is still dappled. Some 20 feet away, the fawn sees me and stops, moving its head up and down, plainly in a conflict between fright and curiosity. Suddenly the wind is right and it catches my scent. Launched by a jump, it floats down the hill on its long legs.

Under Rebecca's tree, droppings continue to fall at the same rate as earlier in the night. At 7:19, a half-chewed fragment of linden leaf drifts down. Rebecca is *still* feeding. I collect my gear and stumble home, thankful to be moving downhill.

My experience with Rebecca was atypical in one sense. As mentioned before, porcupines don't normally rest in the same tree by day that they feed in at night. Apparently Rebecca's feeding tree was large and comfortable enough to serve as a resting tree as well. She returned to it several times during the summer.

Why do porcupines feed at night? An obvious consideration is predator avoidance, though most of the porcupine's natural predators are also active at night. A second possibility that deserves experimental evaluation is a change in plant chemistry from day to night. Tree leaves become saturated with water and may undergo changes in acid-base balance. Whatever the reason for the porcupine's activity preference, it introduced me to the rich life of the summer night.

Linden

Before tracking porcupines through the night, I had been only dimly aware of the linden (*Tilia americana*) as a Catskills forest tree. It is rare along the slopes of Vly Mountain: less than one tree out of a hundred is a linden. In addition, the nondescript bark resembles ash, and the distinctive leaves and fruits are often so high up in the canopy they can be seen only with binoculars. After two summers of radiotracking, I came to realize how much the porcupine's summer life revolves around this tree. In a curious way, the linden began to peer out of the crevices of the forest. One summer morning, during a hike through a distant cove, I stopped in surprise when a sweet fragrance enveloped me. I had caught the bee's message—a linden tree in full blossom. In the Catskills forest, almost all the tree species (and all the most abundant species) are wind-pollinated. The linden is visited by bees, who can find trees widely scattered in the forest. The linden's ability to keep in genetic touch at a distance helps it to persist in the forest at a low density.

But that low density proved no barrier to the tree's discovery by porcupines. Often, as I followed a porcupine at night from resting tree to feeding tree, or from one feeding tree to another, the tree at the end of the journey proved to be a linden. From midsummer on, when beech (*Fagus grandifolia*) and white ash (*Fraxinus americana*) dropped out of the diet, the linden became the single most important food species. During the summers of 1983 and 1984, linden leaves were consumed in 34% of all feeding episodes. Other foods included apples (30%) and two aspen species (big-

Major summer leafy foods of porcupines. Clockwise from upper left: linden (with fruit), bigtooth aspen, quaking aspen, raspberry.

tooth and quaking), which made up 26% of the total. The remaining 10% of feeding episodes made use of yellow birch, shadbush, American elm, and raspberry canes. The remarkable feature of the porcupine's summer diet is that the food species, with the exception of raspberry canes, are rare or absent in the forest (Table 10). The animals must leave the forest to feed on species such as apple.

Linden leaves were consumed in the same manner as beech and ash earlier in the year: small leafy branches were nipped off, the leaf blades removed, and the branch with petioles discarded as a niptwig. Midsummer

Time course of nonwinter feeding, 1983 and 1984. A rich acorn crop in 1984
shortened the period of apple feeding.

nitrogen analyses showed that porcupines select only the most nutritious
part of the tree, the leaf blade, which contains 13.1% crude protein. The
discarded parts (the petioles and twig tips) contain only 3.5% and 4.6%
crude protein, respectively.

Whenever I homed in on an animal's radio signal and finally discovered
where it was feeding, I would measure the feeding tree and label it with a
small plastic marker. All linden trees tend to look alike at night in the beam
of a headlamp. But as I walked around the trunk, marking and measuring, I
often spotted the gleam of a small plastic marker already fastened to the
tree. The porcupines were returning to trees they had visited before.
Though lindens are rare in the Catskills forest, occasionally a feeding tree
was close to another linden that seemed to attract no porcupines at any
time. It appeared that porcupines were discriminating at three levels: the
level of tree species, the level of individual tree within the species, and the

level of plant part in the tree (leaf blade versus petiole). Nitrogen measurements could explain plant part preference: leaf blades contained more crude protein than any other part of the plant. But I could not explain the preference for individual trees. I decided to monitor several linden trees regularly to measure the variation in feeding pressure, then analyze the preferred trees chemically to see what made them attractive.

During the summer of 1984, I made weekly visits to 13 widely scattered trees to measure the extent of porcupine feeding in each tree. The group was expanded to 17 trees during 1985. Niptwig count became my measure. By carefully searching the ground under each tree, I could recover even a single niptwig. The green petioles on the branches served as visual flags against the brown forest floor. In both years, the tempo of feeding started slowly in June, then quickened as the summer developed. Peak feeding intensity was reached in early October, just before leafdrop. Lindens and aspens were among the last tree species in the forest to hold on to green leaves, after the dominant maples and beech stood bare.

The porcupines' selectivity was startling. During the summer of 1984, I found 151 niptwigs under the most preferred tree and 58 under the second most preferred. The remaining 11 trees combined contributed only 25 niptwigs; 8 of them were never used at all, though some grew relatively close to preferred trees. The two most preferred trees accounted for 90% of all linden feeding within the cohort. In 1985 the pattern of unequal feeding preferences continued, with less dramatic inequalities. Porcupines may have used some less-preferred trees because total feeding pressure was greater. (The local porcupine population increased in 1985; see Chapter 10.) Nevertheless, four trees still accounted for 69% of all feeding (Table 11).

My next problem was how to collect leaf samples for a variety of chemical tests. The lindens were 50 to 100 feet tall and lacked branches low enough for climbing or leaf collection. Ladders would not reach and in any case would be too heavy to carry up and down the mountain. Peter Chabora at Queens College told me of researchers in the rain forests of Costa Rica who shot pairs of tied-together steel balls into the canopy to rip down leaves. I designed my own low-tech leaf collector, a pair of 3/4-inch steel washers tied together with twine and shot from a powerful slingshot. Every week, I became a hunter of leaves. I bought washers from a hardware store in five-pound boxes and carried heavy pocketfuls on my expeditions. Typical chemical analyses required two average-size linden leaves per tree. I began my campaign under each tree by preparing six projectiles. A long pull on the slingshot, the washers flew up with a whining sound, and a small thwack of contact in the canopy. For a few moments nothing happened, then I saw my game, a large leaf sailing down in reversing arcs. My eyes never left it until it was on the ground. I bagged it.

The ultimate satisfaction came from capturing a large leaf, sufficient for all the analyses, then hearing the washers fall to the ground near my feet. Such triumphs came rarely; that is why I allowed six projectiles per tree. Sometimes the projectile hit a branch or tore through the canopy without severing a leaf. Sometimes a leaf began to drift down, only to be snagged in a lower branch. Equally frustrating was trying to follow two leaves sailing in separate trajectories, then losing one on the ground because I could not keep my eye on both.

Shooting leaves on an August afternoon, I was nearing the end of my circuit and trying to collect leaves from D', a large, sloping tree on a woodland trail. The sun had just set behind the mountain, and the trail lay in shadow, but the tops of the tallest trees still caught the last rays. I launched my projectile and heard it rise through the canopy with only a tiny tick—no leaf flew down. But as the bright washers kept soaring, they entered the zone of high sunlight and twisted, luminous and free, before arcing back to the shadows. As the missile tumbled and fell, I had an illumination. I realized that the porcupine, too, was a hunter of leaves. Unlike the grazing ruminants of the plains that crop a field of grass and find any number of species acceptable fodder, the porcupine must hunt its food by discovering the rare trees in the forest that will best sustain it. Out of a thousand forest trees in the Catskills, one or two are acceptable lindens and one is a bigtooth aspen. To locate and return to those trees, the porcupine uses all the skills of the hunter: memory, attention to landmark and local detail, persistence. That explains why the American psychologist L. W. Sackett (1913) found that the North American porcupine has an extraordinary ability to learn complex mazes and to remember them as much as a hundred days afterward.

But I was hunting for more than leaves; I was also hunting for understanding. No single factor had leapt out as an explanation for the porcupine's choices, so I examined many possibilities. Were preferred trees richer in nitrogen, in the way leaf blades are richer than petioles? I wasted much effort on those onerous analyses since nitrogen values show a great deal of scatter. Individual leaves from the same tree may differ by several percentage points of crude protein. But in the end, a statistical analysis of results showed no correlation between nitrogen content and individual tree feeding rank. In fact, the average nitrogen content of the trees fell during the course of the summer as overall feeding intensity rose. Are nonselected trees better protected by tannins? I ran two kinds of tannin determinations (condensed tannins and total phenols) and found enormous variation between trees. But again, no correlation could be shown with feeding preference. What about levels of calcium, sodium, and potassium? Porcupines have a strong salt drive. Perhaps they were responding to subtle differences in sodium or potassium levels. That proved another dead end.

Finally, in early October 1984, I looked at the acid-base balance of linden leaves. I had found earlier in the summer that porcupines, when feeding in apple trees, avoided trees with acid (low-pH) apples. I collected leaves from each tree in the group, homogenized a leaf-water mixture in a blender, and measured the pH with a portable pH meter. For the first samples, the pH values showed little variability, falling in a mildly acid range between 5.9 and 6.2. All those came from low-ranked trees. Then a leaf from tree 853, the porcupines' second-favorite tree in 1984, registered a pH of 6.7, nearly neutral. I quickly homogenized leaves from tree A', the animals' first choice, and got a value almost as high. Finally, a pattern was discernible.

My 1984 results were based on a single set of pH readings taken at the end of the feeding season. I repeated pH measurements in 1985, taking readings throughout the summer. The results not only confirmed that porcupines feed most heavily on trees with highest-pH leaves but also that the overall tempo of feeding parallels a seasonal increase in pH.[1] Taking the pH readings at face value, one might assume that porcupines want to limit acid intake, as they undoubtedly do in the case of apples. But the apples that they consume in great quantities show acid contents two orders of

Linden 853 (left of center), the porcupines' first choice in 1985 and second choice in 1984. More than 180 niptwigs were collected under this tree in 1985.

magnitude higher than in the linden leaves. It is therefore more likely that porcupines are responding not to acid content per se but to some associated defense compound in the leaves. Unfortunately, the nature of the compound is unknown at this time.

Whatever the acid status of linden leaves may be, they do not offend

Time course of linden use and average leaf pH in 1985.

The relationship between feeding pressure on individual lindens and pH of their leaf homogenates.

human taste buds. I have eaten linden leaves from both low-pH and high-pH trees and found them indistinguishable. They were surprisingly mild, almost bland in taste. In that respect lindens are very different from the impossibly bitter aspen leaves, which also rate high on the porcupine summer menu.

Aspen

The only trees challenging the linden in importance in the summer diet of
the porcupine are bigtooth aspen (*Populus grandidentata*) and quaking aspen (*P. tremuloides*). Aspens are even more scarce in the Catskills forest
than the lindens. Their aggregate abundance in the forest is approximately
0.1% (one tree out of a thousand is an aspen). Yet 26% of the animals'
summer feeding was on the leaves of these two species. However, fewer
porcupines fed on aspen compared with linden. In 1983, 8 of 9 collared
animals (89%) fed on linden, but only 5 of 9 (56%) fed on aspens.

Aspens are among the most shade-intolerant of all forest species
(Bakuzis and Kurmis 1978). Their seedlings cannot survive in the deep
shade of beech, maple, ash, and red oak. Though bigtooth aspens can
reach full canopy height, they do not replace themselves in the mature forest. Quaking aspens grow only along the forest edges, and porcupines at
times undertake long trips to reach them.

Porcupines show none of the preference for individual aspens that they
show for lindens. They do harvest leaves by the same niptwigging technique and avoid the petioles. As with linden, aspen leaf blades have much
higher nitrogen levels than petioles or twig tips.

Aspens present a danger encountered in few other tree species: brittle
branches. One night I tracked Rebecca to a young quaking aspen growing
on the edge of Roarback Field. After waiting a few minutes for her to resume feeding, I continued up the hill to visit my other animals. Next morning, on the ground under the aspen, I saw a branch about four feet long,
with little sign of leaf removal. The base showed a jagged, splintering
break, not the clean, diagonal cut expected of a niptwig. I was holding the
leader of the tree. Rebecca had climbed into the top of the tree and bent it
past its breaking point. Since I found no quill mass on the ground, she must
have saved herself by snagging another branch as she fell. Her free movements in the days following also suggested no injury.

Apples

Porcupines love apples at any time of the year. One winter afternoon when
I wanted to show a porcupine to two visitors, we made our way up the
mountain, through deep snow, to Finder's den, a low rock outcrop just be-

low the ridge. The porcupine was deep inside the earth and out of sight. I placed two Red Delicious apples in the den entrance, then stepped back to watch. We stood about 12 minutes in the deep silence of a snowy landscape. Then a little movement commenced inside the den. Finder's head emerged from the shadows, picked up an apple, and dragged it inside. We heard the soft sounds of a porcupine enjoying its favorite food. Even captive wild porcupines, which normally turn their backs and bristle all quills at human approach, will turn and take an apple out of my hand.

These apple fiends begin to raid our orchard by early July. The orchard itself, with 16 apple trees and one pear, covers two acres. To the north and west are old fields reverting to woods and containing a dozen-odd wild apple trees derived from the orchard seed source. With a single exception, the apples of greatest interest to my porcupines have proved to be not the orchard fruit but the wild apples. Raccoons like them too. On a bright-starred, moonless night in July, I tracked Squirrel to a wild apple tree in Roarback Field, northwest of the orchard. There was a suspicious amount of movement in the tree, and I turned on my head lantern. Clinging to the branch above Squirrel was a baby raccoon, green eyes gleaming in the light. The two animals were sharing the tree without interfering with each other. In years since, I have found raccoons and porcupines sharing the same apple tree many times, without a sign of discord. Squirrel moved energetically through the apple tree, harvesting apples directly or cutting small niptwigs to gather fruit on short terminal branches. She ate only the apples and had no interest in leaves. In the beam of my lantern, I sometimes caught the dull red reflections of her eyes, sometimes the white top of her head, sometimes a reflection from her radio box. For the most part, she remained hidden behind leaves, and I saw only the branches moving as her feet sought separate footholds for stability.

Later in the month Squirrel started bringing her baby to feed in the apple trees. Mother and baby foraged in the same tree but on different branches. The baby was relatively clumsy; during one 40-minute observation period, it dropped 18 apples to the ground. Squirrel almost never dropped her food. She turned the apple carefully in her paws, biting off small pieces till only the core (endocarp) remained. In the morning the discarded cores displayed her careful workmanship—only the soft outer meat (exocarp) had been removed.

The orchard. Every year, the apple tree to the right of the footpath was stripped of its fruit by mid-August, while surrounding trees stood untouched.

Many porcupines came to feed on apples. I counted at least eight different animals during a summer, including two different mothers with their babies and two adult males. It was not unusual to find two animals feeding in the same tree, and on two occasions I found three. They tended to crowd into a single tree because only a small number of apple trees were acceptable to the porcupines: one tree in the orchard proper and six wild trees on the periphery. The difference between acceptable and rejected apples was obvious from a simple taste test. The rejected apples were sour. Preferred apples were also the first to mature.

In chemical terms, the selected apples had an average pH of 4.07, the rejected fruit averaged pH 2.95. The two classes of apples did not differ significantly in other respects. They had comparable levels of total sugars, crude protein, and sodium-potassium ratios. Porcupines have good reason to limit their acid intake. Excess acid reduces the efficiency of physiological sodium conservation (Rose 1984, Cogan and Rector 1982). As noted in the previous chapter, porcupines feeding on apples showed increased so-

Adult porcupine consumes an apple.

dium drive and lost sodium in their urine. Presumably such losses would have been greater if the animals had not selected the least acidic fruit. To humans, the preferred apples had a bland, mealy taste. To porcupines, they were so attractive that preferred trees were stripped of their fruit by mid-August. The trees stood with a rumpled look, their branches littered with wilted niptwigs. Nearby, trees with more-acidic fruit stood untouched. In years when the mast crop failed, porcupines returned to the less desirable trees in September as apples matured.

Wendell Dodge (1967) has commented on the porcupine's special preference for Red Delicious apples. I bought four strains of apples from a green-grocer and measured the pHs of their homogenates (1:10 in water). The results might have been predicted from the acid-avoidance theory. Red Delicious had the highest pH, at 4.1. It was followed by Yellow Delicious at 3.7, Macintosh at 3.35, and Granny Smith, the most acidic, at 3.1. Red Delicious apples do not differ significantly from other strains in terms of protein content (0.6% for Red Delicious, 0.7% for Macintosh). Raccoons, who are less efficient apple foragers, did not follow the same apple preferences as porcupines.

During the peak apple-feeding months of July and August, porcupines never stopped using tree leaves. The reason may lie in the low nitrogen content of apples (about 0.7% crude protein for apples versus 15% for linden or aspen leaves). In fact, porcupines who fed on apples always fed on linden or aspen leaves during the same night. During 12 all-night observation sessions, animals feeding on tree leaves alone used an average of 1.25 trees per night (range 1–2). Five animals feeding on mast or apple fruit used an average of 3.2 trees per night (range 2–5), always accompanying mast or fruit with tree leaves.[2] The apples' high content of digestible carbohydrates, however, provided an energy source and allowed the porcupines to continue putting on weight during the summer.

The biological function of fruits such as apples is seed dispersal, but at first glance porcupines feeding on apples do little to disperse the seeds. They discard their apple cores directly under the feeding tree, leaving the seeds in the shadow of the parent tree. Presumably porcupines reject the cores to avoid ingesting the cyanide-rich seeds.[3] But that is not the final destination of the seeds. Another animal appears to have arrived at a way of dealing with the cyanide load. On an August day in 1985 when I opened a small dresser I keep in the salthouse, a deer mouse (*Peromyscus maniculatus*) jumped out and ran behind a woodpile. In a corner of the drawer I discovered a platform made of a shredded plastic bag and strips of dried grasses and leaves. In the middle of the platform sat a huge pile of apple seeds, the food cache of an industrious deer mouse.

The nearest source of the seeds was an orchard tree 200 feet to the east, now completely stripped of its apples by the porcupines. The cores dropped below the tree had been carefully opened by the deer mouse, the seeds extracted and carried back to the salthouse. Deer mice have large cheek pouches and can probably carry around a dozen apple seeds per trip (B. E. Horner, personal communication). In this case, the porcupines had made the seeds accessible to the mice; the two species working together formed an effective seed-dispersing team.

I placed the seeds in a plastic bag, to sort and count them. As I worked on the salthouse, the deer mouse kept returning to its food cache. I discovered it had bitten a small hole in my bag and had been carrying away the seeds to a safer location. To compensate the mouse, I left a slightly larger pile of winter rye in the dresser drawer. At home, I counted and sorted the apple seeds. I found a total of 10,253 apple seeds weighing 236.6 g (about half a pound). Mixed in with the apple seeds were 25 larger seeds from other species: sugar maple, wild cherry, plus an unidentified third species. Assuming 5.85 intact seeds per apple core, the 10,253 seeds represented about 1750 apples. And assuming 12 seeds carried per trip, the mouse had made more than 850 round-trips, a distance of 64.4 miles. Also, the seed cache contained few empty seeds—perhaps a dozen in the entire pile. Yet intact apples contained an average of 1.35 empty seeds each. The mouse had not wasted effort.

The story has a few additional layers. Some of the apple seeds had small, neatly drilled holes in the seed coats, the work of a seed predator. And both the seeds and the leaf litter below the cache were overrun by tiny white mites. Are they associated with the seed predators, with surface fungi, or with some other biological enterprise?

The porcupines in the apple trees thus enter a widening web of ecological involvement: the apples, raccoons, deer mice, seed predators, and white mites are all part of a subtly woven set of biological transactions linking the porcupine to the living world around it.

Fall Foraging

At the end of August, as the favored apple trees stand depleted, the forest yields a major new food source: mast in the form of acorns and beechnuts. Even though the porcupines have not climbed beech trees since spring and have climbed oak trees only for occasional daytime rest, the two tree species now assume overwhelming importance for the porcupines, particularly in years of heavy mast crops.

Red oaks and beechnuts produce a small, basal crop of acorns and beechnuts every year. But in certain years all trees in an area fruit massively, and acorns sufficient to establish several forests lie on the ground. Such overproduction is necessary to outstrip the demand of acorn predators: the weevils, chipmunks, gray and red squirrels, white-tailed deer, wild turkeys, raccoons, and porcupines. All descend on the crop with such force that in basal years no acorns may survive. For red oak, 1983, 1986, and 1988 were basal years; 1984, 1985, and 1987 were years of heavy mast crops. Porcupines were able to take a good percentage of the crop in each year, because they got to the acorns before the ground predators did.

Again, porcupines used the niptwigging technique to harvest acorns. (Beechnuts, producing a relatively minor crop every year, are harvested in the same manner as acorns.) The porcupines cut small terminal branches, then scoop the acorns out of the acorn cups or the beechnuts out of the beechnut husks. The residue is discarded. The canopies of large oaks quickly fill up with snagged niptwigs. The giant trees hold enough fruit to keep a porcupine in residence for several days. Smaller trees, especially in basal years, might be cleaned out in minutes or hours.

One acorn-foraging porcupine that I followed through an entire night in late September climbed six different trees, three of them oaks. Mayday, an adult male, had spent the day resting in a large sugar maple. When I reached him at 9:50 p.m., the warmth of the day still hung on the mountain, but Mayday was already crunching leaves in his first feeding tree, a small linden. Acorns are an excellent energy source because of their high fat content, but like apples, they are poor nitrogen sources. That is why porcupines continue feeding on tree leaves throughout their mast harvest, up until leaf-fall. Mayday's feeding had become more frenzied by about 11; I heard branches dropping and the animal moving in the canopy. There was a rich smell of fallen leaves and moisture.

At 12:08, a barred owl screamed out from a tree so close that I felt as though I were sitting inside the horn of a giant loudspeaker, with vibrations rubbing my skin. As I stared into the forest, trying to locate the source of the sound, a large, dark bird landed in the tree behind the porcupine. Its wings were outlined in flight against the transparent canopy, the sky light with stars. Mayday had grown very still. The owl soon left on silent wings, hitting no tree branches as would a wild turkey or grouse. When it reached its new perch, it screamed a single note, with a twist and crackle in the middle, like the first note of a siren. The porcupine did no more feeding in his linden tree.

At 2 a.m. Mayday descended and moved off in the night. I gave him a head start, then followed his radio signal upslope along the ridge. The head start I offered had not been enough. Half a mile farther and 200 feet higher up the mountain, I found the animal in a small red maple, a species never used as food by porcupines. Mayday had climbed the tree to escape me. Again, I waited in the dark. Once Mayday descended to a low crotch in the tree and chattered his teeth at me. Then his courage failed, and he climbed back to the top. Finally, 20 minutes after my arrival, he left the tree. I gave him a 10-minute head start. When I caught up at 3:40 a.m., Mayday had moved a short distance south while remaining at the same elevation. He was up another red maple, his third tree of the night. The tree was good-sized. With all its leaves gone, it appeared hung with stars. I lay down near the tree and watched.

I wondered why he had chosen a tree with no available food. All around us, the area was thick with oaks, the ground littered with niptwigs and empty acorn cups. The answer came quickly. The oaks were already occupied. In one oak, a porcupine was feeding noisily. From another oak came the sound of droppings falling to the ground. Because the oaks retain their leaves, I saw only dim suggestions of the porcupines. I wondered whether such an aggregation was a mating-season phenomenon or whether the cluster of oaks was a limited resource comparable to an apple orchard.

Only 10 minutes after my arrival, Mayday descended and set off noisily through the leaves. I gathered my gear and followed, reaching him at 4:15 a short distance south and at the same elevation. This time he had found his own oak, a vigorous tree growing in a clump next to a small clearing. He fed there for 20 minutes, then climbed a smaller oak tree in the same clump, his fifth tree for the night. After an hour of feeding and resting, he moved again. I followed sleepily, to a sapling-sized oak. It was now 5 a.m., and a first small grayness was stealing into the sky. Standing under the tree, I heard vigorous crunching above, then sounds of a porcupine descending, but the animal came down not from Mayday's tree but from a neighboring oak. An unmarked porcupine stopped about six feet above the ground, stared at me for a moment, then made a snorking sound, like a child imitating a pig. It repeated the snork, then completed its descent and disappeared down the slope. Later in the morning, when I awakened from a nap under Mayday's tree, a red morning sun hung in the trees. Mayday was resting quietly. I started for home.

In mast crop years, the oaks draw porcupines through September and October, until the acorns fall to the ground and are rapidly cleared by deer, turkey, and chipmunk. There is concomitant feeding on the much smaller crop of beechnuts and on linden leaves as a nitrogen source. In 1983, 1986, and 1988, when the acorn crop failed, the oaks lay stripped by September, and the porcupines fell back on late-maturing apples and on linden.

The period of feeding on mast and linden is associated with continued weight gain, and adult porcupines reach their highest weights of the year.

Juveniles maintain a positive weight balance up to the December snows by feeding on ground vegetation such as raspberry and green marsh grasses. By that time, adults have long been denned up or under hemlock cover, feeding on winter vegetation. They will lose weight during the ordeal. Their survival will depend on reserves accumulated through a summer and fall of hunting the rare leaves and rich fruit of the forest.

Notes

1. Correlation between leaf homogenate pH and feeding preference:
   1984, $r = 0.654$, $df = 11$, $P < 0.05$
   1985, $r = 0.737$, $df = 15$, $P < 0.01$
2. $t = 3.25$, $df = 11$, $P < 0.01$.
3. Apple seeds contain amygdalin, a cyanogenic gentiobioside (Conn 1979).

7

The Winter Den

Winter's first, thin coat of snow is a compulsive storyteller. Large and small mammals of the woods who have been skulking and stealing through the shadows are suddenly printed in the snow. Even after the animals are gone, their footprints remain to tell their stories. The density of animal populations revealed by such tracks is a surprise. Deer, fox, porcupine, wild turkey, squirrel, hare and cottontail, grouse, mice, and voles can all be seen reliably. The rare black bear, bobcat, or coyote are lucky finds. On such an afternoon of sparkling early-December snow I found a porcupine track crossing our marsh. It was my first encounter with this animal on its own terms. I spent two days following it in the snow, from its origin to its destination, and I have been following others like it ever since.

A Trail in the Snow

A porcupine trail in the snow can be confused with the track of no other animal. The footprints are large and, like a miniature bear's, plantigrade. That is, the animal steps down on the sole of its foot, not just the toes. In contrast to the large footprint, the stride is short because the legs are short. The animal scuffs its way along, never jumping over a fallen log or a patch of water. There is a rhythm to the movement of the legs, as regular as a sewing machine stitch. When the track is fresh and the snow deep enough, one can see the overlay of a longer periodicity—the side-to-side sweep of the comblike tail.

My individual is easy to follow, because no other porcupines are abroad. The tracks of deer or wild turkey, by contrast, make a hopeless maze as one animal oversteps the trail of another of its kind. The porcupine crosses the marsh and heads gently uphill along an old sawmill road. Periodically it overtreads a deer path, the deer traveling in the opposite direction. The road grades down to Roarback Creek where the creek flows in a deep, steeply banked gully. By following the path, the animal avoids the insecure footing of a straight descent. This is a well-used animal crossing. I can see a number of deer tracks following the same route. The creek's current in early December is relatively gentle, and I step across easily on projecting rocks. But the porcupine has crossed by a bridge I had not noticed: a fallen tree trunk angled across the stream. I can see its careful steps in the snow on top of the log. It then begins the serious effort of ascending the ridge on the opposite side. It climbs the ridge at an angle, lengthening its path but grading it for an easier climb.

After a while, the animal stops at a large beech tree to feed. But it abandons the tree after chewing off only a tiny test piece of bark near the ground, perhaps an inch square, and continues its journey. Its small body fits comfortably under a fallen tree around which I have to detour. It has urinated lightly in the snow. After passing under a tangle of wind-thrown branches, it begins a hard, frontal climb up the slope. The track ascends steadily, then burrows inside a large, hollow sugar maple trunk open at the bottom. The animal has moved in and out repeatedly, dragging out old leaves and other debris as though to clean out the hollow. It is looking for a den. But in the end something about the site proves unsatisfactory, and the porcupine resumes its climb.

Higher up, it briefly explores another old sugar maple, a "General Sherman" tree, with two openings at the base. Winter winds would have whistled through the space. Near the tree, the porcupine intersects the trail of a solitary grouse, walking downhill and dragging its tail in the snow. An evergreen Christmas fern projects its green sawtooth edge above the white ground. The porcupine keeps climbing. It walks around a large-diameter beech tree that carries an old chew mark near the base, the work of another porcupine. It squeezes under a fallen tree, then crawls over another one concealed by snow. For a short time it travels downhill along a lumber road, but soon it seems to recollect itself, leaves the road, and pushes uphill once more. It is entering porcupine country; more beech trees are displaying old chewing wounds on their trunks. The animal stops for a serious meal, chewing a sugar maple in two accessible places, where the trunk forms sharply convex buttresses. One bare patch measures 5 × 40 cm (2 × 16 inches), the other 5 × 18 cm (2 × 7 inches). Small fragments of outer bark litter the snow. After the meal, more climbing. I don't know how the animal felt, but I am overheating and have to open my winter jacket.

A deer track, more crawling under fallen trees, then drama in the snow. The porcupine track intersects the track of a red fox. The deer, squirrel, and grouse tracks gave no indication of porcupine interaction, but the fox is different. The two animals have clearly reached the same place at the same time and have exchanged greetings. Both tracks show milling and turning in the snow, though there are no loose quills or fur to indicate a physical attack. Then the tracks separate and resume their original directions of travel. It is easier for the porcupine to eat trees than it is for the fox to eat porcupines.

I follow the porcupine. More deer tracks, two sets of squirrel tracks, and then my goal—the lair of the porcupine. The animal is inside its chosen den tree, a strange old sugar maple like a giant bird's leg kicking skyward. The thick trunk carries a single eccentric branch at the very top. An opening at the bottom is too small for my head but wide enough for an incautious arm. I reach as far as I can but feel only space above. The porcupine is higher up inside and out of reach. Outside the opening is a spot of urine, pungent and porcupinelike, and two small clusters of scats melted in the snow.

The trail to the den tree has been a virgin trail; each step has been sharply recorded in fresh snow. The den tree is almost at the top of the ridge, and the trail climbs no higher. But a short, curious snow trail follows the isocline to the left. The footprints look blurred, and the ones I can read clearly are leading toward the tree, not away from it. I follow the trail for a few dozen feet before unraveling the mystery.

The tracks are fuzzy not because they are old but because they are superimposed on each other. One set leads away from the den tree, the other, on top, leads toward it. The porcupine has made a round-trip and traveled in its own footsteps. The object of the trip stands less than 100 feet away: a young, rather twisted beech tree about 16 cm (6.5 inches) in diameter. High in the tree, about 10 square centimeters of bark have been chewed away. Above that, a branch has two large bare areas along the upper surface. The snow beneath the tree is scattered with the frizz of rejected outer bark. The animal has used only the inner layer—the phloem and cambium. The porcupine is gone, but the tree shows many feeding scars from years past, most high in the tree. Around the feeding tree, I count 19 other beech trees in a variety of sizes, and 14 show clear marks of porcupine feeding, mostly in the upper crown but often along the trunk. Most of the feeding scars are from past years. One medium-sized tree 25 cm in diameter has been girdled sometime during the past two or three months; a 1-foot strip of trunk has been exposed all the way around the base. The tree is doomed. My first reaction is shock. I get a different perspective a minute later.

At the top of the ridge, I find a scene of destruction. A lumbering operation has reduced almost every sizable tree to a stump. Decaying slash lies tangled everywhere, with thick, young growth squeezing through to reclaim the forest. A super-porcupine has been at work here, one who does not eat the trees he cuts.

On my way back, I pause again at the den and look out across the ridge. The sun has set behind Vly Mountain but still glows red on Cave Mountain and the Jewett range, Beehive and Saddleback Mountains. The landscape projects an incongruous sense of the Grand Canyon: great distances, somber red colors, and the dark shadow in the foreground creeping out across the valley. As often as I have looked out from porcupine dens in the mountains, I have found spectacle. But now the shadows make me hurry on.

To complete my picture of the porcupine's journey, I return next day to the marsh and track the animal backward to its point of origin. The trail leads me across the stream to a small grove of hemlocks and then to the specific hemlock where the animal started. The evergreen branches of the hemlocks had given shelter during the snowstorm. From this lovely spot the animal has moved constantly uphill, crossing a stream and a marshy area twice, moving about 3/4 mile in linear distance and 500 feet in elevation in one long trip, investigating den possibilities along the way, finally choosing one that was both comfortable and close to food.

I return to the den tree 36 days later, this time without a porcupine to guide me. I find all the landmarks along the way: the animal-crossing site across the Roarback, the General Sherman maple rejected as a den site, the sugar maple with the two basal feeding scars (now considerably darkened by exposure), then

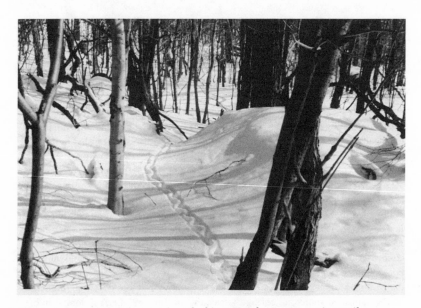

The trajectory of each footstep is etched in snow along a porcupine trail.

the feeding area of beeches with twisted tops, and finally the kicking-leg den tree with the small opening at the bottom. No tracks lead from the den tree—fresh snow has fallen, and a thin layer has infiltrated the opening. The porcupine has moved, and I am unable to follow.

I have spent a long time describing the den-searching porcupine because it revealed to me, in my very first encounter, many of the aspects of porcupine winter behavior in the Catskills. Every element of the story has proved to be significant: the starting point in the hemlocks, the long journey accomplished in a single day, the precise knowledge of local geography, even the little drop of urine in the trail.

In wildlife research, one follows a subject with a will and personality of its own. One must always wonder whether the behavior observed is typical of the species, typical of the individual animal, or not typical of anything, as was a deer I once found who had fallen on snow-covered ice or a raccoon I watched sniffing the tail of a skunk. To evaluate an observation, one must repeat it many times, test it for deviation from random process, and try to see it from the perspective of the organism involved. In the years since encountering the den-seeking porcupine, I have followed hundreds of similar tracks in the snow. Some of my questions have been answered, but a crop of new ones has grown up.

Den-Entering Time

Raccoons, beavers, and woodchucks use shelters year-round. My Catskills porcupines, on the other hand, are den dwellers only during the winter. In that sense, my den-seeking porcupine was out of step with the rest of the population, which had entered winter dens around the first week of November. Some clues to the factors that determine when a porcupine enters its den may be found in sporadic summer denning behavior. Almost all the time, porcupines in the summer months are found out in the open: in a tree when resting or feeding, on the ground when traveling. But on rare instances they may be found in dens.

Early summer view of a porcupine den. While columbines and Canada violets bloom in the foreground, the resident has been absent for many weeks to forage in the open forest. It will not return until November.

On a Mother's Day in early May, my wife, Steph, and I went out to look at the woods and to locate two of our porcupines. The morning was splendid, with thick tree buds casting a dusky light and the first half-open leaves dancing in the sky. Only one factor spoiled the walk: newly emerged blackflies were biting hard on every inch of exposed skin. The female Squirrel was in a well-frequented resting tree, linden number 766. Instead of lying on a branch, she was inside a hole in the tree. My binoculars revealed her hunched up to hide all bitable skin. As I studied her, a blackfly bit my hand, and I watched the skin swell up immediately. Later on our walk, we discovered the large male Mayday in a similar position, in a hole in an old, leaning sugar maple. Fortunately for us and the porcupines, the blackfly season in the Catskills is short. But while the season lasts, the flies are fierce enough to drive at least some porcupines into dens.

Another temporary denning stimulus is rain. The next time I found both animals inside tree dens was almost a month later, in early June. It had rained all day, often hard, and I had held off my tracking in hopes of clearing weather. The rain never stopped, and I went out in late afternoon. Again, I located both animals inside hollow trees. They were probably drier than I was. On another June day years later, a friend and I went out radiotracking during a light drizzle. We found Squirrel lying on a comfortable branch in a favorite resting tree, a large, hollow sugar maple. Suddenly the rain began pelting. Squirrel got up, turned around, and climbed inside an opening high up the tree.

The North American porcupine is a widely dispersed, ecologically adaptable species. Its habitat encompasses not only the familiar woodlands of the north but also portions of the desert such as the Mojave of California. It has been suggested that porcupines survive in the low-desert habitat by hiding in dens from the daytime heat, then venturing out at night to seek green vegetation (Betancourt et al. 1986). That is the strategy of most desert-dwelling mammals. But the den can protect a porcupine against winter cold as well. Heat stress is not a problem in the Catskills; cold stress can be. A number of times I have found my animals driven into temporary dens by sudden cold spells. On the night of October 6, 1984, the temperature on the mountain crashed to an unseasonable 24°F. Next morning, while patches of frost still whitened the ground, I found the females Moth and Cameo inside separate rock dens and Squirrel inside a tree den. A fourth animal, the juvenile Becky, was inside the hollow base of a sugar maple. Three other animals, whom I reached only in the afternoon when temperatures had climbed, were out in the open.

Prewinter denning responses to cold differ in three ways from winter den use. First, prewinter den use is episodic. Subfreezing temperatures drive most porcupines into dens, but they emerge again once the thermometer climbs. In the winter, animals typically remain in dens even when day temperatures rise above freezing. Second, prewinter dens are havens of opportunity, found near favorite roosting or feeding sites. With few exceptions, they lie outside the animals' winter territories and are never used in winter. Third, there are differences in den types. The great majority of prewinter dens in the Catskills are hollow trees; most true winter dens are rock crevices.

The stimulus for entering permanent dens appears to be a string of days when temperatures drop below freezing (Roze 1987). Data from six winters (Table 12) show animals entering permanent dens only after minimum daily temperatures have fallen below freezing for 7 days (range: 3–9 days). The average calendar date is October 29. Early cold spells in 1985 advanced permanent den occupancy to October 15. The particularly warm autumn of 1984 delayed permanent den entrance to November 10. The variation between years was greater than the variation between animals in a given year, suggesting a climatic response.

Den Types

At first sight, the winter dens chosen by porcupines seem to offer little protection from cold. One den type, a live hollow tree, was used by my porcupines 20% of the time. Den trees typically have openings higher on the trunk, and the majority have an appreciable list, making for easy climbing. The opening, whether at the base or higher, is not closed. There is no insulation or nest material inside the den. On the contrary, porcupines may remove windblown leaves and debris. With only its tail presented to potential predators, the occupant can rest easy up inside the tree.

Young porcupine scrambles up a snowbank to enter its den in a hollow tree.

A much more common den type, making up 70% of the winter dens used by my porcupines, is the rock outcrop. The Catskill Mountains are formed of sedimentary sandstone. In the valleys, a thick blanket of gravel and clay overlies the rock. At higher altitudes, the mountains' skin wears thin or disappears, exposing seams of sandstone alternating with conglomerate and shale. In this country of exposed rock and broken boulders, most porcupines spend their winters. Along the rock faces, frost and running water have bitten into the softer shale layers to create fissures. Those reaching 12 feet or deeper into the mountain are the den sites favored by porcupines. During winter, drifting snow covers the opening, leaving only a small entrance. With its back to the entrance, the porcupine sits in the deepest part of the recess.

The innermost region of the den is bare, though much of the rest of the floor is covered by the decomposing droppings of previous occupants. Often the droppings are reduced to a fine sawdust and smoothed by years of porcupine traffic. In moist, temperate habitats such as the Catskills, much of the physical breakdown of porcupine dung deposits is accomplished by a guild of mites, arthropods too small to be seen by the naked eye (Calder and Bleakney 1965). They also help to transmit certain porcupine parasites (Chapter 11). Where water is absent, as in desert sites, porcupine dung is cemented by the animals' urine into a concretelike, durable conglomerate. Betancourt and coworkers (1986), who have studied porcupine dung accumulations in desert caves, report that the material could not be broken by hammer blows heavy enough to shatter the surrounding basalt.

The remaining 10% of the winter dens used by Catskills porcupines is split evenly between hollow logs and human outbuildings (barns, sheds, cabins). The buildings must be situated near the animals' food trees; they need not be unoccupied. One November night, at the height of the hunting season, I was expecting to find the porcupine Moth denned in a hollow linden tree in the middle of a hemlock forest. Instead I tracked her radio signal to a cabin near our own woods. Two vans were parked outside; a dim light was burning. I formed a chilling hypothesis: hunters had killed Moth

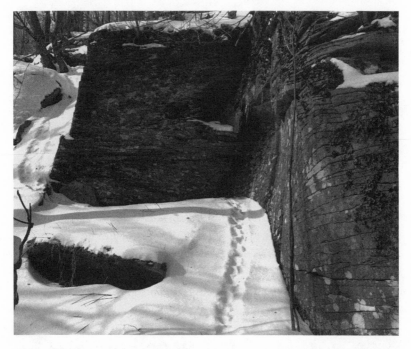

Squirrel's trail to Split Rock den. The jumbled footprints show she has traveled back and forth in her own footprints.

in the woods and taken her radiocollar inside. The radio's motion sensor had shown no sign of activity.

Early next morning I drove to the cabin to confront the hunters. I pounded on the door. No answer. I pounded again. The door creaked open. To my surprise, the head that asked me what I wanted was only knee-high. A hunter had been sleeping on the floor and was addressing me from his sleeping bag. As I stood explaining, more and more bodies emerged. Finally I was facing six men crowded in a little cabin about 16 feet square. They were not pleased to be awakened. They became indignant when I asked if they had shot my porcupine. To demonstrate that the collar was right inside the cabin, I turned on my radio receiver. But it wasn't. The signal was weak and came from a thousand yards away, where Moth lay sheltering under a barn after spending the night under the hunters' cabin. Perhaps the sounds of six hunters turning in their sleep had kept her awake. She never returned to the cabin den, for which I am thankful. I visited the cabin a week later, with a bottle of scotch and apologies. But the hunters had left.

Dens and Heat Conservation

If porcupines enter winter dens to escape from cold, their den choices seem curious. Dens contain no insulation, the entrances are open, and the animals don't huddle up for warmth. In addition, they emerge to feed at night, when outside temperatures are lowest. Without doubt dens could be engineered to conserve more heat, but perhaps other considerations rule that out. Would an insulated den build up an unacceptable level of ectoparasites? Would the insulation foul the quills? Would closing the entrance make sense if it had to be opened every night for feeding? Those questions have not been experimentally investigated.

But in important ways, the dens do protect porcupines against heat loss. Body heat may be lost in four principal ways: by evaporation, conduction, convectional flow, and radiation. Evaporation refers primarily to the unavoidable loss of water through the lungs. Conduction means the direct transfer of heat from one surface to another, as would happen if a porcupine stood on bare stone with its naked footpads. Porcupines minimize conductional loss by resting primarily in the sitting position, the body propped up by the tail, the front paws held against the chest, and hind paws turned partly sideways so the footpads are not in direct contact with the ground. In convection, a fluid such as air or water transfers heat. The principle is familiar to us as the windchill factor—we lose heat more rapidly on a windy day. The air inside a porcupine den is still. Perhaps that is why my den-seeking porcupine rejected the General Sherman tree with its two openings; it would have been drafty. Convectional heat loss would be lowest in rock dens, which have deep and often curving entranceways.

Heat loss through infrared radiation is analogous to the flux of light or ultraviolet energy. The amount of heat lost is proportional to the surface temperature of the radiant body and to the difference in temperature between the radiant body and the heat sink.[1] The excellent insulating properties of porcupine fur (Chapter 3) keep the animal's exterior temperature low, close to that of surrounding rocks and vegetation. Hence, radiational heat loss to the surroundings should be minimal. However, the open night sky can have a far lower temperature and can therefore be an effective heat sink. Shielding from the open-sky heat sink should contribute significantly to heat conservation. Again, a deep rock crevice should be more effective than a log or tree den because deep-earth temperatures may remain above freezing year-round (Calder and Bleakney 1965). Some preliminary experimental data from the Catskills support that assumption.

In February 1988 I installed temperature-recording devices for one-week intervals in a ground den and a hollow-log den. One recorder was placed inside the den, the other outside, out of the sun and one foot above the snow line. For the rock den (occupied sequentially by at least two animals during the winter), a high of −1°C was recorded February 1, when the outside temperature reached 4°C during a midwinter thaw. The den low of −6°C was recorded February 7, when outside temperature fell to −19°C (−2°F). At the time, the inside-outside differential measured 13°C (22°F). For the hollow log (occupied by the male Jasper), the high of −3°C was recorded February 20, when outside temperature reached −2°C; the low of −11°C followed late the following day, when outside temperature fell to −17°C. The maximum inside-outside differential was 9.4°C (17°F), observed February 21.

Roger Powell (personal communication) has recorded inside-outside

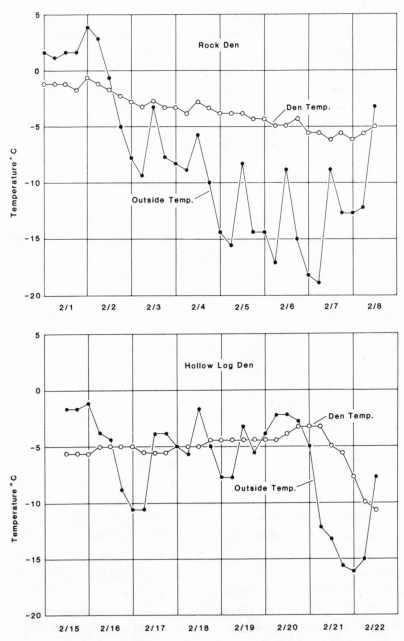

Internal and external winter temperatures in a rock den (top) and hollow-log den (bottom). The inside-outside differential was lower in the hollow-log den.

temperature differentials for three porcupine dens in hollow trees in the Ottawa National Forest, Michigan. Measurements were taken on three days in December 1976, between 9:45 a.m. and noon. The highest differential, observed in two dens, was 7°C (12.6°F) when outside air temperature measured −21°C. Apparently the Michigan tree dens offer the same degree of thermal protection as my Catskills hollow log.

According to Irving et al. (1955), the critical temperature for Alaskan porcupines is −12°C (10°F). When external temperature falls below that, the animals increase their metabolic rates above the basal level to maintain core temperatures of 37.5°C (Irving and Krog 1954). Steven Clarke (1969), working with Massachusetts porcupines, reports a critical temperature of −4°C (25°F). Based on the figure of Irving et al., both dens offer adequate protection, since den temperatures did not fall below −12°C in either case. With Clarke's figure, the rock den is superior, offering adequate protection for 4.5 days out of 8. The hollow-log den would have been adequate for less than 1 day, forcing the resident to burn extra fuel to maintain constant core temperature.

Both types of dens are essentially temperature-averaging devices. But the thermal mass of the rock den is much larger. Only long, severe cold spells could drop its internal den temperature to the critical level. In any case, both den types would protect against convectional and radiational heat loss.

The strategy of limiting radiational heat loss explains a curious observation I made in my third winter of radiotelemetry: some porcupines spend little or no time in winter dens. For the first two winters of observation, all my animals occupied dens. In the third winter I added two animals to the study, Moth and the crippled male Imp. Moth settled into a series of tree dens and the next winter had her adventure under the hunters' cabin, all within the range of normal porcupine behavior. Imp was different. He spent the winter in a hemlock-dominated area, entering his first den very late, on December 16. The den was the crawl space under a barn. The next week, Imp had moved to a neighbor's shed nearby. But he stayed under the shed for only three weeks and then left dens permanently. He spent the rest of the winter in the open, sheltering in or under hemlock trees.

The first time I found Imp in that situation was on a bitter night in January. The temperature had fallen to −28°C (−18°F), and a dry snow lay in drifts. He was under a hemlock, lying on the ground inside a crown of twisted apple branches. He had spent considerable time there. I saw several bedding hollows, such as deer make in the snow, and two large accumulations of droppings. A feeding trail moved off to the right. Imp looked moribund. He did not stir or erect his quills when I approached. A fine coating of snow covered his face, close to the ground. His condition looked so grave and the night was so bitter that I gave him only a 50-50 chance of surviving to morning. When I returned to check on him the next day, I was so uncertain of what I would find that I carried a heavy plastic bag as a body bag.

I reached the large hemlock with the apple thicket at its base. Imp was not inside. I looked up into the tree, dark in the dusk. There, close against the trunk and about 25 feet up, was the black shape of my animal. I thought he looked triumphant. For the remainder of the winter, Imp was always either up in a hemlock tree or in some thicket at its base. His feeding trail in the snow showed the drag mark of his paralyzed foot. He froze to death in March during a severe cold wave, when temperatures fell below those of January.

Because Imp had been crippled, I ascribed his behavior to his injury. And because he froze to death, I assumed that wintering in the open was nonadaptive. But in subsequent winters, two normal animals, the adult males Homer and Killer, went through the same behavior without visible ill effect. For two weeks at the beginning of the winter, Homer occupied rock dens. He spent all the rest of the winter in or under hemlock trees. Killer spent two entire winters in hemlock cover. One difference between Imp and the other males is that the latter wintered in hemlocks that formed a thick, unbroken forest. Imp's hemlocks grew in scattered groves and formed a less effective weather shield.

Evergreen cover offers thermal advantages in the winter. Hemlock needles are layered so thickly in the canopy that they shield a porcupine from the heat sink of the open sky. The trunks and foliage of the hemlocks also act as secondary sources of radiant energy, reradiating at night the energy they have absorbed during the day as well as the long-wave radiation emitted by the snow and surrounding vegetation (Clarke and Brander 1973). Naturalists across the country report that porcupines may spend winters in trees, away from formal dens. In every report that lists the tree

Pins and needles: porcupine in a white spruce. This species may be used by animals as a winter den substitute, and it forms an important winter food in the north.

species, they have been evergreens. Robert Brander (1973) reports that a Michigan porcupine spent 26 consecutive days sleeping and feeding in the crown of a hemlock. Graham Smith (1982) in northeastern Oregon found his animals sheltering from snow and wind in large, mistletoe-infested Douglas firs. The growths created witches'-brooms, whose dense architecture was particularly effective in sheltering the animals. Curtis and Kozicky (1944) list the most common "station trees" in Maine as hemlock and white spruce. In the thirties, Walter Taylor (1935) described the porcupines of Idaho spending much time in the winter in yellow pine, Douglas fir, and white fir.

Animals other than porcupines may depend on the hemlocks' green winter blanket. White-tailed deer converge on local hemlock stands during the winter and leave a maze of trails and sleeping depressions known as a deer yard. Their choice is commonly ascribed to reduced snow cover under hemlocks. Perhaps the hemlocks' sky-sheltering properties are of equal importance.

Spending the winter under hemlocks does not preclude a porcupine's use of a winter den. Moth used a series of hollow trees as dens in a hemlock grove. However, she emerged from her dens earlier in the spring than other animals and spent the interval in hemlock shelter. At least three other porcupines awaited full spring in hemlock groves after abandoning their rock dens for the winter.

Den Fidelity

Because porcupines do not dig or excavate their own dens but depend on ready-made shelters, good dens are often in limited supply. That may be why porcupines return year after year to the same dens. Squirrel, my animal under longest observation, has returned to the same palatial rock den for seven winters. Every other animal observed for more than one winter has returned to at least one den used in the previous winter. Sometimes there are breaks in the pattern of occupancy. Rebecca used den A in 1982–83, but not in 1983–84; she returned in 1984–85 and in the three subsequent winters. Animals returned to both rock and tree dens; outbuildings had less of a magnetic effect, perhaps because they were less intensively used to begin with. Other researchers have suspected but never proved that porcupines return to dens. In Wisconsin, L. W. Krefting recaptured a female in December 1952 that had been captured and marked two years earlier only 100 meters away (Krefting et al. 1962). However, he also found other animals far from sites of initial capture.

Den Change

Krefting's discrepancy is explained by porcupines' regular moves to new dens throughout the winter. I found my animals in new quarters, on average, every 23 days. Thus each animal was associated not with one den but with a suite of dens. The reasons for their frequent moves remain obscure.

One factor that regularly induced movement was disturbance at the den, such as trapping the animal. Of 19 cases when animals were trapped and promptly released at their dens, den change followed in 12 cases. The changes were usually not permanent. Squirrel abandoned her favorite den three times because of flooding by a midwinter snowmelt. Water entered in the back and ran through the den in a stream, scouring it of accumulated droppings. When water flow had abated, Squirrel returned to a clean, dry den.

Disturbance does not account for all the observed moves. Adult males may have greater wanderlust than juveniles or females. Of three adult males I followed for at least one winter, two did not use dens. The third adult male, Finder, used normal dens but changed them every nine days. That rapid rate of change differed not only from the patterns of females but also from Finder's own pattern as a juvenile, when he changed dens at the same rate as females and other juvenile males. Whether the pattern is true of other adult males requires further investigation.

Also requiring further study is the role of food in den change. Do animals change dens because they exhaust the food supply in the vicinity? On its face, that seems unlikely because porcupines often return to vacated dens later in the winter and resume feeding on the same trees they were gnawing before. What cannot be ruled out is that attacked trees throw up a chemical defense against the tree predator, just as they do in response to summer defoliators. The defense may be only temporarily effective and allow the animal to return weeks or months later. The question has not been investigated.

Den Sharing

For most of the winter, porcupines occupy their dens alone, sitting in their dimly lit recesses by day and emerging to feed at night. Activity indicators on their radiocollars suggest that they move little or not at all while in dens. That dozing, banked-down existence may be broken by the arrival of a second porcupine.

One cold December morning, Squirrel's radio signal led me to her favorite winter den, Split Rock den. Instead of the customary single feeding trail in the snow, two trails emerged from the den entrance. One led downhill to a near clump of freshly chewed sugar maples, the other climbed steeply uphill. As I stood examining the feeding sign, high-pitched squawks from within the den broke the winter stillness. They were the cries of an annoyed porcupine, and they did not let up until the beam of my flashlight pierced the interior gloom of the den. In the back of the long passageway stood two porcupines. Squirrel was in the back, apparently barring the passageway. The other animal carried no radiocollar. When I returned a week later, Split Rock den was silent, with Squirrel alone in possession of her spacious quarters.

On average, my porcupines shared winter dens only 12% of the time. There are clear indications that the experience is unsettling to both animals. Porcupines normally urine-mark the snow outside their dens, leaving a series of drips or small dribbles in the middle of the feeding trail. When two animals are in residence, both mark their trails, and the dribbles may grow into ostentatious streaks. Den-sharing seldom lasted longer than a week. In 12 of 17 instances of sharing, both animals abandoned the den, reacting to the sharing as they would to a serious disturbance. Other investigators report similar results. Jacob Shapiro (1949) in the Adirondacks never found more than one animal in a den. Wendell Dodge and Victor Barnes (1975) in western Washington report simultaneous occupation of a den by two porcupines only 4 times, and then only during breeding season. Their study site had a rugged topography with an abundance of den sites. Robert Brander (1973) in Michigan reports dual den occupancy in only 3 out of 46 cases. However, Dodge's (1967) porcupines in western Massachusetts shared dens so often that he describes the animals as "gregarious" during the winter. At the same time, he cites evidence of strife: the animals could be heard squawking inside their dens. The most probable explanation for those anomalous results is that Dodge's study site around Quabbin Reservoir contained few acceptable den sites. The rock outcrops in a rolling countryside contain few cavities, and the shortage may have forced porcupines to share dens.

In about half the cases in my study, only one of the two animals could be identified by its radio signal or by capture. But in the 6 cases out of 11 when both animals could be identified, they formed a male-female pair. The odds of that happening by chance alone are less than 1%.[2] Of further significance, the male and female had previously shared a summer territory. Thus, the male Finder shared both dens and summer territories with Squirrel and Cameo. And Squirrel's den was visited not only by Finder but also by the male Homer.

One anecdote illustrates the reluctance of two males to share a den. In early winter, I captured the juvenile male Pound to attach a radiocollar. To release him, I carried him up the ridge in a wire mesh cage to the region of abundant rock outcrops and den sites. As I toiled uphill through the snow, Pound remained calm and interested, sniffing the air as though to get his bearings. My path took us within 20 feet of Finder's occupied den. As we passed, Pound's reaction was striking: his quills rose slightly, and he emitted a wave of fear smell. He calmed only when we were safely past the den. I released him far away.

The reluctance of porcupines of the same sex to share dens may act as a population-dispersing mechanism in late fall, when animals first search for dens. As a young female wanders in search of an unoccupied tree or rock crevice, she may leave her birth site far behind. She will spend her first winter alone.

Den Abandonment

The days lengthen. Icicles grow over the entrances of rock dens and drip in the warming sun. The snow takes on a coarse, granular texture, and openings melt out around tree trunks. A red-eyed vireo begins to call. The time is coming for porcupines to abandon their dens. In the weeks of late winter or early spring, they can be found on windless days sunning themselves in trees outside their dens. Then, one day, they are a great distance away, feeding on new food sources and embarked on a new cycle of seasons.

The stimulus for den entrance was a string of days with minimum temperatures falling below freezing. The stimulus for den abandonment appears to be a combination of at least two factors. First, daily temperature minima must again climb above freezing. Second, the snow cover must melt off sufficiently to allow easy travel. If either requirement is not satisfied, the animals stay in their dens.

In 1983, temperatures had climbed above freezing by the first week of April, and the snow cover was shrinking daily. Then heavy snow fell for two days in mid-April. The snow pack reached its maximum thickness for the winter and did not disappear again until the last day of April, when temperature minima were well above freezing. All porcupines waited in their dens until the snow was gone. All were found out of their dens at the same time, on April 30 (Roze 1987). In 1985, the opposite situation developed. In a winter with only 35% of normal snowfall, the ground was bare by the third week of March. But porcupines held their places in dens until the first week of April, when minimum daily temperatures had climbed above freezing. The 1983 season had seen the latest date of dispersal from dens; 1985 saw the earliest. But in both years, the same conditions had been achieved: a temperate, snow-free environment. Even as the porcupines left their dark, often cramped quarters, each animal remembered the spot well, because it would be coming back in another winter.

Notes

1. Radiant heat loss, in kilocalories per square meter per hour, is given by the equation $Q_r = \varepsilon\, \sigma\, T_s^4$, where ε is the emissivity, ranging from zero to one; σ is the Stefan-Boltzmann constant; and T_s is the surface temperature in °K (Robbins 1983).

2. $(2 \times 0.34 \times 0.66)^6 = 0.008$.

8

Winter Foraging

On a January afternoon, I walk just below a ridge of Vly Mountain, as wind snatches away the sound of my snowshoes crunching the snow. A sudden rasping sound makes me pause. Not 20 feet away, a porcupine is debarking a small beech tree. It is about 12 feet off the ground, feeding on a two-inch-diameter trunk, working from the top down. A five-foot expanse of bare wood shines above it. The animal is removing the thin bark all the way around the branch; no portion is being rejected. It keeps changing the angle of attack as it chews rhythmically, then seems to lick the chewed area, or perhaps just swallows a mouthful of bark. As I approach slowly, it continues working. It may not have heard me or may not be used to humans walking along the ridgetop. Now I notice that the tree it is working on is stunted and misshapen, as are neighboring beech trees. This is the work of porcupines in winters past. Only when I stand directly below the porcupine and a human bodylength away does it take notice. It stops feeding, moves to the opposite side of the trunk, and erects its quills.

Leaving the porcupine to compose itself, I follow its snow-drifted feeding trail to a rock den 40 feet downhill. A flat, deep entranceway disappears inside the mountain. The view from the cave entrance is framed by large trees on both sides. Saddleback Mountain rises in the background. Below it lies the dark hemlock forest, bordered by white fields and a twisting country road. Through windblown snow crystals, the mountain has been joined to the earth and sky. Perhaps from a porcupine's vantage point, a wandering human in this landscape is too minor an element to react to.

Feeding Diversity

My hilltop porcupine was atypical in only one respect: it was feeding during the daytime. But like others in the area, it was a chewer of tree bark, a maker of snow trails, and an invader of available shelter. Winter food of porcupines is easily identified; the patches of missing bark in the tops of

Porcupine feeding sign in hemlock. Hemlock bark is not used because of its high tannin content. Instead, animals nip off terminal branches and consume needles and small twigs.

trees can be spotted from hundreds of feet away. In addition, they may use twigs, buds, and the needles of evergreens. Because of the visibility and economic importance of their feeding mode, porcupine winter food choices have been amply documented. The specific makeup of the winter diet seems to vary from community to community. For example, Tenneson and Oring (1985) compared porcupine feeding patterns at two sites three kilometers apart in Itasca State Park, Minnesota (Table 13). The French Creek porcupines used white pine, elm, and linden for 90% of their diet. For their Green Lake neighbors, the same species accounted for only 23% of the diet. It is significant that the three food species made up 24.8% of the forest at French Creek but only 10.4% at Green Lake. With populations only three kilometers apart showing such diversity of feeding behavior, it is not surprising that the porcupines of Idaho, New Brunswick, and Arizona should show even greater differences in winter food preference (Table 14).

Selectivity

Glancing at Table 14, one might conclude that porcupines are not selective about winter food choice. That would be wrong. In the Catskills, sugar maple is a preferred winter food, while red maple is almost never touched. Likewise, white ash, whose young spring leaves are highly preferred, are never attacked for their bark. The same is true of apples. Although the fruit (but not the leaves) are prized in August and September, apple bark is almost never touched in the winter. Hop hornbeam, a common species at lower elevations, is never sampled in the summer and used only sparingly during winter. Clearly, porcupines are both selective and opportunistic in their winter food choice.

Nutritional Ground Rules

Some general principles can help to rationalize the complex and contradictory picture of winter feeding behavior. Daniel Janzen (1979) of the University of Pennsylvania has pronounced a maxim relevant to the situation: "One beast's drink is another beast's poison." A given plant species is not universally acceptable to all animals. Red maple twigs, rejected by porcupines, are important winter browse for white-tailed deer. Apple bark, almost never touched by porcupines, is eagerly sought by field voles and cottontails; apple twigs are browsed by deer. Likewise, white ash twigs attract deer, who cannot reach them in the trees but travel long distances to feed on windthrows and logging slash. (The greater range of species options available to deer is counterbalanced by their inability to climb trees and chew bark.)

Every plant-herbivore system is a mutually interacting system. Plants respond to herbivore attack by erecting defenses in evolutionary and ecological time. Examples of evolutionary plant defenses are the physical defenses such as thorns, silica crystals, and leaf hairs. Chemical defenses may be either long-term (evolutionary) or short-term (ecological) in nature. They include compounds such as tannins, terpenes, alkaloids, cyanogens, salicylates, and a host of others. A herbivore can use the stored resources of a plant only if it can overcome the plant's physical and chemical defenses. Animals differ little in their basic metabolic requirements. They differ enormously, in both qualitative and quantitative ways, in their ability to overcome plant defenses.

In mammals, the primary organ of detoxification is the liver. Here toxic molecules are broken down or conjugated with carriers such as glucuronic acid to make them suitable for excretion. In herbivorous mammals, gut microorganisms play an equally important detoxification role. One spectacular example comes from the work of Milton J. Allison (1987), a USDA microbiologist at Ames, Iowa, and R. J. Jones and R. G. Megarrity (1986) from Queensland, Australia. They noted that goats in Hawaii could safely feed on *Leucaena leucocephala,* a small leguminous tree that produces the toxic amino acid mimosine. Cattle in Florida and Australia were poisoned by the same tree. Allison and his coworkers showed that a unique bacterium in the goat rumen degrades a toxic mimosine metabolite known as 3,4-dihydroxypyridine (DHP), protecting the goats. When Australian steers were inoculated with rumen fluid from the Hawaiian goats, they acquired the same DHP resistance as the goats.

The gut microorganisms of ruminants such as goats and deer inhabit the rumen, situated at the head of the small intestine. In porcupines, the gut microorganisms are concentrated in the caecum, at the end of the small intestine. That positional difference as well as qualitative differences in gut microflora may account for differences in food tolerances between porcupines and ruminants. In addition, indirect evidence suggests that the gut microflora may vary from one porcupine to another.

Detoxification is only part of the task of the gut microflora. Its other function is digestion. Plants lock up much of their carbon stores as structural carbohydrates, in cellulose, hemicellulose, and pectin, which are inaccessible to the digestive enzymes produced by the mammals themselves.[1] Hence all herbivores depend on the digestive enzymes of their gut microflora. The cellulose-digesting ability of porcupine caecal bacteria was demonstrated in 1949 by A. Balows and M. W. Jennison.

The porcupine's diet must supply two necessities: energy to drive the life processes (derived in large measure from cellulose digestion), and nutrients to replace worn-out body components. Most important of the nutrients are nitrogen (needed to build proteins and nucleic acids) and certain minerals. In terms of nitrogen, the porcupine's diet is distinctly inadequate. Better-quality winter foods contain nitrogen in the range of 1% by dry weight. Most tree bark falls below that level, with 0.5% a typical value. Animals cannot maintain constant body weights at that level of nitrogen intake. As a consequence, all porcupines I have examined lost weight during the winter. They survived only because they had built up reserves during the summer and fall.

If nitrogen and metabolizable carbon are low in winter foods, why don't the animals simply eat more? There is no lack of bark in the forest. The problem is processing time. The bacterial digestive processes of the caecum are relatively slow; it takes approximately two days for food to pass through the digestive tract. A faster passage would not give caecal bacteria sufficient time to do their work.[2]

Feeding Technique

Porcupines typically feed at night. With the settling of dusk, they shuffle out of their dens, urinate at the entrance, and snowplow their way toward a feeding tree, usually less than 300 feet away. Sometimes the animal feeds at the base of the tree, but more commonly it climbs into the crown and eats the bark of upper branches. With thick-barked trees such as adult sugar maple, it feeds in two phases. A first pass of the incisors shaves off the dead outermost cork layers—they fly in all directions and fall on the snow below. On the second pass, the porcupine harvests the inner bark, shaving it down to the cambium, grinding it with the cheek teeth, and swallowing it. Usually, bark on the outer branches is thin enough to be harvested in its entirety, in a single pass.

The pattern of tooth scrapes left on the trunk by an adult porcupine displays the animal's craftsmanship. The bark is removed only down to the cambium; the remaining surface is plywood-smooth, more finely finished than the work of beaver. The porcupine removes the bark in small triangular patches, each patch composed of five or six scrapes converging on an apex, like sticks in a tepee. The apex represents the position of the upper incisors, held fixed against the bark. The lower incisors scrape, moving over a fresh path as the lower jaw swivels in a narrow arc. Examined care-

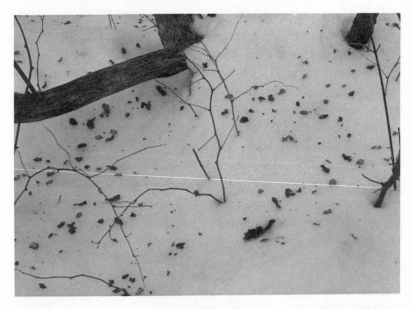

Outer bark, rejected by the porcupine, falls as frass in the snow. Animals feeding on thin-barked branches consume the entire bark.

fully, the anchor points of the upper incisors can be seen as spaced indentations around the edge of the open scrape. The final pattern on the trunk conveys rhythm, economy, and elegance. The animal does not scrape the same surface twice, does not leave residual strips of bark, and does not vary the depth of its scrape.

As I walked one day through persisting March snow, I came across a pair of chewed yellow birch that violated all those norms. The feeding job was strikingly messy. The animal had wasted effort by going over some areas twice, had elsewhere left scraps of inner bark on the trunk, had scraped at varying depths, and showed a chaotic, unrhythmic attack. A faint feeding trail led to a gray boulder on the edge of a clearing. I peered into a shallow recess underneath. At the far end, the darkly furred form of a small porcupine lay pressed against the rock. Capture was easy—the juvenile male was too small to put up a fight. It weighed 1.9 kg, just over 4 pounds, and carried one of my tiny numbered tags in its right ear. I had tagged it the previous summer, when it was only a few weeks old. It was now spending its first winter on its own. Like many a human baby, it remained a messy eater.

Juvenile's feeding sign: a messy job.

Adult feeding sign: even, rhythmic tooth scrapes.

Feeding Specializations of Individuals

The porcupine's feeding trail in the snow is a notebook of information. When I began to examine a series of such feeding trails, I was struck by something curious. Each animal was feeding on only one (sometimes two) species of trees, encountering and rejecting trees along its feeding trail that other porcupines might find entirely acceptable, might in fact be using as *their* species of choice. The top map on page 135 illustrates the distribution of trees along an actual feeding trail. The circles represent 17 trees attacked by the porcupine, some with only a light test bite, others heavily chewed. One small tree, 6.6 cm in diameter, had been stripped bare from top to bottom. All 17 trees were of a single species, beech. I counted all trees inside the trail, plus all trees within 3 meters (about 10 feet) around it, and assumed that they were available as feeding choices to the porcupine in question. The area encompassed 158 trees, with 87 beech, 37 sugar maple, 28 hop hornbeam, and 6 white ash. Of those four species, beech and sugar maple are highly preferred winter foods for the porcupine population as a whole, hop hornbeam is used rarely, and white ash never. The odds of attacking 17 beech trees by chance alone are less than 5 out of 1000, much lower than biologists like to accept as due to chance.[3] It is more reasonable to assume, therefore, that the porcupine is actively selecting beech to feed on.

Now consider another porcupine, observed a year later and about one mile away. This animal picked its way downhill, traveling in the snow shadows of two large boulders and a rock outcrop, then fed on 7 sugar maples strung out on a line. The 28 trees within 3 meters of the feeding trail included 16 sugar maples and 2 each of red maple, striped maple, mountain maple, hop hornbeam, beech, and white ash. Porcupines regularly feed on sugar maple, striped maple, mountain maple, and beech. Hop hornbeam and red maple are rarely touched, and white ash is rejected. The probability of randomly selecting 7 sugar maples in this feeding area is greater than 0.5, or not low enough to rule out random selection.[4] Nevertheless, the second porcupine selected a diet that did not overlap the diet of the first porcupine.

The two porcupines discussed here (and all others examined) selected feeding areas in which their preferred tree species was the most abundant

Porcupine foraging area (stippled) with looped feeding trail. All trees selected are beech.

Porcupine foraging area (stippled). All trees selected are sugar maples.

species. The first porcupine, feeding on beech, encountered beech 55% of the time while feeding. The second porcupine, feeding on sugar maple, encountered sugar maple 57% of the time. That could mean that a porcupine's feeding choice is dictated by surrounding forest composition, or it could mean that porcupines select areas enriched in the preferred tree species. To explore the question, I selected control areas for each feeding area and statistically sampled their species composition. Control areas, 30 meters from the feeding areas and at the same elevation, measured 30 m by 30 m; 100 trees were sampled in each. Sample comparisons of forest composition in feeding and control areas are given in Table 15. Because the control areas were larger and more evenly distributed, they reflected more accurately the local forest composition. The comparisons suggest that porcupines are selecting patches of forest that are richer in the desired food species. The differences are statistically significant and are large enough to reflect active choice, not random fluctuation in forest composition. Why should the porcupine make that choice? Perhaps for the same reason it travels in its own footsteps and does not venture far from the den to feed: its body is poorly designed for travel in deep snow. By selecting a winter foraging area where the desired species is dominant, it can reach its food in fewer footsteps.

and Sunquist found that individual animals had "modal trees"—species in which they spent the majority of their time, feeding as well as resting. No two animals with a common home range (other than mother-infant pairs) shared the same species of modal tree. Montgomery and Sunquist point out that such specialization reduces competition within the species. The role, if any, played by individual gut microflora remains to be elucidated.

Winter Range

Porcupines feed a short distance from their winter dens, as first noted by J. D. Curtis in Maine in 1941. Curtis found that 35% of all feeding occurred within 100 feet of the den, 59% within 200 feet, and 83% within 300 feet. In addition, porcupines move relatively short distances when changing dens. Both behaviors reflect the animals' difficulty in traveling in the snow. The combination of feeding movements and den-change movements defines an animal's winter range. During the normal snowy Catskills winters, my porcupines showed a drastic decrease in movements compared with summer activity. For the first three years of radiotelemetry, their winter ranges averaged 7.4 ha (18.3 acres), and their summer ranges 64.9 ha (160.4 acres). That represents an 89% decrease in movement.

But during the winter of 1984–85, my porcupines wandered all over the mountains, testing and abandoning far-flung dens. Their winter ranges averaged 59.9 ha, a value statistically indistinguishable from normal summer range. The difference was snowfall. The weather station at Prattsville, eight miles away, recorded only 35% of the snow falling in previous winters. For much of the winter, the mountains were bare. The following summer, New York City's Catskills reservoir system came close to drying up, the city declared a drought emergency, Mayor Koch did a rain dance at the Ashokan Reservoir, and the city's water commissioner was forced to resign. Perhaps if he had been aware of the unusual winter behavior of porcupines, both he and the city might have taken more timely action.

Those dramatic porcupine responses to snow cover help resolve a discrepancy in the literature with respect to winter range. Dodge and Barnes (1975) radiotelemetered 18 porcupines in a Douglas fir–western hemlock forest in western Washington. The animals were tracked for up to 432 days

A porcupine must snowplow a trail in heavy snow.

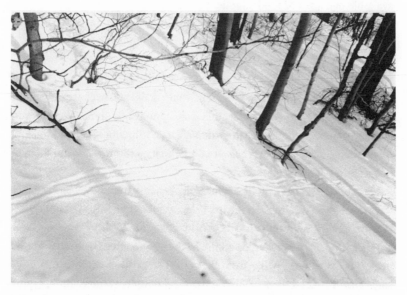

Modes of traveling in the snow: tobogganing down a hillside. A glaze of ice lies under a thin surface powder.

each. They showed no difference between summer and winter movements. No other radiotelemetry study at this time has followed porcupines through a winter-summer cycle, but all other authors report decreased movements in the winter on the basis of trapping data. The discordant observations of Dodge and Barnes are probably best explained by local weather. Their western Washington State study site lies in the western foothills of the Cascade Range. The falling snow is relatively wet there and freezes to form a hard crust. The crusted snow offers no impediment to porcupine winter movements, unlike the deep, fluffy snow of the Catskills, in which porcupines can sink up to their bellies. Dodge and Barnes point out an additional factor that favors an unchanged winter range in their animals. Den sites and winter foods are evenly distributed throughout the study area. The porcupines are not forced to assemble in specific locations such as upper-elevation rock outcrops where den sites may be found.

One may conclude that porcupines decrease their movements in winter not because of cold but because of snow. Their short legs and naked foot-pads are more useful on other substrates. In addition, porcupines in some locations may be forced to curtail winter travel because of restrictions on available den sites or food supplies.

Influence on the Forest

Because porcupines feed close to their winter dens, and because they return to the same dens year after year, they can significantly influence the structure and composition of the surrounding forest. Porcupines don't affect the woods in the same way that beavers do, who may fell trees or kill them by flooding low-lying sections.

Porcupines seldom kill a tree outright. When a tree dies, the death follows from basal girdling. To measure the extent of tree killing, I tallied 812 feeding trees in current use over two winters. Only 38 (4.7%) had been girdled at the base and therefore killed. The species composition of girdled trees was indistinguishable from that of all trees used (61% beech, 29% sugar maple, 10% others). Girdled trees did not, on average, differ significantly in diameter from the overall tree population used for feeding

(14.7 cm for girdled versus 14.0 cm for all trees used). There was, however, an upper limit to the size of trees girdled. The largest tree girdled was 40.4 cm in diameter. Many feeding trees were larger, up to 84.4 cm for a sugar maple. Porcupines presumably avoid basal feeding on the giant trees because the thick outer bark must be laboriously removed to reach the edible inner regions.

In my survey, the girdled beech trees did not succumb immediately. Beech tree No. 225 (18 cm diameter) was girdled in the winter of 1978–79. Against all expectation, it flourished during the summer of 1979, only to be girdled again during the winter of 1979–80. That kind of resistance is probably a result of the interlocking root systems of beech trees. When girdling prevents a beech tree from nourishing its own roots, its neighbors may offer assistance.

Most porcupine feeding occurred in the crown of the tree. Of the 812 trees examined, 248 showed some degree of feeding (often only a small test bite) on the lower 2 feet of the trunk. When I counted only heavy feeding (removal of more than 100 cm^2 of bark or girdling of the tree), I found that 84 trees (10.3%) had suffered significant basal damage. The bulk of serious feeding took place in the upper regions of the trees, usually among the small branches of the crown.

It can be argued that porcupines are long-term agents of ecological diversification. Their winter habit of seeking out forest patches enriched with preferred trees should make it easier for rare tree species to invade such feeding areas. Unmolested by the porcupines and unsuppressed by the original dominants, the added species should contribute to the diversity and stability of the forest. The porcupine's suppression of the forest canopy should also encourage the understory, with advantages to a range of animals such as the ruffed grouse, snowshoe hare, white-tailed deer, moose, mourning warbler, yellowthroat, and a variety of other songbirds and small mammals.

Like the beaver, the porcupine is a manager of its habitat. Its management efforts are restricted to small patches of forest in the vicinity of the winter dens. Because the sites are often in rugged and inaccessible terrain, they are seldom seen by human visitors. But to many of the permanent residents of the forest, the porcupine's patches offer food and home.

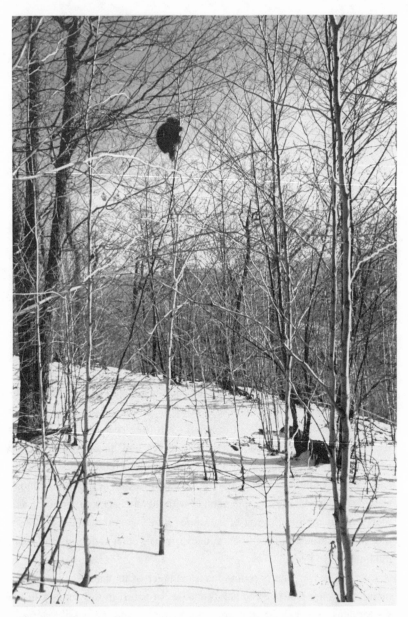

Finder in the top of a beech sapling. Most winter feeding of porcupines takes place in the canopy.

Notes

1. Cellulose is a polymer of glucose in beta 1-4 linkage. Hemicelluloses are predominantly polymers of five-carbon sugars. Pectin is largely a galacturonic acid polymer in alpha 1-4 linkage. Starches are polymers of glucose in alpha 1-4 and alpha 1-6 linkage (Robbins 1983).

2. I have measured gut passage time by placing wild porcupines on a 100% apple diet. Animals feeding in the wild produce bulky droppings. The low-fiber diet of apples produces much smaller droppings. The transition time between the two dropping types is approximately 48 hours.

3. $\chi^2 = 8.38$, df = 1, $P < 0.005$.

4. $\chi^2 = 1.9$, df = 3, $P > 0.5$. Not significant, assuming only the four palatable species are subject to attack.

5. The work of R. E. Hungate (1966) has shown that among ruminant herbivores at least, there may be a match between dietary plant species and specific gut microorganisms. For example, the protozoan *Ophryoscolex purkynei* does better on grass than on an alfalfa diet. *Diplodinium dentatum* is intolerant of clover, unlike *Epidinium* species, which prefer red clover and starchy foods. Hungate has shown further that certain protozoa are mutually intolerant. For example, *Polyplastron multivesiculatum* is intolerant of *Epidinium* species and *Eudiplodinium maggii*.

.9.

Reproduction and Maternal Care

Somewhere ahead, a porcupine is screaming. I walk through a leaf-bright October forest, tracking Rebecca. The sound starts again, close. She is up a young oak tree, a dark mass near the end of the branch, and a second porcupine sits next to her. At 5:25 p.m., the sun has already set, but the western sky glows brightly and the near-transparent October canopy affords a clear view. An autumn bite is in the air. In the Catskills, mid-September to mid-October represents the peak of the porcupine mating season. Through my binoculars I study Rebecca and her suitor. He looks coal-black, in contrast to Rebecca's more silvery hue. They seem to be equal in size.

The male advances toward Rebecca, and she retreats to the tip of the branch. Her back is turned to her would-be lover, and as he tries to reach her, she gives him little slaps with her tail. The male retreats—porcupines are as vulnerable to quills as other animals. Rebecca is howling, the waves of sound washing through the empty woods. Her suitor answers more softly. He reaches out his paw to her tail, but she slaps again.

At one point, Rebecca seems to be weakening: her tail is half-raised. The male immediately puts his head down and tries to sniff her rump. Then he elevates himself on his haunches as though to say he is ready. But Rebecca is not.

The male is enterprising. He retreats to the trunk of the oak tree, climbs up to the next branch, and heads out over Rebecca, trying to reach her from above. But the distance is too great, and he returns to his starting point.

Rebecca rebuffs him the way a buffalo rebuffs her male: she sits down. Then she gets up and turns to face him. She has retreated to the outermost limits of the branch and utters small cries as the male presses in. Surprisingly, he moves back toward the trunk to wait. I have been watching for 15 minutes. The woods have fallen absolutely still.

Rebecca's next action seems totally inappropriate. She nips off a twig and begins to feed. The red oaks are still holding their acorns, and porcupines have been mast-feeding for weeks. But as Rebecca feeds, the male keeps drawing closer and interrupting her. *He* is not hungry. When the male approaches again, Rebecca squawks and whirls to face him. She keeps trying to feed but drops her branch. The male retreats slightly and waits, rounded up and dark. Rebecca turns her back, which the male accepts as encouragement. He touches her gently on the rump. Rebecca jerks, spins around, and screams. The male shuffles all the way back to the trunk, descends to the next lower branch, and tries to find a pathway up from below. There is none. He comes back to his previous position. The light is getting dusky now, and my breath is more visible in the cold, but the porcupines look fluffed out and warm.

The male approaches again with reassuring chuckling sounds but is thrown back by a scream. At 6 p.m., as Rebecca goes on feeding, the male creeps up from behind. Rebecca turns and cries out, but her cry is softer now. In the dusky light, I can't be sure what happens next, but she appears to offer him the branch she has been feeding on. They feed on the same branch at opposite ends. Then Rebecca nips off another branch. The two feed side by side, about two feet apart.

Now the male approaches quietly and lowers his head to sniff the spot where Rebecca has been sitting. She continues feeding. I become aware of the moon shining through the trees above the ridge. At 6:20 the animals have stopped feeding and sit quietly next to each other, rounded out against the cold. Ten minutes later, they have become two black knots against the darkness of the trees. The moon catches a slight haze in the air and hangs like a paper lantern above them. I turn home. I expect that the persistence and gentleness of the male will prevail in the end, but at the same time, I realize I have not been admitted to a mystery. Despite years of study by a series of naturalists, many aspects of porcupine reproductive behavior still retain this quality of half-revelation.

Male-Female Interaction

Reproductive activity is both more and less important in the life of the porcupine than in the life of the human being. It is more important because an adult female like Rebecca can expect to spend 11 months a year either pregnant or lactating, year after year with no time off to rebuild body reserves. On the other hand, Rebecca is unlike humans in that she may copulate only once a year, during the 8- to 12-hour period that she is in heat and solicits the male. But 12 hours out of the year represents only a small percentage of her time.

The male, who does not normally spend any time with the female, must find that tiny window of opportunity. As a female approaches her estrus, the membrane that had obstructed the vaginal orifice weakens and dissolves. The vagina begins to secrete a thick mucus, apparently serving as an olfactory cue for males. They follow the faint odor trail to its source. During the mating season, males wander more widely than in the months before. For instance, Homer's home range for July-August 1983 (before mating season) measured 19.9 ha (49 acres), but during mating season, in October-November, it grew to 100 ha (247 acres). In fact, mating-season

Rebecca (farthest on the branch) rebuffs her suitor.

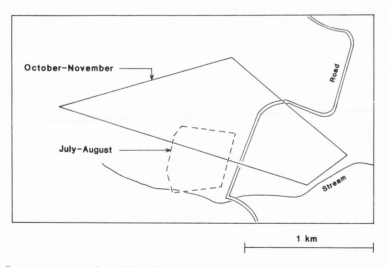

Range expansion of an adult male during breeding season (October-November).

wanderlust may explain the larger overall home range of dominant adult males. Home ranges of subadult males do not expand at mating time. When Finder was 1 year old, in the summer of 1983, his July-August home range measured 13.3 ha; the October-November range actually shrank, to 9.0 ha (see map on page 148).

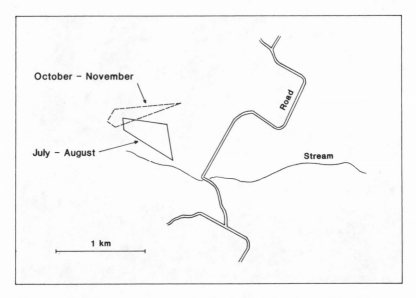

Absence of breeding-season range expansion in Finder, an immature male.

As the males wander, pre-estrous females send olfactory signals. A female advertises her reproductive status by the odor of her urine as well as by the vaginal mucus. With the vaginal closure membrane gone, the mucus can mix with the urine, and a male can check her condition simply by sniffing the urine under her tree. More important, the urine spattering down through the canopy will generate an odor cloud that will alert males far away.

Most of the time, the male following an odor plume arrives too early. Though the female's urinary and vaginal secretions have started to signal, she is not yet receptive. The male therefore begins to guard her. He climbs into her tree and waits on a lower branch, sniffing periodically to check her status. Sometimes he gently nudges her from behind, forcing her forward on the branch so he can sniff the surface she has been covering.

The guarding behavior may last several days, and it may involve more than one male. I got an illustration on a late-September evening as I followed Rebecca through another mating season. This time, Rebecca was up a giant yellow birch with the male Taylor, so close on the same branch they were touching. Neither animal had its quills erected, but Rebecca seemed annoyed. She gave small, sharp squawks, more than once a minute. When

Rebecca turned her side to the male, he pushed his head into her lower belly. She squawked but did not budge. Taylor pulled back, then plunged his head once more into her belly, keeping it there a long time. At 7:15, Rebecca increased the frequency of her vocalizations till she was calling almost continuously, but softly. At 7:35 she stopped. It was now so dark I could not see the animals. Around 8:30 a wind picked up and masked any sounds coming from above. Chilled to the fingers, I left. On my way home, I noted that the small immature male Goff was in a tree about 100 feet to the east.

When I returned the next evening, Rebecca and Taylor had moved up-hill, almost to the top of the ridge. Even from a distance, I could hear squawking. I found both in a giant oak tree, but on separate branches. I couldn't guess what Taylor had been doing to elicit the protest, but all was silence when I reached the pair. On this second day of signaling by Rebecca, two other males were relatively close. Goff had moved downhill and was now about 600 feet away. Rebecca's adult son Ram was on the other side of the ridge, about 500 feet away. For a moment I thought I may have spotted another male, a large, compact shape clinging to a sapling. Then, like a magician, it bent its head, raised two giant wings, and flew noiselessly away to the east—a barred owl. I hurried on to locate other porcupines, working into the night. At 1:40 a.m., from far away, I heard the high-pitched screams of porcupine, coming from Rebecca's position.

On day 3 Rebecca had moved a short distance from her previous position and was up a large oak tree, alone. But the number of her admirers had increased. A booming radio signal came from the adjacent oak tree, which held Killer, a powerful male. Killer was looking rather sorry. A second male was guarding him. Killer was as far out on a branch as he could get, his tail turned to his pursuer. I saw at least two white quillshafts embedded in the other male's muzzle. I recognized the animal. It was not Taylor but Mayday, a large male who had dropped his transmitter four years previ-ously, retaining the nylon collar around his neck. The collar emphasized his muscular build and suggested a determined nature.

Under the tree I found a storm of loose quills, some commingled with tufts of hair. Some quills were kinked and toothmarked, suggesting that the victims had extracted them from their own skins. Many more quills lay under Rebecca's tree 30 feet away. A great battle between males had taken place here; the screams of the previous night had probably come from the males, and the battle was not yet finished. Long-courting Taylor had been vanquished, but Killer and Mayday remained so involved with each other that they had left Rebecca alone in her tree. Evidence showed the struggle had taken place on the ground. In many places, the ground cover had been torn up, with quills driven into leaves and twigs. Weapons had included the formidable incisor teeth; large tufts of hair had been torn out along with quills. The tufts had come from the sides and upper back, where the quill defense was less effective. I collected 1474 quills, with many more escaping my notice among dry leaves and twigs.

Rebecca's first suitor, Taylor, had fled about 200 feet away, on the other side of the ridge. He had been involved in the melee; there were seven dozen loose quills under his tree. They had been combed, shaken, or pulled out of his coat, not lost during primary battle. Goff and Ram were even farther away than on the previous day.

On day 4 Rebecca's mating encounter remained unresolved. She had moved about 200 feet west, taking Killer and Mayday with her. All three animals were up the same tree, a large, sloping sugar maple. Rebecca was

The residue of battle: 1474 quills lost by three males in competition over a female.

resting on an outer branch; the two males remained preoccupied with each other and sat on a separate branch. Mayday, with foreign quills still projecting from his muzzle, was on the inside, guarding Killer. But Killer was no longer dangerously far out on the limb and showed little fear of Mayday. I found 6 quills under the tree. Two showed toothmarks, indicating they had been pulled out of the skin by the porcupines above.

I don't know who finally inseminated Rebecca, but it is clear that male porcupines vary considerably in their reproductive success, more so than females (Tables 16 and 17). Whereas essentially every female bears one young a year, some males may produce no offspring, others may sire several. Mating success in males is positively correlated with weight (and probably age) of the male and with the size of his nonwinter territory. (Finder is excluded from the analysis in Table 16 because he suffered a serious fall from a tree in 1986, which appears to have left him permanently impaired. He had a high mating success in the previous year and a much larger home range.) Apparently the female's long preovulatory signaling facilitates the variation in male reproductive success. Because the males receive sufficient advance notice, all receptive females are likely to be located, and several males can assemble and either leave the scene or do battle for supremacy. The female is therefore assured of mating with the strongest, most persistent male. In fact, it is possible that a single dominant male may inseminate all the females within his home range. It is probably significant that Rebecca's 1987 territory lay partly outside Killer's 1987 range, calling his authority into question.

However, the female cannot be raped. The consummation of the sex act takes place only when the female is receptive; most successful copulations are thought to take place on the ground. Both Albert Shadle (1946, 1951, 1952; Shadle et al. 1946) and Wendell Dodge (1967, 1982) have described the process of copulation in the porcupine, the former in a laboratory setting, the latter in the wild.

Perhaps the strangest aspect of the interaction is male urine-hosing of the female. The male approaches on his hind legs and tail, grunting in a low tone. His penis springs erect. He then becomes a urine cannon, squirting high-pressure jets of urine at the female. Everything suggests the urine is fired by ejaculation, not released by normal bladder pressure. Porcupines with everyday full bladders don't squirt their urine, don't have erections, and don't aim at females (Shadle 1946, 1951; Dathe 1963; Dodge 1967).

Shadle, observing the process in caged animals, noted that the urine salvos were so powerful that drops of urine splattered on the laboratory floor 6.5 feet away. In less than a minute, a female may be thoroughly wetted from nose to tail, especially her belly and sides. If the female is not ready, she may vigorously shake off the urine and walk or run away. If she is ready, she does not object. The urine hosing may begin in the tree; then the pair descend to the ground, where more showers may follow.

Finally the female assumes the traditional copulation posture of mammals: she elevates her hind quarters and curves her tail back over the quill rosette. If the female is insufficiently aroused, the tail may be only partially elevated and may require pushing aside by the male. He can now penetrate without fear of impalement. He rests his forepaws against the quill-free undersurface of the tail or lets them hang loosely. Dodge (1967) states: "Sexual contact is very brief, with a violent orgasm, after which the male drops back and proceeds to groom and cleanse himself. After short periods of rest, the play is pursued again until one or the other climbs a tree where he or she will scream at the other member, thus ending further mating attempts."

According to Shadle, each sex act lasts 1 to 5 minutes, but repeated copulations may stretch the interaction out over several hours. In the end the male lies exhausted, though the female may solicit additional copulations. Within hours a half-inch-diameter vaginal plug, with a bluish white, starchy appearance, forms in the vulva. The vaginal plug, a reproductive feature of many rodents, is apparently formed by enzymatic action on the semen and is therefore a male product. Though its role in porcupines has not been studied, proposed functions in other animals include gradual release of spermatozoa as the plug disintegrates, prevention of semen loss, and blockage of copulation by other males (Voss 1979). A further possibility in the porcupine is that it may reduce the female's ability to signal to other males.

Male Reproductive System

In addition to the strange courtship by urine, male porcupines show a number of further reproductive idiosyncrasies.

The baculum (described in Chapter 3) keeps the penis normally retracted within the penile sheath, where it lies flexed like a partly folded jackknife

Tip of porcupine penis in cutaway view (after Hooper 1961). B, baculum; U, urethra; S, surface spines of glans; SU, sacculus urethralis; BS, basal spines in sacculus.

(Mirand and Shadle 1953). The flaccid length is about 7.5 cm, the same as the depth of the vagina. Erection is accomplished in two ways. A rapid muscular contraction straightens out the penis, everting it beyond the penile sheath. That happens not in minutes, as in humans, but in two to four seconds. Further erection is accomplished by the same mechanism as in other mammals: the influx of blood into the three central chambers (the corpora cavernosa). The baculum has little to do with keeping the penis erect; its average length is only 1.2 cm (0.5 inch).

The glans (tip) of the porcupine penis is covered with low spines about 0.3 mm thick and 1 mm long. Most are conical, but some are double- or triple-crested. Mirand and Shadle, who described the spines, report they are made of a horny material and arranged irregularly on the surface. Undoubtedly the structures add something to the female's sensations during coitus, but it is not known whether they help induce orgasm or go farther and induce ovulation. Such spines are common among hystricomorph rodents, for example guinea pigs, agouti, paca, and nutria.

A bizarre accessory of the penis that Mirand and Shadle failed to describe is a small, eversible sac, the sacculus urethralis (Pocock 1922,

Hooper 1961). When the penis is viewed from the tip and the glans is slightly retracted, two openings appear: the urethra above (dorsally) and the sacculus urethralis below. Both openings are visible to the naked eye. The low prickles, which cover the glans, end at the urethral opening but cover the inner surface of the sacculus urethralis. At the bottom of the sacculus sit two larger spines, each about 2 mm long. During full erection, the sacculus everts, and the large spines as well as surface prickles are brought into view. Eversion of the sac is controlled by the amount of blood in the engorged penis as well as by longitudinal cords at the base of the sac. The function of the sacculus remains unknown. The male porcupine shares the extraordinary structure with other New World and Old World porcupines and with hystricomorph rodents in general. It is perhaps significant that in so many of the species with a sacculus, large spines are situated in the bottom of the sac. They should provide strong vaginal stimulation during intercourse, in addition to effects of the smaller surface spines of the glans. The sacculus may therefore function as a housing for penile spines too large to fit comfortably on more exposed regions of the glans.

Sperm production typically requires temperatures lower than body core temperature. For that reason, the testes of sexually mature mammals are housed in the relatively cooler environment of the scrotal sacs. The so-called porcupine scrotal sacs are not histologically similar to scrota of typical mammals, but they appear to have a similar physiological function (Pocock 1922, Weir 1974). Embryonically, the mammalian testes develop inside the abdominal cavity, near the kidneys. They then descend into the scrotum through the inguinal canals. Mirand and Shadle showed that in porcupines, the testes descend at least twice. The first time is in the embryo. But within 8 days following birth, the testes travel back into the abdominal cavity. The second time is at the onset of sexual maturity. For my male Finder, that occurred at the age of 24 months. When examined in March 1984, at the age of 22 months, Finder's scrotal sacs were empty. In May, when Finder was 24 months old, I was amazed to find a swelling, but on one side only. The right testis had descended; its mate was still in the abdomen. In August 1984 Finder had two plump swellings around the cloaca; both testes were down. For the male Ram, one testis had descended at 25 months, with the other only half-descended.

Since the onset of his sexual maturity, I have captured Finder 13 times, at all times of year, and the testes have remained in their scrotal sacs. The same has not been true of other adult males examined, including Ram. Their testes have remained abdominal from roughly January to July, descending to the scrotum from August to December. My observations agree with those of Dodge in Massachusetts, who found testes abdominal through most of the year, descending to the scrotal pouches during breeding season. Reasons for the variation between males are unknown, and other porcupine populations have not been studied from this perspective.

Female Reproductive Tract

Because female porcupines almost invariably produce a baby every year, despite a relatively brief annual receptive period, it has been suggested (without proof) that the act of coitus itself induces ovulation. That is the pattern in many rodents, as well as ferrets, rabbits, and others (Weir 1974). Wendell Dodge (1967) suggests another explanation for the high fecundity: females may be cyclic ovulators. If a female is not fertilized during her first ovulation period, she may recycle a month later, as in the case of human females. Dodge's hypothesis is supported by his histological examination of porcupine ovaries and by a stretched-out mating period in his New England porcupines (September to January).

Among my Catskills porcupines, the peak mating period spanned mid-September to mid-October (Table 18). Of 33 male-female interactions observed over four years, all involved guarding behavior in a tree or male-female joint presence in a den. In no case was the copulation proper observed. According to the recycling theory, the December interactions represented last-chance copulations for females who had failed in October or November. In at least one case, that was not possible. On December 31, 1985, I found Squirrel in a den with a male. If that were the time of copulation, her baby should have been born around July 30, 1986. But I found her with an approximately 2-week-old baby on June 7, suggesting conception at the end of October or beginning of November. Her December encounter may have been just for warmth. On the other hand, Squirrel's 1984 mating-season encounters lend support to the recycling theory. She was with males on September 16, October 13, and November 11, roughly on a 28-day schedule as suggested by Dodge. Unfortunately the date of birth of her baby cannot be fixed because it was discovered late in the summer.

Some strong if circumstantial evidence for recycling comes from an observation by Betty Lou Burge (1966) of a young captive female porcupine. The porcupine passed a vaginal cast on September 8, 1965, and again 28 days later, on October 6. Each cast resembled a small (7.5 cm long) translucent sausage casing. The cast represents the intact epithelial lining of the vagina, which proliferates extensively and is sloughed off intact following estrus. Burge allowed the animal free access to a male and on August 10 observed copulation, 28 days before the passing of the first cast. The female delivered a baby on May 15, 1966, suggesting another mating at the beginning of October. Since the animals were not observed around the clock, additional copulations were possible. The interpretation is that the female went into estrus on August 10, September 8, and October 6, with copulations each time but successful fertilization only on the last try.

Pregnancy and Birth

The term of pregnancy of the porcupine is one of the longest known in the animal world. At 210 days, it approaches that of the human, whose body mass is ten times larger (Shadle 1948). Possibly a shorter term cannot be managed on the porcupine's winter diet, when females are losing weight even as their fetuses are growing. But the timing of the mating season and pregnancy accomplishes two goals. By finishing more than 90% of all matings by November, porcupines exploit the autumnal mobility of males. Once December snows have fallen, the movements of all porcupines are reduced by about 89%, and males may no longer be able to follow interesting odor trails. Second, the timing of births for early May assures mothers of a rich diet for milk production while babies find the enriched diets they need for rapid weight gain. Hence the embryo that implants in October is implanting at the optimal time. During the winter, when essentially all females are pregnant, they conserve their energy, shelter deep in the earth, and try to maintain body weights on inadequate diets. The fetus is growing inside the mother's body but remains small. During the last month of pregnancy, in April or May, a rich spring diet suddenly becomes available, and the fetus roughly doubles in size.

At birth, the baby is well developed and weighs around 490 grams (about 1 pound). It is completely covered with fur and quills but comes into the world much like a cat, wrapped in its caul (the amnion). Inside the caul, the quills are soft. After delivery, the mother licks off and eats the caul. It contains valuable minerals and protein; its removal also keeps odor-cued predators such as foxes and weasels from locating the baby. Though the baby's quills harden during the first hour and it defends itself with vigorous tail flicks, its best defense at that time is to hide.

My closest experience with birth in the wild came on May 5, 1986, when I found a porcupine baby that may have been only hours old. I had searched for babies all day. In the morning I had radiotracked Moth to an impenetrable tangle of slash; all her behavior indicated she was hiding a baby there and not stirring far from its side. In the afternoon, higher up the mountain, I spotted an unmarked porcupine on the ground, about 100 feet ahead. The animal was conspicuous against the browns of the forest floor; the wildflower peak at that altitude would still be some weeks ahead. I out-ran the porcupine, captured it, and examined it. It was a 3.9 kg (8.6 pound) female, and it had recently given birth. Its vaginal closure membrane showed a small cross-shaped scar in the process of closing up again. I milked a nipple and expressed a small drop of milk. But though I searched every fallen tree trunk and rock crevice, I could not locate her baby. I pressed on and located two more animals.

My last visit of the day was with Rebecca. She had descended to the bottom of the valley, where cutleaf toothwort bloomed in green islands among persisting browns. I reached her just as she was ascending a medium-sized red maple. That meant she had been spending time on the ground, a suspicious behavior. She climbed slowly and stopped about 10 feet off the ground at the first small branch. There she remained clinging vertically to the tree trunk. She had to have a baby nearby. Almost immediately, I saw it. Instead of hiding in some crevice or shadow, it lay in plain view, pressed against the exposed root of a beech tree adjacent to Rebecca's refuge, a small black mass against the gray of the bark.

It was the smallest porcupine I had ever seen. It did not run when I reached for it. I gathered it inside a paper lunch bag and weighed it: 450 grams on my spring scale, almost exactly 1 pound. Then I examined it more closely. The head seemed out of proportion, taking up almost half the body. At first it watched me through eyes bright and open under the long eyelashes, then through eyelids closed down to a squint, as though hiding. Its incisors were fully erupted, but they were as narrow as little needles and totally white, lacking the orange enamel of adults. As I held it, it began to chatter its teeth in the traditional warning of porcupines, but the teeth didn't make contact and there was only a vibrating silence. It also made small slaps with its tail, shedding diminutive all-black quills that looked like tiny splinters and measured only 5 mm long. The baby was entirely black; none of the quills carried the white contrast coloration. I smelled it up close. It was odorless, lacking the pungent signature of the adult porcupine. Pink skin gleamed through sparse belly fur. The sex was female. The footpads were tiny versions of the adult's. From its navel, a shriveled umbilical cord still hung. I estimated its age at about one day and wondered whether Rebecca's halfhearted climb was due to exhaustion or to maternal conflict. During the entire episode, she watched intently but made no sound and did not move to rescue her baby.

I put the baby back at the base of its beech tree, and it made a pathetic attempt to hide, pushing its head partially under a root but leaving the rest of the body exposed. It lay still, then opened one eye to see if I was gone. I went, after making one more observation. Nowhere in the vicinity could I find an accumulation of porcupine droppings such as adults leave when they lie in one spot for a few hours. In a number of mammals, the mother stimulates defecation of young offspring by licking under the tail, then eating the feces, thus robbing a predator of a valuable cue. I have found the same cleanliness around all baby porcupines discovered in the woods. Only when the baby is old enough to climb do tiny droppings begin to accumulate under the tree.

At the time of discovery, I didn't have a chance to examine the mother. Two weeks later, I weighed her at 5.5 kg (12.1 pounds). Assuming that as her weight at the time of delivery, the baby represented 8.2% of the mother's weight. For comparison, a 7.25-pound human baby delivered by a 125-pound mother represents 5.8% of the mother's weight. Because of such high maternal investment, twin births appear to be at least as rare among porcupines as they are among humans. Of 24 porcupine babies I have encountered over the years, all have been singlets. Albert Shadle (1950) states that of several thousand births reported, not a single twin birth has been found. Wendell Dodge (personal communication) also has never observed a twin birth.

Rebecca's baby grew rapidly. It essentially doubled its weight in two weeks. Later in the summer, the weight gain slowed but nevertheless remained well above the rate shown by its mother (Table 19).

Lactation

One reason for the differential weight gain must be that the mother is feeding on tree leaves, the baby on tree leaves plus milk. Even though the porcupine bears only one offspring at a time, it has four nipples, one pair under the armpits and the other pair abdominal. (Over the years, I have discovered two females with an odd nipple count—each carried five. And two other females, a mother-daughter pair, had only two nipples each.) According to Shadle (1950), the baby takes turns nursing at all four nipples. The mother squats on her haunches and tail, allowing the baby to nose about her belly (which is quill-free). When the baby locates a nipple, it tugs at it for a few seconds, then goes on to another, and another, and another, and back again to the first. A baby eventually establishes a fixed sequence of nipple usage, with only an occasional variation. A nursing baby accompanies itself with soft cooing, grunting, and smacking of lips and often works its small paws through the hairs around the nipples. Having exhausted the milk supply, it wanders off to play or sleep.

Shadle observed captive animals. I have observed nursing in the wild, by surprising a mother and baby at night. The mother was Squirrel; I reached her at 2:10 a.m. on an August night. Her baby was 15 weeks old, weighed 2.5 kg, and was able to climb large trees and travel long distances with its mother. The two had been resting on the base of a J-shaped cherry tree, which was only 30 degrees off the horizontal. As I arrived, mother and daughter scooted up the tree, with Squirrel in the lead. Squirrel had chosen her nursing station well; thick surrounding vegetation blocked cold night breezes, and a shadbush feeding tree was available nearby. At 4:30 a.m., a squeaking and mewing broke out in the treetop. Then I heard the scraping sounds of porcupine descent and saw two dark masses descend to the lower, sloping portion of the trunk where the animals could rest comfortably. If I had stood up, I could have touched them. Now nursing began, and it was a musical affair. There is evidence that in some mammals the baby's vocalizations during suckling stimulate milk let-down (Tindal and Knaggs 1970). Both Squirrel and her baby were vocalizing continually, the baby in a higher register, the mother answering in contralto. The sounds had the incongruous quality of metal zippers riding up and down. At one point, the baby made a soft *mmmm* sound, which I associate with mother-searching. At no point did the vocalizations take on the sharper edge of anger. The music continued uninterrupted for 30 minutes, when I stood up and sent both animals fleeing up the tree. After a few minutes, the nursing sounds resumed in the upper branches, then died off. A short time later, thrushes began their morning chorus.

A lactating mother gives little indication of her condition. For a week or so following delivery, the areolae around the nipples are pink and swollen, and milk can be obtained by gently pulling the nipple, as one would pull the teat of a cow. Porcupine milk, even then, is produced sparingly. It appears as a glistening white drop at the tip of the nipple, not as a stream. But within two weeks the swelling subsides, and milk can no longer be obtained manually. That does not mean the porcupine has stopped lactating. To test for lactation at that time, I use the oxytocin method. Oxytocin, a hormone released by the posterior pituitary, lets down milk when the baby begins to suckle (Tindal and Knaggs 1970). It can release only preformed milk and does not by itself stimulate milk synthesis. The test is performed by injecting a small amount of the hormone in a leg or arm muscle. Within a minute the areolae swell as lactiferous ducts send down milk. When the nipple is gently pulled, milk floods the tip.

My use of the oxytocin method showed that porcupines in the wild spend a surprisingly long time lactating. Unfortunately, it is difficult to trap the female just after birth (to fix the starting point) and just before dispersal of the offspring (to fix the end point). Table 20 therefore gives figures both for observed (minimal) periods of lactation and estimated (most probable true) periods. The estimated days of lactation are obtained by extrapolating back to the probable date of birth and forward to the last observed contact between mother and baby.

Since Acidie's baby, when first captured on June 22, 1985, already weighed 1 kg, it had to be around three weeks old. Hence the term of lactation for Acidie would be around 113 days. Likewise, Rebecca's baby probably stayed with its mother at least another four weeks (since the other babies did so), hence the estimated term is 110 days. Squirrel's 1986 baby was at least two weeks old when first discovered. In addition, Squirrel was observed in the same tree with her baby as late as September 13, when she was presumably still lactating. Hence her estimated term is 112 days. Squirrel's 1987 baby was approximately one week old at time of first capture. It stayed with its mother until September 26, when it dispersed. Thus 30 days must be added to the period of confirmed lactation in 1987. Moth's 1988 baby was approximately one week old when first captured. The best estimate for the five mother-offspring pairs listed is therefore 127 days of lactation.

That is a staggering figure. The average period of gestation for the porcupine, as established by Albert Shadle, is 210 days. When that is added to 127 days of lactation, the female is spending 337 days a year (11 months) either being pregnant or nursing a baby. Shadle, who kept a porcupine colony at the vivarium at the University of Buffalo and allowed the animals to breed, found mothers nursing their offspring for 90 to 150 days. With the latter figure, a female would spend 360 days a year either in pregnancy or lactation. Shadle believed that such long periods of lactation would not be observed in nature. Yet the behavior of Catskills porcupines has been little different from the captives'. Ecologists point out that a long period of maternal care is needed to compensate for a poor resource base. A folivorous (leaf-feeding) diet is among the poorest available in nature; porcupines are therefore following ecological prediction in their extended maternal care.

In contrast to the observations of Shadle and my own study, B. C. Farrell and D. P. Christian (1987) have observed much shorter periods of lactation in a laboratory setting. For three females observed, the average period of lactation was 72 days (range: 68–78 days). The animals were maintained on a diet of rabbit chow. It is possible that the rich commercial diet and the reduced metabolic demands of living in 16-cubic-meter cages allowed the mothers to finish earlier. Their infants, however, weighed proportionately less at weaning than did infants in the wild. Farrell and Christian report juveniles averaging 44% of maternal mass at weaning. My available data, for four mother-infant pairs, gives a figure of 53% (range: 39%–75%).

What is surprising is that the wild females who spend 337 days a year in pregnancy and lactation do so year after year, with essentially no years off for recovery. A survey of three females over six years shows a minimum of 15 babies produced (Table 17). The data include two question marks. No baby could be found for Rebecca in 1983, yet that May she was behaving as a typical young mother, hovering around a hollow den tree and seeking salt. She probably produced a baby and lost it at an early age. Squirrel's 1984 maternity status is more questionable. No baby was ever found, and she did not salt-chew extensively, but she behaved suspiciously in mid-June. Unfortunately, I was not using the oxytocin test in 1983 or 1984 to establish lactation status. Rebecca did not produce a surviving baby in 1987, as shown by direct observation and confirmed by the oxytocin test. That year her weight surpassed Squirrel's for the first time, demonstrating the cost of lactation. Squirrel was heavier than Rebecca every year from 1983 through 1986, and again in 1988. Moth was the lightest of the three in every year of observation.

Mother-Infant Relationships

For the first six weeks of life, a baby porcupine is too weak to travel long distances, and the mother does not move far from its side. Young babies cannot climb trees above sapling size because for the small animals the trunk of a large tree is essentially a flat wall. As a result mother and baby meet only at night. During the day, when the mother sleeps in some large resting tree, the baby is hidden on the ground below.

I have found young babies installed in every sort of hiding place. Squirrel's 1983 baby was hidden in a rock crevice about 100 feet downhill from the mother's resting tree. Rebecca's 1986 baby, at the age of three weeks, lay pressed into a small cavity under a fallen tree trunk, its dark back an extension of the shadow. Rebecca was high up in a tree about 25 feet away. Acidie's 1985 baby lay in plain view on top of a rotten log, looking like a dark knot on the surface. And Moth's 1986 baby remained inaccessible for weeks inside a jumble of tree-crown slash until its curiosity betrayed it when it climbed out to explore. But the most common hiding place by far was the hollow base of a tree. Mothers often spent the day resting in the tops of such hollowed trees. By shining a flashlight inside the recess, I often discovered the baby within. That was how I first found Rebecca's 1985 baby, Moth's 1984 baby, the three-week-old baby of Squirrel in 1983, and others through the years.

C. A. Tryon (1947), who delivered a baby porcupine by cesarean section and raised it to the age of two years, comments that the baby's first instinct was to follow any moving object. Presumably the babies sleeping in the hollow base of their mother's resting tree followed the mother to the tree, found themselves unable to climb, and hid themselves in the inviting dark recess.

When mothers forage in treetops at night, the babies also follow to the feeding tree, then lie down at the bottom to wait. Baby and mother always come together at night; their resting positions during the day show increasing separation as the baby grows older, travels greater distances, and chooses different resting trees for daytime sleep. At night, it is the mother who travels to the baby, sometimes from half a mile away. The mother moves rapidly to the rendezvous, suggesting that she is following landmarks and not an odor trail. If mother and baby are foraging in separate trees at night, the mother seems to have a good idea of just where the baby is.

Rebecca did the night I radiocollared her baby Becky. On an August night, I tracked Rebecca to an apple tree on the east edge of Roarback Field and discovered Becky rapidly climbing a large tree on the other side of the field. The baby was now able to keep up with its mother and carry out most adult tasks. She remained silent throughout her capture, even when I carried her off for overnight observation and radiocollar attachment. At the capture site next morning, I found evidence of a mother's concern. On a flat rock at the base of Becky's tree lay a pile of fresh porcupine droppings, where Rebecca had waited for hours for her baby to return. I released the baby under the tree, and she scrambled up to the top. That night, mother and baby were together again, feeding in separate linden trees a few dozen feet apart.

Mothers never defend their babies, even when capture occurs in sight of the mother. One reason may be that animals like Rebecca, who wear radiocollars, have been recaptured so many times over the years that they may feel some loss of confidence. Naive porcupines may act more aggressively; I have been charged twice by naive porcupines disturbed in their dens.

Both charges stopped short. Also, Catskills porcupines may be timid because they are generally smaller than porcupines in other parts of their range. John Bryant of the University of Alaska tells me that Alaskan porcupines, who are larger than those of the Catskills, frequently charge when provoked. Finally, the porcupine baby itself is not defenseless. It is born fully quilled and with defensive reactions well developed. In a sense, its long residency in the uterus represents a form of maternal protection. By midsummer, its rapid growth has probably made it as effective as its mother against small predators.

Separation

With nightly contact with its mother, and with gradually increasing travel together, a baby's independence grows. At three months, it may begin to spend occasional nights a short distance from its mother. On the following night, the two are found together again. The accompanying figure shows the growing independence of Bus, Squirrel's female offspring of 1983, and Pleiades, Moth's male offspring of the same year. I established nocturnal separations of the animals by means of a measured-thread device. (Thread unwinding from a spool activated an odometer.) After a while, the forest floor was covered by a giant spiderweb of nylon threads. The data show that mothers and offspring seldom separated through August and the first two weeks of September. During subsequent weeks, which coincided with the peak of the mating season, mothers and infants were rarely found together but remained relatively close to each other. Long-distance separation occurred at the end of October.

An indicated separation for a night does not prove that the mother never met her baby that night, since I did not monitor the two for all the hours of darkness. The question is important because I found that a mother who does not provide milk for three nights in a row stops lactating.

During their time with their mothers, Bus and Pleiades learned the identity and location of the rare food trees. They learned the locations of dens and other shelters and hiding places. After separation, their learning would come through their own efforts. They set out energetically to survive the biggest test of their lives: their first winter alone.

Nocturnal separation (in meters) between two mothers and their offspring. Both babies showed increasingly longer separations as the summer progressed, with permanent loss of contact in mid-October. The female offspring (B) left her natal range permanently. The male (P) entered a winter den on his natal range.

Social Structure

A porcupine leads a solitary existence throughout much of its life. Nevertheless, it participates in complex and predictable social interactions, as these two examples of male-male meetings illustrate.

Strangers

The first story begins after midnight in July 1983, as my daughter Rachel and I are observing Rebecca's feeding activities in a spreading wild apple tree above our wellspring. The tree stands in a small clearing; unbroken forest begins just to the north and west. We are prepared to listen to feeding sounds from the apple tree. Instead, as soon as we sit down, we hear a distant, high-pitched screaming from the woods to the west. Any sustained disturbance in the night forest is strange, and I wonder what animal might scream so persistently. Suddenly I know. These are the howls of a porcupine. We gather our gear at once and set out in the direction of the tumult. When screams are ringing in our ears, we turn off the trail and look up. A drama confronts us.

The lower branch of a small ash tree holds two porcupines, about 12 feet off the ground. The first, the size of an adult male, is about halfway out on a branch, facing a second porcupine, which is hanging upside down at the end of the branch, in imminent danger of being thrown to the ground. Its quills are maximally erected, its tail points toward its adversary. It is the animal that is screaming without interruption. I see that it is wearing a radiocollar, so I quickly tune my receiver. The distressed animal is Woodruff, a giant male I collared two months previously, when he weighed a whopping 7.7 kg (17 pounds).

Under the combined illumination of two bright headlamps, the dominating porcupine breaks off his attack and retreats to the trunk of the tree. He looks muscular, and to my eye triumphant, but I see in my binoculars that Woodruff has inflicted some pain. The attacker's muzzle is filled with quills; many appear to be broken off halfway. After a short pause, he begins to climb up the trunk, his back partially erect. Woodruff remains hanging and continues to scream, with interspersions of tooth-chattering, for about 10 minutes. Then the cries grow less intense until he falls as silent as his opponent. He rights himself on the branch and moves back toward the trunk. As he sits hunched, I see the marks of battle.

167

A large white quill has been driven into his upper lip. I also see three white quills in the chest and one in the arm. Woodruff remains at the base of the branch, reluctant to climb after his opponent or descend toward the two humans.

There are no loose quills under the tree to indicate previous thrashing on the ground and no niptwigs to indicate feeding. I find several dense, fat droppings of the type that Woodruff usually produces, evidence that he has spent several hours in the tree. The fight tree is about half a mile east of Woodruff's previous position and perhaps a quarter mile out of his normal range. I surmise that he left his home range either to visit a salt source or to feed in an apple tree and was caught by a resident male. The experience must have been terrifying for him; in more than 300 captures, I have never heard a porcupine scream in that manner.

Woodruff never again returns to this section of the woods. Next day, he has retreated to his usual haunts high up the mountain. As I study him in my binoculars, I see he has already removed all visible quills. He stays in the high mountains for the rest of his life, until killed by a hunter the following winter. On autopsy I find four large quills buried in the body fascia, a permanent residue of his encounter.

Woodruff's battle with the uncollared porcupine, although spectacular, fits our understanding of much of male mammalian behavior (including human male behavior). It also fits other reports of porcupine intermale aggression. Wendell Dodge has stated that male porcupines in captivity may kill other males. And R. B. Brander (1973) has described porcupine interactions at a salt source as "agonistic," accompanied by a great deal of vocalization. Outright battles were avoided by withdrawal of subordinate individuals. Brander does not specify the sexes of his animals, but the large individuals were probably male.

Friends

The second example of male-male interaction follows an entirely different script. This story begins well after midnight in August 1986 as I capture a giant porcupine at the salthouse. His eartag identifies him as Killer, a male I tagged the previous summer. I want to take him to the city for a feeding study. By the time I have made a physical examination and placed him in a cage, it is 3:30 a.m. I want to drive to the city at once, to take advantage of the cool of the night. When I pass once more by the salthouse to lock up, I find another porcupine chewing the salt sticks on the east wall. It is much smaller than Killer and offers little resistance as I grab it. I make a quick physical exam. It is a young male, with eartag No. 58 in its right ear. I have captured Ram, Rebecca's baby of the previous year.

Capture of the 15-month-old male crystallizes something in my mind. Two radiotagged babies had dispersed out of their natal territories at the end of their first summer of life; both were females. Studies of male dispersal have suffered from experimental glitches, but they suggest that males do not disperse. I have captured Ram inside his natal territory.

I decide to include him in the feeding study. I put him in a separate cage in the back of the station wagon and drive off at once, arriving in New York at 6:30, in full daylight but before sunrise. Of the two males, the smaller one is more alert and aggressive, clinging to the sides of his cage and giving small warning screams when I come close. I install them in adjacent cages in an ivy-covered recess behind our house. Here they will be shielded from the August sun but get some cross-breeze. I fall into an exhausted sleep.

When I wake at noon and check the porcupines, I am shocked to find Ram's cage open, the animal gone. The door-retaining spring lies on the ground, worked loose by the captive. I search all nearby trees and find nothing. Where would a porcupine go in New York City? I walk along the railroad tracks to the Ravine, a wild stretch of old willows and box elder, and try to view it through the eyes of a Catskills porcupine, used to resting in cool forests and feeding on linden, aspen, and apple. I don't recognize a single possible feeding species. What can Ram find here to relieve his hunger? What if he encounters a family dog? New York City dog owners don't expect their pets to return home with a muzzle full of quills. What if a child tries to play with him? What if he gets in the way of a car? I search a long time but return home empty-handed. I feel devastated. I have sentenced the small animal to death.

After nightfall, my neighbors Don and Joan Curran tell me they saw a porcupine moving near a fence on Depew Avenue. They clapped their hands, and the animal ran to the other side, under Mrs. Turner's pine trees. "But of course," Don adds, "we know there are no porcupines living in New York, so it had to be something else, perhaps a raccoon." A small feeling of relief comes over me. The animal is still in the neighborhood. I plan to resume my search the following day, but that proves unnecessary.

During my search, I have left Killer in his securely fastened cage outside the house, with a handful of apples for food. I check him for the last time at 12:30 a.m., only to find two porcupines in the beam of my flashlight. Killer is noisily demolishing an apple inside the cage, and the little porcupine is clinging to the wire mesh outside, as though drawn by the big male's company. I run into the house, grab my rubber gloves, and have Ram captive again in a minute. His coat is dusty, suggesting he has spent time in some ground-level hideout, not up a tree as I had expected. His mouth is dry, and he is hungry when I offer apples. The sudden reversal of fortunes is stunning, but so is the behavior of the two males. Far from trying to kill each other, they have reacted as friends. I keep them for ten days in adjacent cages; their behavior never deteriorates. Is it possible the animals have known each other before?

I conclude they have. At the end of my feeding study, I equip both males with radiocollars and release them in the mountains at the site of initial capture. My tracking during subsequent months reveals that they not only inhabit broadly overlapping territories but sometimes occupy the same tree. At times I find them using the same tree on alternate weeks or resting in trees near each other. At the end of September, I find both up a large oak tree near the top of the ridge; Rebecca is in a tree directly below the pair. On November 29, Killer is up a leaning linden tree, Ram inside its hollow base. There is never any hint of friction between the two. They separate only in the winter, occupying different dens or hemlock trees.

Male Territoriality

At the time of his urban adventure, Ram was still a juvenile with unde-scended testes. Killer's and Ram's territories overlapped the territory of Taylor, an adult male almost as large as Killer (see map on page 173). Killer and Taylor have at times rested peacefully in adjacent trees and in the same tree in successive weeks, but they have never, in my experience, occupied the same tree at the same time. Still other males shared the ter-ritory of Ram, Killer, and Taylor. An unidentified male was guarding Rebecca in a ridgetop sugar maple during the 1986 mating season while Killer and Ram remained a short distance away (in opposite directions) and Taylor was much farther away. Another male, a juvenile, was captured in 1987. There may be still others.

Generalizations

The following generalizations concerning porcupine territoriality have emerged from my studies.

- Females exclude other females from their territories; male ranges may overlap extensively with those of other males. A single male may over-lap the territories of several females. That agrees with den-sharing pat-terns during the winter (Chapter 7), when identified den-sharers con-sisted of male-female pairs.
- Certain males show little overlap with others. For example, Finder was never found close to Killer, Ram, or Taylor.
- Females inhabit territories of roughly equal size. Male home ranges may vary considerably in size, with smallest ranges occupied by juveniles and subordinates, the largest ones by dominants. Home ranges of domi-nant males overlap up to five females.
- Males expand their natal territories as they mature. Females disperse as juveniles.

Hypotheses

The data available are consistent with the following hypotheses.

- Though porcupines are largely solitary, males interact amicably within loose associations. Dominance hierarchies determine access to estrous females (Chapter 9). Competition for females has been observed directly and is also suggested by the higher body weights of males compared with females. Males from different associations may be intolerant of each other, as were Woodruff and his antagonist. It is not known whether such antagonism is a group behavior or is limited to dominant males.

- Members of a male association cooperate because they are genetically related. They may share a common mother, a common father, or both. As yet no direct evidence, such as analysis of DNA fingerprints or enzyme polymorphisms, supports this hypothesis. However, the failure of young males to disperse and the stability of adult female territories over many years suggest that local males share maternal genes. Whether they also share paternal genes depends on the term a dominant male can control his extended harem.

- Conversely, adult females behave agonistically toward each other because they are unrelated and must compete for scarce resources. For that reason, females are more territorial with each other; their territories are relatively small and defensible. Female intolerance extends even to mother-daughter pairs once daughters become independent and mothers enter their fall mating period.

Those hypotheses are still preliminary; their confirmation will require additional data. I will first present the existing data on which my conclusions are based and then discuss the implications of my hypotheses and compare porcupine social structure with that of some other mammals.

Female Territoriality

Female porcupines show strong site fidelity. Year after year, each can be found foraging in her own core section of the woods, resting in established resting trees and feeding in the same lindens, apples, and aspens. Year-to-year changes in territorial boundaries tend to be minor compared with

Female nonwinter ranges, 1983. Though neighboring territories overlapped extensively, their core areas showed little overlap.

Female nonwinter ranges, 1985.

Nonwinter ranges of males Killer, Taylor, Ram, and Finder, 1987. In contrast to female ranges, male ranges overlap and show considerable variation in size.

Nonwinter ranges of females Rebecca, Squirrel, and Moth, 1987.

changes observed in males. But even males remain true to a core area, returning year after year.

The maps on pages 172 and 173 illustrate changes in nonwinter territories of the females Rebecca, Squirrel, and Moth. Neighboring ranges overlapped extensively in 1983, even though the core areas remained exclusive.
Fewer data points are available for Moth than for the other two females
because she was radiocollared in midsummer.

Females defend their core areas against other females. It is difficult to
catch them actually battling in the woods, though I have found circumstantial evidence that they do. Since defense of territory is a form of competition, one might ask what happens to the size of female territories if the
level of competition is stepped up by an increase in population density.
Without being aware of it, I was studying just such an experiment in 1983.
A violent scabies epidemic ran through my study population and reduced
its density. The epidemic burned itself out in 1984, and the porcupine
population rebounded. The change in population density was accompanied
by complementary changes in size of female territories. In 1983, males
and females had roughly equal home ranges (65.2 ha for females, 71.6 ha
for males). Over the following five years, the average female home range
contracted to 23.2 ha; the average male home range remained constant
(Table 21). During the same period, population density approximately tri-
pled (Table 22).

Another way in which the territorial instinct is manifested is through
homing behavior. Animals removed from their territories will return when
given the chance, as did the adult female Gro. When I found her in early
April 1983, she was so weak and unresponsive that she seemed near death.
I picked her up without resistance and carried her to the cabin without
anesthetizing her. She had lost 30% of her summer weight—a dangerous
condition—and she was overrun by lice. But on a diet of apples and chow
in the city, she regained her strength and weight. In May I returned her to
Lexington and released her into a countryside of wildflowers, bursting
buds, and birdsong. I made one mistake. Instead of returning her to the site
of capture, on top of the mountain, I released her behind our cabin, far to
the east of her normal territory and in an area she may have never visited.
Rather than heading uphill to her home territory, she traveled farther away.

A week later she was in a beech-hemlock forest 1.4 miles to the east, where she remained two weeks. But when I visited her on May 30, I found the ground under her rest tree strewn with many dozens of porcupine quills, far more than would be expected from loss in grooming. Because the quills were widely scattered, they could not be explained by the porcupine's falling out of the tree. I concluded that Gro had fought with either a would-be predator or a resident porcupine. From the number of quills lost, I also concluded that the fight had been a serious one.

Apparently Gro had been unsettled by the experience, because a week later she abandoned her location in the hemlocks and moved two miles west, climbing more than 1000 feet in altitude. I found her on a southern ridge of Vly Mountain, feeding in a beech tree. Two weeks later still, she traveled a mile north to Jaeger Ridge, completing a large circle back to the heart of her 1983 territory. I found her resting in an ash tree, with niptwigs scattered on the ground. But again, dozens of quills were strewn under her tree. Such quill-scattering is extremely rare, perhaps because porcupines are relatively invulnerable to local predators. In my eight years of radio-tracking porcupines, I have found only five massive quill-scatters; two came from Gro, and within a three-week period. In both cases, Gro was a new arrival, first as a strange porcupine in the hemlock forest and then as a long-absent owner in her old territory. I therefore guessed that both altercations involved other porcupines, probably the resident female in the hemlock forest and a usurping immigrant in Gro's former territory. Following her return, Gro never again left her traditional boundaries, and I found no further evidence of battle.

Porcupine territorial constraints break down in two situations: feeding in apple trees and chewing salt at the salthouse and outbuildings. In both cases, several porcupines may visit at the same time even though their territories do not overlap at other times, perhaps because apple trees and salt sources represent limited resources that belong to no porcupine in particular. That is to say, no porcupine feels invaded when it finds another porcupine using the resources; both are visitors. (That does not prevent some expressions of irritation in the form of squawking.) The behavior may be facilitated by the location of the orchard and the salthouse outside the forest proper.

Juvenile Dispersal

Juvenile dispersal is defined as a one-way movement of a sexually immature animal away from its mother's territory (natal territory). A great deal
of social structure derives from the pattern of juvenile dispersal; it deter-
mines who inherits the parental territory and who leaves home. The pattern
among porcupines is unusual among mammals: female offspring leave,
males stay (Greenwood 1980). The evidence for the pattern is based on the
following case histories.

- As already mentioned, Rebecca's 1985 son, Ram, was recaptured in
  1986 inside his mother's territory. After radiotagging, he has lived inside his mother's summer territory, with range extensions to the west.
  Though he matured sexually in the summer of 1987, his range showed
  little change until summer 1988.
- Moth's son Pleiades, radiocollared in July 1983, separated from his
  mother in October but remained within her territory. In November he
  entered a rock den where he either dropped his radiocollar or froze to
  death in January 1984. The den emitted a weakening radio signal for a
  year and a half afterward, but I was never able to recover the transmitter.
- Squirrel's 1988 son, Quill, has remained in his mother's territory at least
  through December 1988.
- Moth's 1988 son, Woolbear, has likewise remained in his mother's territory through December 1988.
- Rebecca's 1984 daughter, Becky, was radiotagged in August 1984. In
  September, she left her natal territory and traveled 1.5 miles west across
  two mountain ridges, establishing a new territory in a hemlock forest far
  from her mother. Her radio failed in November 1984 and further contact
  was lost.
- Squirrel's 1987 daughter, Eft, dispersed on September 26, in a heroic
  one-way trip to the east. Along the way she crossed a county road, a
  state highway, and a good-sized stream. She then climbed Saddleback
  Mountain and came to rest 4.2 miles from the center of her natal territory. She spent the winter exploring a series of dens; her radio failed in
  March 1988.
- Bini's 1987 daughter, Chili, dispersed on September 25 and traveled 1.3
  miles northwest, across the ridge of Vly Mountain, to a winter territory

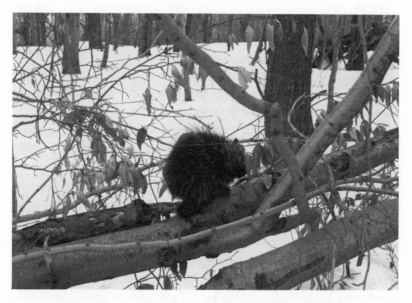

A newly dispersed juvenile is fending for herself, feeding on beech slash.

near that chosen by Becky three years previously. She survived her first winter alone and at the time of this writing has become a mother.

In summary, the evidence for female-biased juvenile dispersal in porcupines is based on the life histories of seven radiocollared animals, four males who remained in their natal territories and three females who dispersed. The probability that such an outcome might result from chance alone is 0.028 (Fisher's exact test). Since that is rather close to the cutoff point of 0.05 that biologists like to use to measure significance, I will add one more life history, of a more circumstantial nature than the preceding four. Topmost was an infant male I radiocollared in June 1983. A month later I replaced the collar with an eartag so I could use the collar on another porcupine. Though I had spotted Topmost's mother in a tree, I was unable to capture her; hence I could not establish her territorial boundaries. In March 1984, I found Topmost undersized, emaciated, and overrun by lice; he also suffered from some disorder of the digestive system that caused him to produce droppings of wildly variant size. I kept him for two weeks for observation and fattening up, then radiocollared and released him at the site of capture. Over the next year, his territory partly overlapped his 1983 positions (the natal territory). Unfortunately, because he was followed for only a month in 1983, the natal territory is defined by only five radiopositions. Two fall inside the 1984 territory, one lies on the border, and two fall outside. That degree of overlap is roughtly consistent with Ram's 1986 territory, which also projects beyond its natal territory by about 50%. If Topmost's dispersal history is added to the seven others, the probability that observed female dispersal is due to chance alone drops to 0.018.

What prompts the juvenile females to disperse? In some mammalian species, such as the wolf, dispersal follows aggression from resident pack members (Mech 1987). That does not happen in the porcupine. As noted in the previous chapter, the juvenile, whether male or female, becomes increasingly adventurous as the summer progresses, straying ever farther from its mother at night. Finally contact between the two is broken completely; females disperse while males remain in their natal territories. The break comes during the fall mating season, when females stop lactating and go into estrus. The night before Chili dispersed, I was sleeping in the woods near her feeding tree. Her mother's signal was coming in weakly, from far away. Twice during the night Chili gave a mewing call that juveniles use to solicit suckling. Her mother did not respond. The next day, Chili began her three-week journey to the west. Hence the mother's influence on juvenile dispersal is, at most, indirect. The urge to disperse appears instead to follow an inner development signal (or ontogenetic switch, in biological jargon). Such a mechanism appears to operate in other mammalian species as well, including ground squirrels, *Spermophilus beldingi* (Holekamp 1986); prairie dogs, *Cynomys ludovicianus* (Fagerstone et al. 1981); and others.

Though juvenile females disperse during the breeding season, they do not generally breed during their first year. Of 14 females examined in 1988 (9 adults, 5 dispersed juveniles), all adults were lactating but only 1 of the 5 juveniles was producing milk. The sole exception was Chili, who gave birth to a male infant around June 15. That means she conceived her baby around November 15, some 50 days after leaving her natal territory. Therefore, even if a female breeds during her first year, there is little chance she will mate with her father. Average dispersal distance for the three dispersing females was 3.7 km (2.3 miles), corresponding to 3.9 male territory diameters.

Adult Dispersal

All of the dispersal episodes mentioned so far have involved juveniles. Only dispersal by juveniles is likely to prevent inbreeding. To complicate matters, porcupines can also disperse as adults. Whereas juvenile dispersal is predictable, female-biased, and triggered by an ontogenetic switch, adult dispersal is rarely observed, male-biased, and triggered by sexual competition. Four of my adult males (out of 17 males radiocollared for an aggregate of 16 porcupine-years) made permanent, long-distance movements. They left established territories and never returned. Hence one can expect adult males to disperse at roughly four-year intervals.

The first male disperser was Eight, a medium-sized animal captured and eartagged in July 1983. Almost a year later, in May, I radiocollared him while he was molting and looking scruffy. For two months he ranged in a long, narrow east-west territory. Then in July, he disappeared over the high ridge of Vly Mountain. Though I could pick up his signal at the top of Vly Mountain for several weeks afterward, the signal disappeared when I descended into the valley. I concluded he had crossed over the next range of mountains 3.6 miles to the west. Then there was only silence at his frequency, despite long expeditions to locate him. The second permanent relocation involved the adult male Homer. When first captured in July 1984, he held a territory almost totally overlapping that of Finder. In December 1984, Homer walked approximately 2 miles east to a hemlock forest, where he spent the winter. When spring came, Homer stayed in the new area, expanding his territory to the south. My histories of Eight and Homer are too skimpy to guess why they left their established home ranges.

Matters are different with the third known male disperser, Finder. Born in the summer of 1982 and radiocollared during his first winter, he became sexually mature in 1984 and achieved dominant status by 1986. During 1986 he achieved the impressive body weight of 8.0 kg (17.6 pounds), occupied a large nonwinter territory (70.2 ha), and had good mating success (I observed him guarding three different females during the mating season). Finder's world came crashing down the following summer, in 1987, when a new and powerful male, Jasper, appeared in Finder's territory. Jasper was full-grown when I first encountered him. Though I had never captured him before, I now began to capture him regularly, leading me to believe he was an immigrant into the area. Jasper displaced Finder from his dominant position, despite Finder's slight weight advantage. An accident may have contributed to Finder's decline. During the summer of 1986, he suffered a serious fall that left him temporarily unable to climb. Though his injuries healed and he resumed climbing, he may have been permanently impaired.

I did not witness the showdown between the two males, but during the breeding season of 1987 I saw its aftermath. Finder's home range showed little of the expected breeding season expansion and remained at 37 ha. Concurrently, Jasper ranged over most of Finder's former territory. Several times in the fall I found the defeated male inside a den when other porcupines were still resting in treetops; at those times Jasper would be nearby. Most important, Finder lost his harem. He failed to guard a single female during the mating season, while Jasper visited at least three—as many as Killer, the dominant male to the south.

In the spring of 1988, Finder left the land of his birth and began moving east. By May he had reached the banks of the Schoharie, the major stream in the region and an impassable barrier during the spring runoff. He moved slowly along the riverbank, staying in tree cover, moving about 1 mile per week. The rate of travel was well under his capacity; in the past he had been able to cover that distance in a single night. By June 12, Finder had reached the outskirts of Prattsville, 4 miles linear distance from his original home range but representing a 7.1-mile travel path. I saw him there for the last time, up a white ash tree that offered both food and rest. The following week, there was silence at his radio frequency despite a 100-mile search of every hilltop and valley in the area.

The fourth adult to disperse was Rebecca's 1985 son, Ram. As noted earlier, he spent the first three years of his life within his natal range. He often rested in trees his mother had used and several times sat with her in the same tree, though never during the mating season. By June 1988, Ram had attained the respectable weight of 5.05 kg yet had never been observed guarding a female. The local male who enjoyed that privilege was Killer, whose home range was four times larger than Ram's. On July 2 the younger male began a one-way journey by traveling up the mountain, higher than he had ever climbed before. He crossed the ridge and drifted across the Little Westkill valley, then started up the next mountain on August 1. I reached him there on a hot summer day, resting in the shade of a hemlock. A nearby·clearing offered a distant, hazy view of Vly Mountain, to which Ram never returned. The following week, his radio signal disappeared.

The behaviors of Finder and Ram illustrate once more the flexibility of response that is a hallmark of the porcupine. Whereas juvenile dispersal appears to be a wired-in behavior that functions to limit inbreeding, adult dispersal is a plastic response to competition. A male, defeated in battle or repressed by a powerful dominant, need not spend the rest of his life as a bachelor. He may opt to emigrate and find fulfillment in woods far distant from his birth. But it is a journey full of risk, which may end not in fulfillment but in death.

Dispersal Data from Other Studies

An illustration of a different set of dispersal behaviors comes from a study by Dodge and Barnes (1975) in western Washington State. Their study followed 18 radiocollared porcupines for periods of 28 to 432 days. Three of the animals showed unusually long movements during the study: a subadult male moved 31.1 km, a subadult female 6.8 km, and an adult female 6.1 km. In contrast to my own observation, this study shows dispersal by males as well as females, and by adults as well as subadults. The subadult classification of Dodge and Barnes includes animals less than two years old; my own classification of juvenile refers to animals less than a year old. The sample sizes from the Washington study are too small to permit generalization, but several possibilities must be considered to explain the discrepancy with my own study:

- Porcupines of western Washington may behave differently from porcupines of eastern New York, perhaps because of differences in food supply. However, the two populations showed similar home ranges.
- The pattern of juvenile dispersal observed in New York may reflect only a female bias, not a 100% certainty of male nondispersal.
- Dodge and Barnes do not relate the movements of juveniles to movements of their mothers. Did something happen to the mother of the sub-

adult male? If a mother is killed, there may be nothing to keep a baby attached to its natal territory. Because of such uncertainties, it is difficult to compare the two studies.

Discussion

The picture of porcupine social structure drawn from my data is that of an animal largely solitary throughout its life yet strongly attached to a piece of land (its home range) and having well-defined relationships with other porcupines. Why are porcupines solitary? Many herbivorous species forage in herds. Folivorous or partly folivorous herd species include the howler monkeys of the New World (Terborgh and Janson 1986) and the gorillas and colobine monkeys of the Old World (Struhsaker 1975, Curtain and Chivers 1978). On the other hand, other folivores such as the indri (Terborgh and Janson 1986), the sportive lemur, the koala, the phalangerids, and the three-toed sloth (Montgomery and Sunquist 1986) are either solitary or restricted to mother-offspring groups.

One of the proposed benefits of group living is defense against predators. A group has more eyes and ears to detect a predator and possibly more muscle to repel an attack. But the porcupine defense is so powerful against all but a handful of predators that an early warning is not necessary, and a single porcupine can be as effective as a herd. The strategy of self-reliance is carried so far in the porcupine that even juveniles a few weeks old can defend themselves to some extent. They have to—their mothers leave them alone during the day. Another proposed benefit is defense against aggressive conspecifics. Groups of male common chimpanzees (*Pan troglodytes*) may attack individuals or smaller groups from another clan (Wrangham 1986). There is no evidence for such predatory group behavior in the porcupine. Although male-male and presumably female-female battles may ensue, all encounters seem to be one on one. Herd living may also increase the animal's ability to discover food. Catskills porcupines become feeding specialists during the summer, when high-quality linden and aspen require diligent searching through the forest. Although those foods are rare in the forest, they do form a reliable supply. Once a porcupine has learned the location of a tree, it can with certainty navigate a return, even a year afterward. The porcupine substitutes a fine-grained knowledge of its home range for the lottery of new discovery.

At the same time, porcupines avoid all the costs associated with herd living: the requirement of increased home range, the predictable decrease in individual food intake, and the increased load of parasites and disease. It should be clear, however, that even though porcupines spend most of their time alone, they nevertheless live within a complex social network. That is particularly true of males, who recognize numbers of other males, as well as females, within their range.

The female-biased juvenile dispersal observed in the Catskills is so atypical among mammals that it deserves comment. Dispersal of offspring is the norm in both the plant and animal world. The benefits of dispersal are large and widely recognized: a reduced chance of inbreeding, an increased frequency of encounters with members of the opposite sex, reduced levels of competition, and access to suitable empty habitat. But philopatry (residence in the natal territory past the age of independence) also offers important benefits to a porcupine (Waser and Jones 1983): acquaintance with relatively scarce den sites, acquaintance with scarce feeding trees and salt sources, avoidance of predators and territorial residents during dispersal. Porcupines solve the dilemma by having it both ways. Females disperse during their first year and reap the benefits of dispersal; males remain in natal territories and reap the benefits of philopatry. Because their sisters disperse, the likelihood of inbreeding for males is also reduced. (How they avoid inbreeding with their mothers remains a mystery.) Juvenile dispersal is particularly important to long-lived animals such as the porcupine, because a female that fails to disperse risks mating with her father.

Sex-biased juvenile dispersal is relatively common among mammals and birds. What sets the porcupine apart is that among the species studied, mammals overwhelmingly favor male dispersal. (The situation is reversed in birds.) Of the 4000-odd species of mammals, about 70 have been studied well enough to establish the predominant dispersing sex. In only a handful of species is that sex female: chimpanzees, both *Pan troglodytes* and *P. paniscus* (Pusey 1979, 1980; Goodall 1983, 1986); mountain gorilla, *Gorilla gorilla beringei* (Harcourt 1978, Stewart and Harcourt 1986); white-lined bat, *Saccopteryx bilineata,* a small bat from Central and South America (Bradbury and Emmons 1974; Bradbury and Vehrencamp 1976,

1977); African wild dog, *Lycaon pictus* (Frame and Frame 1976; Frame et al. 1979); mantled howler monkey, *Alouatta palliata* (Glander 1980, 1984); red colobus monkey, *Colobus badius* (Marsh 1979); and hamadryas baboon, *Papio hamadryas* (Sigg et al. 1982). The North American porcupine must now be added to that short list.

Half of the female-biased juvenile dispersers are folivores: the porcupine, the red colobus (Oates 1987), the mantled howler (Milton 1980), and the gorilla (Oates 1987). The resource base of a folivore is relatively thin, as discussed in Chapter 6. However, the rare lindens and poplars sought by the porcupine have the advantage of predictability; their produce can be counted on, and their locations can be learned. Therefore, they can be defended. In the porcupine, resource defense (territoriality) is observed only in females. That is to be expected, because the females depend much more on their resource base than do the males. The long and draining period of pregnancy and lactation means that the female cannot share her resources with another female. It is also a possible explanation for the porcupine's anomalous juvenile dispersal pattern. Although female territoriality and male tolerance are unusual in mammals, the system is hardly unique. The widely distributed meadow vole (*Microtus pennsylvanicus*) (Madison 1980, 1985) and the red-tailed squirrel (*Sciurus granatensis*) of Panama (Heaney and Thorington 1978) show similar territorial relationships.

Several other features of the porcupine social structure are logically consistent with female territoriality. In juvenile dispersal, one would expect the dispersing sex to be the one that would bear the heaviest costs in case of inbreeding. Since a female bears only a single young per year, but a male may sire several progeny, she would lose more heavily if she mated incestuously with her father. Because porcupines are long-lived and because dominant males may maintain their positions over long periods, as in the case of the great apes, such a mating might be all too probable for a nondispersing female.

That brings up the symmetrical problem of how a nondispersing son avoids mating with his mother. In 1987, the question was academic for Ram. Though his testes were descended and he was physiologically capable of fatherhood, he distanced himself from his mother while Taylor, Killer, and Mayday fought over her. Killer outweighed Ram by a factor of

1.7, suggesting that it would be years before Ram reached a social rank that allowed him to even consider incest with his mother.

It is also possible that the animals know their relatedness and avoid incest. Such inbreeding avoidance has been demonstrated in Belding's ground squirrel. Paul Sherman, who over 11 years has observed thousands of matings in that long-lived species, has never observed a brother-sister or mother-son mating (Holekamp 1986). Belding's ground squirrels, like most mammals, show predominant male dispersal. Similar incest avoidance is shown by black-tailed prairie dogs (Hoogland 1982).

Another intriguing consideration is the sex ratio of 1.91 (63 females, 33 males) among the porcupines I have examined. A number of other sources have found a female-biased sex ratio in the porcupine (Table 23). That ratio nicely complements female territoriality and female-biased dispersal. A mother producing female offspring will export her daughters and therefore face no competition for food or den sites. Even a son costs less than full price; its adult home range will spread over the ranges of adjacent females.

Female-biased dispersal is the norm in some human societies as well. For example, anthropological work by Wood, Smouse, and Long (1985) shows that among the Gainj- and Kalam-speaking peoples of highland Papua New Guinea, a daughter is far more likely (67%) to leave her parents' parish upon marriage than is a son (16%). The reason is rooted in the social structure of the tribes; the New Guineans practice tropical swidden agriculture, with land owned by fathers and passed on to sons. Undoubtedly, if land were owned by mothers and passed on to daughters, it would be the sons who dispersed.

In the case of human societies, we assume that social structure is the independent variable, with such reproductive behavior as dispersal following in consequence. For porcupines, the arrow of causality can point in either direction. Does female resource defense dictate female dispersal, or does the reverse hold true? But for humans as much as for porcupines, no rigid biological determinism is likely to explain all of social structure and reproductive behavior. For both species, there remains the option of flexible response to compelling circumstance.

.11.

Parasites

On a bright October daybreak in 1981, the Catskills foliage is glowing almost fiercely, and leaves continue to glow while falling on the trails. From outside the cabin, I am astonished to see a porcupine under the oak tree directly below, its orderly quill rows a rebuke to the chaos of fall. I see an opportunity to radiotag another animal for my studies. With a live trap and my thick rubber gloves, I race down the hillside to head it off before it can climb a tree. It does not move as I run up, but turns its back and erects its quills. I place the open door of a live trap in front, prod it gently with a stick, and have it trapped in seconds. The ease of capture should make me suspicious, but I don't discover the true condition of the animal until I examine it inside the cabin. A white halo surrounds the mouth, as though it had pushed its face inside a flour bag. The possibility of scabies comes to mind, but I have not yet seen the full horror of the disease.

I anesthetize the porcupine and turn it on its back to determine the sex. The entire abdominal area, normally dark and covered with short fur, is a mass of thick white encrustations, like bracket fungi on rotten wood. Deep red fissures between the encrustations cut into the skin. The left heel looks elephantine, swollen with two white callosities, making it impossible for the animal to climb a tree. If it tried to climb anyway, the stretching of the underside would open the cracks in the abdominal wall. The claws of the hind feet are abnormally long, as though from disuse. I cannot determine the sex; the genital area is totally encrusted. Only later do I discover it to be a female. I name the animal Scapo, for scabies porcupine.

I have no medication on hand to treat the disease, and in any case I suspect it is too late. I attach a radiocollar anyway, to follow the behavior of a gravely sick animal, and I keep her in the cabin overnight for observation. The disease has not affected her appetite or her ability to digest and excrete. In her cage, she reduces a large apple to a few seeds and flakes from the core, and she leaves an abundance of droppings, rather small but normal-shaped. Back at the capture site, I try to discover what she was feeding on. Though acorns are falling from surrounding oak trees, they appear to be untouched. The porcupine has been feeding instead on a small stand of raspberries. The berries themselves are long gone, but the still-green leaves and shoots remain porcupine delicacies. Several leaves are nipped down to their petioles.

I release my captive the following morning. She is eager to get away but can move only in an awkward, three-legged gait, holding her swollen left hind foot off the ground. Her quills are strongly erected along the back and tail. She passes several climbable trees and heads toward our woodshed about 15 feet away. There she squeezes between the foundation and an open steel drum I use to root tree seedlings. In that poor sanctuary, Scapo seems to go into shock. Her quills no longer fly up when I approach and place an apple on the ground. The only signs of life are the shallow breathing movements of her sides.

On the morning of release, the woods have lost the splendor of the previous day. A high wind has screamed through the night and ripped much of the foliage from the trees. Great openings have appeared in the forest canopy, and gray clouds race across the sky. Soon frost will kill the remaining green forage, and the porcupine will enter her most difficult period of the year. She is so exhausted, I fully expect to find her in the same spot next week, dead. But when I return in the afternoon, the apple I left has been eaten. Scapo is going to fight for her life.

My work in the city leaves time for mountain visits only on weekends, so I next encounter Scapo a week after the release. Early on Saturday morning she is just where I left her a week before; she wasn't there when we arrived the previous night. From above, she looks healthy. Her sides heave rhythmically; her long quills and hair glisten with molten microcrystals of snow. Yet a subtle indication of sickness remains: there is almost no quill erection as I stand over her. As an open-air den, Scapo's space between the woodshed and the steel drum offers some real advantages: acorns lie scattered over the ground around her, and the woodshed shields her from the wind. Watching her, I feel a surge of simple happiness. Last week I gave the animal no chance to live. Today, the odds have shifted, and the victory is mine as well. But I am to discover at what cost her life is maintained.

The next day is mild and sunny, and when I return from an expedition at noon, Scapo has left her open-air den to forage on the ground a few feet away. Her technique is like that of no other porcupine I have seen. She keeps her malformed left hind foot off the ground and slowly, by a motion almost reptilian, half walks, half crawls with her remaining feet. To feed she pushes against the ground with her snout and picks up the food directly with her mouth. I watch for an hour and a half as she slowly crisscrosses a small area near the woodshed. When she finishes and moves back against the side of the woodshed, I walk down to investigate. The ground is littered with the splintered skins of red oak acorns. Acorns are always a major fall food of local porcupines, and this year the red oaks are producing a rich mast crop. They are also an important resource to local white-tailed deer, black bears, raccoons, eastern chipmunks, and wild turkeys. A healthy porcupine has an advantage over all those animals because it can climb the oak trees and harvest the acorns before they fall. Scapo is clearly not in a condition to climb trees and will have to depend on ground foods for sustenance. Although a good bushelful of acorns lies on the ground about her, she will have to compete for them with other, more efficient harvesters. A chipmunk works from the rock slope below the cabin, industriously hiding acorns underground. More serious competitors appear at night. Deer come with the first darkness, not bothering to run away when I stand outside the cabin. Moving just outside the cone of light, they wait for me to leave. I hear their snorting when I open the kitchen window an hour later. With competitors like that, what will happen to Scapo when the last acorns have been vacuumed off by deer? Most troublesome of all, what will happen when the snows come? Can she feed on tree bark at ground level? Can she travel in the snow? Can she survive without a proper den? I decide to intervene.

A week later, I bring a bottle of hexachlorobenzene lotion. In humans, a single application over infected skin kills all scabies mites. I hope it does the same for the porcupine. I go searching for the animal. The open-air den is deserted. It is now November, and under the oaks the riches of last week's mast crop have been depleted, with most acorns chewed to shells and slivers. A few widely scattered acorns remain intact, but Scapo is not equipped to search them out. They will be small morsels for deer. With my radio, I find Scapo in minutes, a short distance downhill at the top of Roarback Field. She rests on the ground, under a small white spruce. Her disease has worsened. The white halo around her mouth has begun to encrust, and scabies has leaped to a new, vital area; white halos now encircle both eyes. She will soon be blind. She protests my close examination with small, repeated jerks of her back and tail, though the quills show only minimal erection. To apply the lotion to her belly, I flip her on her back with a small stick. She has almost no strength left. She shields her belly with her hind feet, but I have no difficulty swabbing the belly and crusted hind foot. When I try to cover the area around her mouth, Scapo bites the sponge and tries to push it away with her front paws. I am finished in a minute. The animal gets back on her feet and painfully moves away. At night, she is in her old quarters by the woodshed. I leave two apples and a peanut butter sandwich. All are gone the next morning.

The calendar reads November 2, but the mildness and sweetness of the day say early September. My daughter Rachel discovers the porcupine in the grass between the woodshed and the garden. Scapo is rubbing her jaw on the ground. Whether she is cropping grass shoots, searching for acorns, or just rubbing an itching jaw, I cannot tell. I bring her peanut butter toast and two apples and, from three body lengths away, watch as she slowly consumes them. I watch for an hour and a half, warm in the afternoon sun, and hear a long-forgotten sound, the song of crickets, a fragment of summer returned. Milkweed is blowing in a gentle breeze. As a single seed wings past Scapo, she makes a sudden, energetic snatch, catches the seed in her mouth, and crunches out the brown center. While she feeds, I carefully move closer till I am only a body length away. She tolerates me as long as an apple remains in her mouth. When it is gone, she clacks a warning with her teeth, waits, then clacks again. She crawls about 20 feet away, just inside the forest edge, and rests her head on a small pillow of moss. She lies there the rest of the afternoon and into the night as we prepare to drive back to the city.

I return at midnight a week later and find the mountainside changed. A thick, fine-grained snow is flying, accumulating in field and forest though melting on still-warm roadways. Scapo is in a new den perhaps 200 feet away from the woodshed, an enormously thick, hollow-trunked ash tree. While snow is swirling outside, the inside of the tree remains dry and earth-warmed. Most important, the hollow has a ground-level entrance. Scapo has made the tree her own; the pungent odor of porcupine rises to the opening and proclaims ownership. I leave an apple as a housewarming present. Next afternoon, the snow continues to fall. Scapo remains inside the hollow ash, consuming the apple. No tracks lead out from the entrance; she is waiting out the snowstorm before venturing forth. The storm is intensifying, and I must cut short my visit. It is the last time I see Scapo alive.

On my next visit, deer-hunting season is in progress. A layer of snow covers the ground and displays the footprints of trespassers crossing our land. My radio apparatus picks up Scapo's signal at close range. At first the antenna appears to point to the hollow ash tree, but at the tree the signal continues from beyond. There are no tracks, no sign of recent occupancy. But as I continue, I run into unmistakable porcupine sign, a row of seven beech trees all freshly chewed along the base. I recognize Scapo's work; she has been unable to climb and feed in the crowns of the trees. Only a small amount of bark has been removed from each tree, a patch about the size of a human palm. It is far less than amounts taken by healthy porcupines, and less than needed to sustain life. Across the lumber road I find another debarked tree, a young linden. I feel a foreboding. The pattern of chewing seems demented. Instead of concentrating on a single patch of bark, the tooth marks form a narrow band all the way around the tree, without penetrating to the inner bark. I imagine Scapo pushing herself around and around the trunk, scraping the bark with her incisors. It is her death tree.

The nature of the radio signal has changed. It is booming, telling me I am extremely close to the source. Then I see it: fine porcupine hairs projecting above the snow. I uncover the thickly quilled back of Scapo, lying with her eyes closed. The body seems fresh, the limbs not yet locked into rigor mortis. I examine her belly and see that the terrible scabs have been responding to my lotion. There are no open sores, and much of the belly is covered with fresh, hairless skin. Only the left hind foot remains unusable. Her weight is only 3.2 kg (7.1 pounds), a full 2 pounds less than five weeks previously. She has starved to death.

While the nutritious herbs and acorns of October were available, Scapo's handicapped condition permitted an adequate calorie intake. The winter snows sealed her fate. Tree bark has a low nutritional value, and a porcupine must eat large amounts to survive. Her weakened condition did not allow that. Yet she had not spent her final weeks in resignation. With determination and ingenuity, she sought out foods that she could eat, found shelter she count enter, and succeeded far beyond reasonable expectation.

Scabies Epidemiology

Scabies appears to be a relatively new disease among porcupines. In 1933, William L. Jellison of the University of Minnesota listed all then-known parasites of the porcupine: one species of louse, one species of tick, a flea, five nematode species, four species of tapes, and a tongue worm. *Sar-*

Scapo with scabies encrustation of legs and lower abdomen. She is unable to climb trees and can travel only with extreme effort.

coptes scabiei, the causative organism of scabies, was not on the list. The first mention of scabies in the porcupine appears in 1958, in a paper by two scientists from the University of Maine (Payne and O'Meara 1958). In 1967, Wendell Dodge wrote that scabies was epidemic among his porcupines in western Massachusetts. They were dying in their winter dens, and some of those still alive were so severely afflicted that their abdominal walls had been perforated and intestines exposed.

No other parasite afflicts the porcupine with equal severity. Though an animal may carry hundreds of lice and thousands of intestinal nematodes, it appears alert and looks healthy. In fact, one wonders whether some of the apparent parasites may not confer a benefit on the porcupine. But in the association between *Sarcoptes* and the porcupine, the parasite grows unchecked into the skin, causing such debilitation that the porcupine dies. One is reminded of the horrible first passage of the plague through fourteenth-century Europe, or of the still-unpredictable scourge of AIDS. Perhaps in time *Sarcoptes* will evolve into a form as benign as the present nematodes and surface lice, but today the association between porcupine and mite remains in its early, lethal stage.

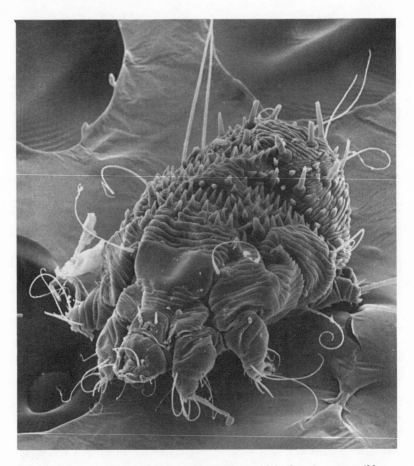

Scanning electron microscope view of Sarcoptes scabiei, *the mite responsible for porcupine scabies. The mite burrows through the skin, setting up a hyperkeratotic response that leads to breaks in the body wall and death of the porcupine (Emko Nonaka).*

My experience with Scapo raised a question. If the scabies mite is spread by body-to-body contact, as textbooks of parasitology assert, how does it infect a solitary species like the porcupine? Porcupines aggregate only under clearly defined conditions: as mother and baby during the summer and, briefly, as mates during the mating season. At less predictable intervals, porcupines may share a den. In my experience, only a single male and female are involved, though under more crowded conditions several animals may share a den (Chapter 7).

Porcupines need not touch each other in a den to transmit scabies; indirect proof comes from my own intimate encounter with a denned porcupine. On a cold February afternoon, I followed a porcupine trail into what looked like a small hole in a snow bank. I labored down the hill in my snowshoes, collected a snow shovel and flashlight, and returned to the den site to learn what an active den looks like. In the snow bank, I found a rock outcrop about 15 feet wide. Below it stretched a broad but fairly low opening, like a front porch. The den proper was in the back, with a narrower opening about a foot in cross section and extending about three feet into solid rock. At the end I saw the white-tipped tail of a porcupine in the beam of my flashlight. The den was absolutely bare; the porcupine was crouching on cold rock. The porch area, where I was lying on my belly, was more cluttered. In front of the den opening lay a neat, foot-high pile of porcupine droppings, with droppings from past years on the bottom and fresh ones on the top. Scattered across the porch was a layer of other droppings, mostly old, and occasional dried leaves blown in by autumn winds.

I crawled in as far as I could to photograph the porch area and the inner den and spent perhaps a quarter hour in the same horizontal posture as the porcupine. Then I carefully shoveled snow back around the opening and exposed rock, leaving a single entrance as before. The porcupine did not find the disturbance intolerable; fresh tracks emerged from the den for several weeks afterward. Meanwhile, however, my encounter had not quite ended. A few days later, I began to itch around the chest, under the arms, in the sides. I suffered for a few days, then sought counsel from my wife, who is a doctor. She found small inflamed spots on my chest and sides and announced, "You have the scabies." Fortunately, human scabies, caused by the same organism that attacks the porcupine, is easily treated. A single application of hexachlorobenzene lotion eliminated the infection.

I tried to live-trap the porcupine, to make a physical examination. The trap malfunctioned, and a week later the animal left the den for good. Since it carried no radio, I could not follow it. Still, I have little doubt I picked up the sarcoptid mites from the floor of the porcupine porch. The mites had crawled toward body warmth through my thick layers of clothing. Direct transmission was impossible, since I had never touched the porcupine.

My experience suggests that porcupine dens, which may be used by more than one animal in succession, may transmit *Sarcoptes* and perhaps other parasites from animal to animal. It also suggests an adaptive value to the den-cleaning activity of the porcupine. If leaves and other debris were not removed from the dens, it is possible the levels of infestation might be still higher. I tried to confirm my den-transmission theory with a standard ecological technique called a Berlese extraction. About 100 g of den droppings are loaded into a large funnel with a screen across the bottom. The bottom opens into a small collecting flask containing glycerine and 70% alcohol. The top is warmed with a 10-watt bulb. Over a week, as the debris slowly dries from the top down, the tiny arthropods migrate lower until they tumble down into the collecting flask. The technique therefore extracts only the living organisms of a litter sample. They may then be mounted on slides and microscoped for identification. I was surprised by the richness of microanimals: insect larvae, rove beetles, tiny wasps, fleas, springtails. But the overwhelming majority of arthropods were mites (eight-legged relatives of ticks and spiders). From one den alone, I recovered 10 species of mites, with 46 individuals in total. None were *Sarcoptes,* nor did I find *Sarcoptes* in any of four other dens examined. That was not surprising in view of the small number of dens examined and the lack of assurance that any was inhabited by an infected porcupine. I could not recheck the infected den, since I was running the experiment a year later.

Two years after my unfortunate encounter with porcupine-den *Sarcoptes,* another opportunity to test the den-transmission theory presented itself. I captured a scabies-infected porcupine by climbing after it into a hemlock tree, then brought the animal back to New York for observation and treatment. I kept it in a wire mesh cage in a cool basement, collected the droppings on newspapers placed under the cage, and extracted the droppings in a Berlese funnel as before. This time, in the artificial conditions of captivity, only two mite species appeared, and one of them was the molelike, skin-burrowing *Sarcoptes:* one adult and six larvae. Clearly the mites were not passed with the feces—the organism is an ectoparasite. The mites had dropped down from the skin and fur of the infected porcupine, surviving off their host's body for the several days it took to collect the sample and make the extraction.

My studies of porcupine scabies have ended because the disease has run its course in my population. The cases I encountered are listed in Table 24.

Since my last encounter with a scabious porcupine, I have made more than two hundred and fifty captures and physical examinations; not one animal has been found to suffer from scabies. The disease, at least in my Catskills population, has returned to its pre-1958 status: not observed in porcupines. As noted in the previous chapter, the local porcupine population density has risen significantly since 1983 (Table 25). Supporting evidence that the post-1983 rise in population is real comes from the parallel contraction in female territories (Table 22) and from increased intensity of linden use in 1985 (Table 11). Apparently the scabies mite, during its residency in the area, was controlling the local porcupine population. But a parasite that is too devastating to its host is ultimately a badly adapted parasite. On a solitary species like the porcupine, the host that *Sarcoptes* kills is likely to be the last host it will have. The remaining porcupine parasites all interact more gently with their host.

The Porcupine Louse

This little brown insect, which lacks wings and eyes and travels up and down porcupine hairs somewhat like the porcupine travels up and down trees, is probably found at some time on every porcupine, often in unbelievable numbers. When I found the female Gro debilitated and near death at the end of the winter, her fur seemed to carry an excessive louse population. At times a dozen or so of the little insects were visible on the surface, their small light-brown bodies conspicuous against the black fur of Gro's belly and neck. At home I sprayed Gro thoroughly with 1% malathion in water, wetting her back and tail as well as her underparts. A day later, the newspaper under her cage turned brown with an accumulation of hundreds of louse corpses—I estimated at least 500 bodies. I changed the papers and found an additional hundred or so corpses 24 hours later, perhaps combed out by the porcupine. No more than a tiny fraction of that large population had been visible while the lice were actively foraging in the porcupine fur.

The porcupine louse, *Trichodectes setosus,* was formerly known as *Eutrichophilus setosus* (Morse 1903). The earlier name was aptly chosen. "*Eutrichophilus*" means "good lover of hair." The living insect can be

Scanning electron microscope view of a porcupine louse on a porcupine hair. The head with antenna appears at left; four of the six legs are visible (×120).

observed under a dissecting microscope. It will not run away if one or two porcupine hairs are introduced into its surroundings. The insect can form a loose pincers around the hair with its front pair of legs, then use the remaining sharp-clawed legs to run rapidly up or down the hair. At other times, all legs are in motion. On reaching the end of the hair, it climbs off, mills around in a confused way, then climbs back and runs the other way. If five or six insects have only a single porcupine hair available, all will cling to the same hair and clamber over each other as they try to move up or down. The lice can also form a pincers around the hair with their mandibles, holding on with their mouthparts instead of their legs. That may be a feeding behavior; the mandibles may be used to scrape off surface grease or loose skin cells. I have placed the lice on the hairs of my own forearm and found them polite guests; they do not bite, although they are equipped to do so. All I felt was a busy wriggling on the skin, as they moved ceaselessly among the hairs. The lice seek body heat. Undoubtedly the reason so few can be seen on the typical porcupine is because they huddle against the body for warmth. On porcupines I have found frozen in their dens, the lice have also frozen to death.

Porcupines probably acquire their lice while nursing against their mothers' bellies. All juveniles a few weeks old or older that I have examined have carried lice. The insects are more conspicuous in the shorter, darker fur of juveniles than on the adults. At that time, the eggs of *Trichodectes* can also be seen, glued to individual hairs like tiny white balloons. Perhaps another reason the lice are so abundant on juveniles is because the mothers molt every spring. As the adults shed their winter fur, the lice may have nowhere to go but to the fur of the juveniles, who won't be molting until their second year.

It is difficult to tell whether the porcupine louse is a true parasite, because the critical studies have never been performed. I suspect that it is in fact a commensal (neutral effect) or a mutualist (beneficial effect) on the porcupine, rendering the service of cleaning. By scraping off excess grease and loose skin cells, the louse may prevent clumping of body fur, thus enhancing the fur's insulating function. At the same time, the lice would leave intact the protective grease layer around the quills, which are too thick for them to travel on. Such cleaning would be doubly valuable to an animal with a diminished ability to clean itself. Arguing against that view is the abundance of lice on emaciated or underweight animals. The true role of *Trichodectes* therefore requires further study.

Ticks

Ticks are the giant relatives of mites and the arthropod equivalent of leeches. Of 70 ticks recovered from my Catskills porcupines, 67 were identified as *Ixodes cookei* by Drs. Milton Nathanson of Queens College, Durland Fish of New York Medical College, and Robert Dowler of Fordham University (Table 26). The remaining ticks were identified as *Ixodes dammini* (2) and *Ixodes texanus* (1). *I. cookei* is associated with medium-sized mammals such as skunk, raccoon, and woodchuck. It is therefore not a specific porcupine parasite. *Ixodes texanus* is somewhat more specialized, concentrating on raccoons. *I. dammini* is known as the deer tick. Adults

Scanning electron microscope ventral view of the head of a porcupine tick, Ixodes cookei. *The barbed hypostome anchors the tick in the skin of its host. Two lateral palps have a chemosensory function (×110).*

feed on white-tailed deer (*Odocoileus virginianus*) and often on humans. Larvae feed on small mammals such as the white-footed mouse (*Peromyscus leucopus*) and on birds (Main et al. 1982, Anderson and Magnarelli 1980, Carey et al. 1980). The deer tick has also gained notoriety as the carrier of Lyme disease, caused by the spirochete *Borrelia burgdorferi*. Acarologists in Connecticut have shown that some *Ixodes texanus* and *I. cookei* harbor rockettsiae responsible for Rocky Mountain spotted fever (Anderson et al. 1986, Magnarelli et al. 1985). Whether the disease is transmitted to porcupines remains to be studied.

An adult *Ixodes*, when engorged with blood, can reach almost 1 cm in length. When the great gray-blue body hangs from a porcupine's belly or armpit, the porcupine makes no effort to scratch or otherwise remove the parasite. Ticks do their job slowly and painlessly but leave visible scars after dropping off.

Catskills porcupines are essentially free of ticks from December through March. The first great wave of tick infestation (the spring wave) strikes in

April and May, when up to 50% of the animals may be parasitized at any one time. Cumulative rates are higher, since often a porcupine may be found free of ticks but bearing numerous scars of previous attacks. The attack rate drops to about 20% in June, then picks up again from July through September (the summer wave). A quiet period is observed during October. Then the third, smaller (autumn) wave strikes during November. The wavelike pattern suggests synchronized molting and feeding cycles, with the spring wave made up of overwintering individuals. Andrew J. Main and coworkers (1982) at the Yale University School of Medicine describe a similar multiphasic life cycle for Connecticut *Ixodes dammini*.

Though less than 50% of the porcupine population carries ticks even at the peak of an infestation, individuals may carry heavy parasite loads. One female carried 12 ticks in May. Another carried 17 in July. They may represent hatches from a single egg mass or an aggregation phenomenon. On average, females were twice as likely to carry a tick as males (0.94 tick per female versus 0.47 tick per male on a year-round basis). The difference is not statistically significant, but it tilts in the expected direction, since females spend more time on the ground because of nursing and maternal care. It is perhaps significant that the most highly infected male ever discovered (with 7 ticks) was Finder, who had been spending all his time on the ground while recovering from a tree-fall injury.

Ixodes ticks do not infect porcupines across their entire species range.

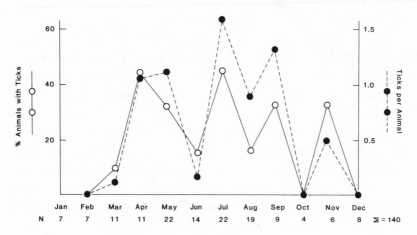

Time course of porcupine tick infection.

Farther north, in Nova Scotia, the predominant tick of porcupines becomes *Dermacentor variabilis,* the dog tick (Dodds et al. 1969). In Alaska, no ticks have been recovered as porcupine parasites (Jellison and Neiland 1965).

Tapeworms

Essentially all adult porcupines carry tapeworms. Evidence comes from the white proglottids universally present in porcupine droppings and from the studies of parasitologists. Reino S. Freeman (1952) reports 23 of 24 porcupines examined carried tapeworms. The remaining animal, though parasite-free on inspection, had been passing proglottids when first captured.

Since porcupines do not eat their own droppings, tapeworms must invade new porcupines through an intermediate host, an oribatid mite. Oribatids are the most common mites found in the debris of porcupine dens. They can be recognized by their convex, highly sclerotized (darkened) outer shell, which gives them the appearance of tiny beetles. As they scavenge through decomposing porcupine droppings, mites ingest tapeworm eggs, which develop into infective cysticercoid larvae in the mites. Porcupines become infected after accidental ingestion of mites that have crawled onto green vegetation surrounding the den. In fact, the mites (14 known species) are obligate intermediate hosts for the tapeworms. Porcupines do not get infected by direct ingestion of the tapeworm eggs. Freeman collected and dissected 520 oribatids from the vicinity of porcupine dens and identified 12 infected individuals. In 929 mites collected far from porcupine dens, only one was infected. For good measure, Freeman also dissected and examined more than 400 porcupine lice and found no tapeworm larvae. The oribatid intermediate is common to all three anoplocephalid tapeworms found in porcupines (*Monoecocestus americanus, M. variabilis, Cittotaenia pectinata*). The *Monoecocestus* tapes are almost exclusively associated with porcupines; *Cittotaenia* is rare in porcupines and better known from hares, including European species (Mead-Briggs and Page 1975; Freeman 1949).

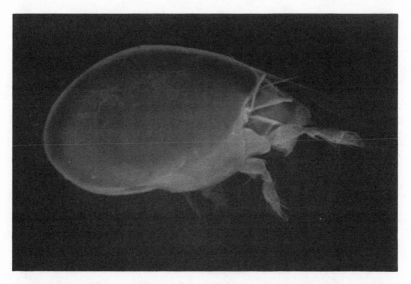

Scanning electron micrograph of an oribatid mite. Oribatids, which are shielded by a pigmented carapace, are secondary hosts for porcupine tapeworms (×170).

Like many other aspects of porcupine natural history, the biological costs of the parasites have not been evaluated. On the one hand, even heavily parasitized porcupines appear to be vigorous and in good health. On the other hand, an uncontrolled natural experiment suggests that costs may be involved. In 1947, C. A. Tryon reported on a porcupine delivered in mid-May by cesarean section and raised by hand. Its initial growth was slower than observed in wild animals, perhaps because it was not getting its mother's milk. But the growth rate picked up in midsummer; by August the baby weighed 3 kg, and by December its weight exceeded 5 kg. In contrast, baby porcupines in the wild first gain weight quickly and then, by late August, reach a plateau. Weights achieved by the end of the first summer fall below 3 kg. Several factors may suppress growth rates after midsummer. The quality of available food is declining (as shown by declining nitrogen levels), and mother's milk becomes unavailable by October. But another factor may be the acquisition of parasitic tapeworms by early August. (Freeman showed that adult tapeworms are found in porcupines 70 days after ingestion of infected mites.) Porcupines acquire intestinal nematodes even earlier. Curtis and Kozicky (1944) report an average of 766 tape-

Weight gains in captive (solid circles) and wild (open circles) juvenile porcupines. The rapid early-summer weight gain observed in wild porcupines plateaus around August, when they acquire their tapeworm parasites.

worms per porcupine, with a high count of 1528. The tapeworms and nematodes should be absent in the hand-reared porcupine. Thus, even while wild porcupines appear healthy and vigorous, they may be sacrificing a significant fraction of potential growth to their intestinal parasites.

Nematodes

One invertebrate zoologist has stated that if all life on earth were swept away except for the nematodes, the former plants, animals, rivers, and soils would still be decipherable from the characteristic massing of their erstwhile nematode inhabitants. The statement is particularly apt for the porcupine, which is known to be a host to at least four species of nematodes: *Wellcomia evaginata, Dipetalonema arbuta, Dirofilaria spinosa, Molinema diacantha.*

Most nematodes are worms of microscopic size. *Wellcomia evaginata,* however, must be considered among the whales of the nematode world.

The worms are over 2 cm (1 inch) long, relatively stout, and conspicuous because they are continually shed with the feces. Occasionally a passed nematode may string two droppings together (Dodge 1967). In terms of body structure, the most remarkable feature of *Wellcomia* is a long lateral outpocketing (evagination) that terminates the female genital tract. The vaginas of female nematodes typically open laterally; in this case they extend outward to give the nematodes an unwormlike shape.

The *Wellcomia* may be present in enormous numbers. Olsen and Tollman (1951) found 30,500 in a single porcupine; Curtis and Kozicky (1944) report a high count of 5184 in a single animal. The nematodes are distributed throughout the small and large intestine but not in equal densities. In one postmortem examination, I found only 6 in the lower segment of the large intestine, but there were so many thousands in the upper segment and caecum that they looked like a short-noodle soup. They became much less abundant in the small intestine and were absent from the stomach. The observed intestinal distribution of *Wellcomia* correlates with the location of the gastrointestinal sodium pool (Chapter 5), which raises the intriguing possibility that the nematodes may play some role in body sodium regulation. *Wellcomia* nematodes are also found in South American and Old World porcupines but in few other mammals (Hugot 1982, Olsen and Tollman 1951). The same pattern does not hold true with the lice, who may play a less essential role. The possibility of *Wellcomia*-porcupine mutualism deserves further investigation.

In addition to the highly visible and abundant *Wellcomia* nematodes, porcupines also carry much smaller, hairlike nematodes of the genera *Dipetalonema*, *Dirofilaria*, and *Molinema*. The filariid worms *Dipetalonema arbuta*, described by P. R. Highby (1943a,b), may be found free in the abdominal cavity. Highby showed that they are transmitted by the bite of one of several species of mosquitoes of the genus *Aedes*. According to C. M. Bartlett, the first four molts of the parasite are found under the skin, close to the site of injection by the mosquito (Bartlett and Anderson 1985). The fifth-stage molt migrates to the final site: the peritoneal cavity, the pericardium, or the brain of the porcupine. Other filariids are transmitted by ticks.

In comparison with man, porcupines are hyperparasitized. A single animal may carry tens of thousands of nematodes, a thousand lice, 400 tapeworms, plus assorted ticks, fleas, mites, and tongue worms. Some of them are unique to the porcupine, suggesting an ancient relationship between parasite and host. Both the intensity of infection and the specificity of the interaction suggest mutual benefits to parasite and porcupine. It is possible that when their relationships are fully explored, some of the parasites will be reclassified as symbionts or mutualists.

.12.

Porcupines of the World

Porcupines other than *Erethizon* inhabit every continent of the world except Australia and Antarctica. They form two geographical and ecological groups, the New World and the Old World porcupines. The New World porcupines weigh 3 to 10 kg, are arboreal, and feed on tree products including leaves, fruit, and bark. Old World porcupines may weigh up to 30 kg, are ground-dwelling, and dig for foods such as bulbs and tubers or feed on fallen fruit. They typically carry more-formidable as well as more-specialized quills. Both groups are classified as hystricomorph rodents, are active at night, have long gestation periods, and bear small numbers of precocial young. They are long-lived. Current scientific opinion favors a common evolutionary origin for the two groups.

New World Porcupines and the Origins of *Erethizon*

When the North and South American continents collided three million years ago, waves of animal migration swept in both directions across the newly formed isthmus of Panama. Most of the march was from north to south, the route of the deer, the horse, the raccoons, the cats. Even the llama reached its present South American home from the north (Simpson 1980). But a number of South American animals traveled the other way. Their descendants include the opossum, the armadillo, and the porcupine.

The North American porcupine (*Erethizon dorsatum*) has traveled farther north than any of the other immigrants, yet it retains close relatives in the south—the prehensile-tailed porcupines of the genera *Coendou* and *Sphiggurus*. It is unlikely that the porcupine making the great transition looked like the present-day *Erethizon*, because no *Erethizon* fossils are

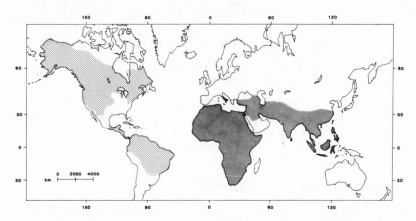

Distribution of New World porcupines, family Erethizontidae (open stippling), and Old World porcupines, family Hystricidae (close stippling). Erethizon dorsatum *is the only porcupine of North America and has the northernmost species range of all the porcupines.*

known from South America. Michael K. Frazier (1981) of the University of Florida has suggested a possible ancestor or close relative in an extinct porcupine, *Steiromys.* Others suggest *Coendou* as the direct ancestor (White 1970), although Frazier concludes that no *Coendou* fossils are known from the north. The close affinity between *Erethizon* and the porcupines to the south should provide added incentive for their study.

The New World porcupines include four genera in addition to *Erethizon: Chaetomys, Echinoprocta, Coendou,* and *Sphiggurus.* The first two contain only a single species each. *Chaetomys subspinosus,* the thin-spined porcupine, is listed as endangered by the U.S. Department of the Interior and was feared extinct in its Brazilian coastal forest habitat. That forest is today 95% destroyed by lumbering and agricultural clearing. *Chaetomys* had not been sighted there since 1952 when, in 1986, it was rediscovered by Ilmar B. Santos, a Brazilian biologist, who made a preliminary study of its habits (Besch 1987, Raeburn 1987). The cat-sized animal is nocturnal and lives in trees. It is covered by soft, brown spines resembling the bristles of a broom and moves with the help of a partially prehensile (grasping) tail. Scientists are unsure whether to classify the animal as a true porcupine or as a separate form related to spiny rats. *Echinoprocta rufescens,* the upper Amazonian porcupine, is not well known in terms of habits and biology. Its tail is hairy, nonprehensile, and about the same length as *Erethizon*'s. *Echinoprocta* may or may not be arboreal and is found in the mountain forests around Bogotá, Colombia.

J. H. Honacki et al. (1982) list 5 species in the genus *Coendou* (*C. bicolor, C. mexicanus, C. pallidus, C. prehensilis, C. rothschildi* and 4 species of *Sphiggurus* (*S. insidiosus, S. spinosus, S. vestitus*, and *S. villosus*). But the two genera are so poorly differentiated that many authorities lump *Sphiggurus* as a subgenus of *Coendou* (Nowak and Paradiso 1983). J. F. Eisenberg (1978) has suggested there may be as many as 20 species in the group. *Coendou* and *Sphiggurus* are distributed from Mexico through Central America, and in South America as far as northern Argentina. Little is known about their natural history. That is regrettable not only for its reflection on the state of Central and South American biology but also because *Coendou* is thought to be the closest living relative of the North American porcupine. A comparative study would shed light on both forms. No studies have so far been published that reveal ecological differences between the *Coendou* species or, for that matter, between *Coendou* and *Sphiggurus*.

G. G. Montgomery and Y. D. Lubin (1978) of the Smithsonian Institution report on a preliminary radiotelemetry study of *Coendou prehensilis* from Venezuela. Transmitters were attached to the tail with adhesive tape and stayed in place no longer than two weeks. Only three animals were followed; their weights ranged from 3 to 5 kg. They were nocturnal, sleeping in trees during the day, usually 6 to 10 m above the ground, shielded from direct sunlight. They changed position every night, moving 200 to 400 m (maximal movement 950 m per night). Home ranges were large, up to 38 ha during the two weeks. Male and female ranges overlapped, with male ranges the larger. The observations are surprisingly consistent with behavior expected in a similar sample of North American porcupines. Since *Coendou* anatomy shows more extensive arboreal adaptations, one might have expected the animals to spend little time on the ground and to have smaller territories. One explanation for the large observed territories might be that the study site was in the llanos, a semiopen countryside where the porcupines might be forced to move longer distances in search of suitable trees. Arboreal adaptations in *Coendou* include a prehensile tail; prehensile extensions of the front and rear footpads, which according to

Coendou prehensilis. *The distal end of the tail can grasp small branches and lianas, allowing the animal access to the outermost regions of food trees (Jessie Cohen).*

Pocock (1922) are movable and enormously increase the supporting area and gripping power of the foot; and muscular and skeletal adaptations for climbing, described by McEvoy (1982).

A more extensive ecological study by Estrada and Coates-Estrada (1985) on forest mammals in southern Mexico shows that the local porcupine, *C. mexicanus,* has a smaller home range (10 ha), a near-total dependence on the middle levels of the tropical rain forest, and a diet consisting of approximately 80% fruits and 20% leaves. It recognizes as palatable the same leaf trees as the howler and spider monkeys. A study of *Coendou prehensilis* from French Guiana finds a primary dependence on the immature seeds of leguminous trees (Charles-Dominique et al. 1981). The porcupines are superb arborealists, able to reach the smallest branches and lianas and strip a tree of all its seeds. The authors speculate that *Coendou* are such efficient seed predators that the trees have evolved synchronous flowering and seed production to swamp their predators.

In the absence of detailed field studies, studies of captive animals may illuminate the biology of a species. One such study was carried out by

Roberts, Brand, and Maliniak (1985) at the National Zoo in Washington, D.C. The eight-year project followed a colony of captive *Coendou prehensilis* under zoo conditions. Five of the animals were wild-caught, 13 were born in the zoo. They were clearly nocturnal. Gestation was comparable to that of *Erethizon:* 195–210 days. All litters consisted of one young. At 415 g, the newborn was well developed and represented 8% of maternal weight. Infants carried a full coat of quills, had strongly prehensile tails, and had well-developed claws. They climbed readily if disturbed but generally lay quietly in one spot for the first two to three weeks of life. They nursed every 4 to 6 hours, for 1 to 3 minutes at a time; that provided 100% of their food for the first 4 weeks of life. During that time, they gained weight at the rate of 12 g per day. For the next 4 to 15 weeks, infants continued to nurse but also fed independently, with a weight gain of about 10 g per day. After 15 weeks, they foraged independently, reaching adult size at about 16 months and sexual maturity at 19 months. The porcupines are long-lived. One female, at 11.5 years, remains reproductively active and has produced 10 young in 8.5 years.

Perhaps the most striking *Erethizon-Coendou* difference emerging from the study is the slow growth rate of *Coendou* infants compared with *Erethizon*. Even under zoo conditions, where the mother's diet should be optimal, it takes more than a month for the baby to double its birth weight. *Erethizon* babies double their birth weight in 2 weeks. Roberts and co-workers suggest that the difference is related to differences in the forest habitats of the two species. The temperate North American forests of *Erethizon* are highly seasonal, offering a small window of opportunity for the growth of young animals. The more constant conditions of the *Coendou*'s tropical forests allow a more gradual strategy. In addition, the observations of the Roberts group suggest that *Coendou* breeds throughout the year, in contrast to the seasonally synchronized breeding of *Erethizon*. The North American porcupine has a higher metabolic rate, which makes the rapid growth possible.

Although *Erethizon* and *Coendou* inhabit different kinds of forests and follow different ecological strategies, they are closely related as New World hystricomorph rodents and share many features of anatomy and behavior, especially in reproductive strategies. In both genera, the female has a vaginal closure membrane that dissolves during estrus and parturition.

The male has a sacculus urethralis and showers the female with urine prior to copulation. There is a long gestation period (210 days in *Erethizon* and 200 days in *Coendou*), resulting in a single, well-developed young (450 g in *Erethizon*, 415 g in *Coendou*) and followed by prolonged lactation (127 days in *Erethizon,* up to 105 days in *Coendou*). Both animals are long-lived (to 18 years in *Erethizon,* over 14 years in *Coendou*). Such similarity is not surprising in view of the close evolutionary relationship between the two genera.

It is unfortunate that more is not known concerning the natural history of *Coendou* and *Sphiggurus*. How are the species ecologically differentiated? How many species are there? What kinds of social systems do the animals have? (The Roberts group notes a series of complex vocalizations and scent-marking behaviors that suggest social interactions, but their natural patterns cannot be determined in a zoo setting.) How do *Coendou* interact with other leaf- and fruit-eaters such as howler monkeys, sloths, and leaf-cutting ants?'Who are their natural predators and parasites? All those questions require more study.

Old World Porcupines

Shakespeare's reference to the "fretful porpentine" (Hamlet Act 1, scene 5) is not to the North American porcupine but to its Old World cousin. Likewise, the porcupine emblazoned on the royal coat of arms of Louis XII of France (1462–1515) is the Old World form. So is the porcupine described by Pliny the Elder and by Aristotle before him (*Historia Animalium*). Old World porcupines have long lived in association with humans and have perhaps evolved with them. That may be why they have none of the boldness and self-confidence associated with the American animal. They are furtive, fast-moving animals specialized for ecological roles different from those of *Erethizon* and *Coendou*. Erna Mohr (1965) refers to them as the ground porcupines, as distinct from the tree porcupines of the New World. Mohr recognizes five genera of Old World porcupines: *Trichys, Atherurus, Hystrix, Acanthion,* and *Thecurus*. But Honacki et al. (1982) list *Acanthion* as a subgenus of *Hystrix;* I shall follow their nomenclature (Table 27).

Trichys

Trichys is considered the most primitive (least specialized) of the Old World porcupines. It is small for a porcupine (1.7 to 2.2 kg adult weight), with a ratlike look enhanced by short quills hidden among the guard hairs and fur. The quills have the quality of stiff bristles, more like the quills of the spiny rats than of the higher porcupines. When frightened, the animal stamps its feet and flares out its quills. A distinctive feature is the tail, long for a porcupine, covered with scales for most of its length, and ending with a tuft of bristles. They cannot be shaken to produce a sound as in *Atherurus* or *Hystrix.*

When the animal runs along the forest floor, it holds the tail aloft like a flag. Curiously, about 30% of museum specimens lack the tail entirely. There is a region at the base of the tail where it breaks easily. Various theories have been offered to explain the tail loss. One guess is that males hold the females by the tail during mating. (There are more tailless females than tailless males.) Another theory suggests that the natives collect *Trichys* tails for some purpose and break them off intentionally. What the special purpose is has not been declared, nor have accumulations of *Trichys* tails been discovered among the villagers. An alternate possibility is that the tail may simply be sacrificed to predators the way some lizards sacrifice their tails to birds; the *Trichys* tail, however, cannot be regenerated once lost.

Trichys are forest dwellers and reportedly more nimble in trees than other Old World porcupines. They are nocturnal and spend the day in an underground den. They are long-lived under zoo conditions; an animal at the San Diego Zoo was still alive after ten years of captivity (Mohr 1965).

Atherurus

The two brushtail porcupine species tend to be larger than *Trichys* but not as large as *Hystrix;* adult body weights range from 1.5 to 4.0 kg. They are equipped with three kinds of quills as well as an assortment of hairs, bristles, and vibrissae. The quills covering most of the back and sides are flat to hourglass-shaped in cross section and have feathery edges. The feathered (barbuled) edges are better developed on the African species, and the barbules seem to act like sawteeth. They clearly do not have the same function as the scales on the tips of New World porcupines, which work to drive the quill deeper into the body of the victim. Among the barbule quills, and

A barbulated quill from Atherurus africanus.

The tail of the African brushtail porcupine produces a threatening rattle. It is composed of stiff bristles and platelet quills.

on the African form only, emerge short, thick quills that are circular in cross section and may be lost during molting. The Asiatic form carries no circular quills. Brushtail porcupines are named for the large brush at the end of the tail, composed of stiff bristles and platelet quills (quills modified for rattling) (Mohr 1965). Vibration of the tail produces a dry, rattling sound that functions as a warning signal.

As in *Trichys*, the tail of *Atherurus* may break off easily. The zone of breakage occurs approximately a third of the way down the tail, where the barbule quills end and the tail carries only a few short bristles underlaid by scaly rings. The incidence of tail loss in *Atherurus*, however, is much lower than it is in *Trichys*. Of 94 brushtail porcupine museum specimens I have examined, only 4 showed basal tail loss.

Reproduction in *Atherurus africanus* has been studied by Rahm (1962). The gestation period is 110 days; the single young weighs about 150 g at birth. Births are scattered throughout the year. By the second day, the newborn is able to leave its mother, go for a walk around the neighborhood, and find its way back. The mother nurses for two months, but babies begin taking solid food within three weeks.

Brushtail porcupines live in all the tropical forests of their species ranges, up to elevations of about 3000 m. They are active nocturnally. During the day, they shelter in hollow logs, rock crevices, eroded cavities in stream banks, and similar sites. They prefer not to dig their own dens but select natural cavities that may be enlarged and modified (Mohr 1965).

Louise Emmons (1983) of the Smithsonian Institution has studied the African species by radiotelemetry. She describes the animals as nervous, fast-moving, and largely subsisting on fallen fruit. Though principally ground-dwelling, they will swim or climb a tree to escape pursuit. They are extremely wary of humans, perhaps because of strong hunting pressure. Adult males average 3.4 kg in weight and are slightly heavier than females. Babies take 2 years or longer to reach adult size. The animals are not crepuscular; they emerge from their dens only when it is completely dark. On dark nights, the activity pattern is trimodal, with two rest periods per night. On moonlit nights, all animals spend more time resting, and the activity pattern becomes bimodal, with a single rest period around midnight. They move along well-defined trails through the undergrowth. Males average 2333 m of travel per night on dark nights, females 1953 m per night.

*An African brushtail porcupine hides in a tree hole
(Louise H. Emmons).*

Moonlight reduces movements for both sexes. Home areas average 13.3 ha, with no significant male-female difference. Emmons speculates that 13 ha may be the minimum area required for feeding on fallen fruit, to insure adequate amount and diversity of that resource.

The most tantalizing of Emmons's findings is that the home ranges of her study population fall into three separate zones of occupancy. Zone 1 is used by one male and one female, zone 2 by three males and two females, and zone 3 by one male. The usage patterns of the three zones are mutually exclusive. Emmons calls zone-sharing animals members of a clan. With Francois Rousillon, Emmons has collared 18 additional animals and found them all to be members of clans (L. H. Emmons, personal communication). The home range of any individual could be predicted from its capture site. Clans consisted of about 3 females and 5 to 7 males each.

Emmons studied a few captive animals. In captivity, three males shared the same den and often rested in physical contact. During encounters, animals groomed each other and made auditory displays of dominance and submission. An adult female appeared to dominate all three males. The males almost immediately killed a juvenile female placed in a connecting enclosure.

Though the African porcupine is found alone in 89% of all sightings, it lives within strong social constraints and is well aware of other porcupines in its forest zone. Its social structure deserves further study.

Hystrix and Thecurus

It is unfortunate that much less is known about the natural history of the remaining Old World porcupines, the five species of the genus *Hystrix* and three species of *Thecurus*. But for *Hystrix* the situation is rapidly changing, with strong research efforts now coming from several laboratories. Though the natural history of these porcupines remains incompletely understood, much has been learned from studies of captive individuals.

Hystrix cristata, *the crested porcupine (San Diego Zoological Society).*

Hystrix and *Thecurus* adapt well to zoo conditions and reproduce success-
fully. However, zoo studies must be accepted with caution. In addition to
the usual distortions of captivity, *Hystrix* and *Thecurus* as well as *Atherurus*
may hybridize in captivity, so identification may be difficult. Whereas
brushtail porcupine species are externally well differentiated, the other species may not be. If hybrids are shipped to other zoos without adequate
background information, they may escape detection (Mohr 1965).

The best-developed senses in *Hystrix* are hearing and smell. Erna Mohr
writes that when a single peanut is dropped to the ground several meters
from a group of dozing animals, they wake up and go in search of the mor-
sel. Though the peanut may be in plain view, they locate it by sniffing. The
animals also have well-developed sensory bristles covering the entire body
but concentrated around the mouth and eyes. Such tactile information must
be especially valuable to nocturnal cave dwellers.

Reproductive Systems   The sexes are hard to distinguish externally, as is
also true in *Trichys* and *Atherurus*. Males and females differ little in terms
of size, weight (females tend to be slightly heavier), and external markings. A true scrotum is not present. The penis may be palpated in its sheath
and everted by pressure from behind. At rest, the opening of the penis
points backward. *Hystrix* (and all other hystricomorph rodents) have a sacculus urethralis as part of the male reproductive system, with two large
bristles at the bottom of the pouch. The bizarre structure, shared with the
New World porcupines, so impressed Stuart Landry that he argued for a
common origin for the New World and Old World hystricomorphs long
before the mainstream of biologists felt ready to do so (Landry 1957, Tohme
and Tohme 1981, Dathe 1937, Pocock 1922). Another hystricomorph feature of the Old World porcupines is the presence of small prickles on the
surface of the glans penis. Two additional *Hystrix* structures that echo
structures found in New World porcupines include a baculum (shovel-
shaped and about 3.4 cm long in *H. africaeaustralis*) and a copulatory
plug formed by the male (freshly ejaculated semen quickly sets to form a
gel) (Van Aarde and Skinner 1986, Tohme and Tohme 1981, Mohr 1965).

The female reproductive system likewise follows typical hystricomorph
patterns. A vaginal closure membrane disappears temporarily at estrus and
at childbirth (Van Aarde 1985, Weir 1974). *Hystrix* species have relatively

long gestation periods (94–112 days), produce small numbers of precocial young (1–3 young per litter with an average of 1.5, weighing 310–370 g), and have long periods of lactation (49–140 days). In all those patterns, the *Hystrix* species resemble the North American porcupine. Such heavy parental investment in a small number of offspring should lead to a high probability of survival for each offspring (Mohr 1965).

Digestive System   All Old World porcupines have the same dental formula as the New World species: (I 1/1, C 0/0, P 1/1, M 3/3) × 2 = 20. That is, each quadrant of the adult jaw carries 1 incisor, 1 premolar, and 3 molars. *Hystrix* species show one important dental difference from New World porcupines and from the Old World genera *Atherurus* and *Trichys:* their molars are rootless and continue growing throughout life. They help the animal macerate the sand-covered bulbs and tubers it digs out of the ground as part of its diet (Alkon and Saltz 1985, Gutterman 1982, Mohr 1965). The Cape porcupine, *Hystrix africaeaustralis,* is known for its habit of collecting bones (often scavenged from hyena feeding sites) and taking them back to its den for gnawing, apparently to correct calcium and phosphate deficiencies in its diet (Duthie and Skinner 1986).

The tongue carries a rasplike array of "horn teeth." Mohr believes they aid in mincing of fine foods but may also be related to grooming. *Hystrix* spend a great deal of time licking themselves and each other; perhaps a tongue passing over the roughly quilled exterior must be armored.

The *Hystrix* digestive tract contains a prominent caecum, filled with microorganisms that help break down complex carbohydrates. The animals produce hard, dry droppings that resemble date pits (Van Jaarsveld and Knight-Eloff 1984, Mohr 1965).

Quills   The quills of *Hystrix* include some of the most formidable structures known in the porcupine world. I use one pencil-thick quill of *H. indica* as a slide pointer. Quills of that size have been known to kill leopards, pythons, and other would-be predators. The stout defense quills are about 18 cm (7 inches) long. In *Thecurus,* the quills are thicker than the diameter of the front incisors. Much longer but thinner are the flexible, slightly curved outer quills. *Hystrix* are large animals; adults may weigh up to 30 kg (66 pounds). When the quills are fully erected, the animal appears

10 cm

Development of rattle quills in Hystrix. *The quills are carried on the tail and deliver an audible threat signal.*

even larger and more formidable. The illusion of size is enhanced by erectable bristles of the mane or crest present in *H. cristata, H. indica,* and *H. africaeaustralis.* During a confrontation, the porcupine moves rapidly sideways or backward, trying to impale its enemy.

   Hystrix contain two other types of quills: the flat barbule quills of *Atherurus* and the hollow, open-tipped rattle quills in the tail. A rattle quill begins development as a normal, spine-tipped quill. During maturation, the tip separates cleanly and the spongy inner contents are lost. Left behind is a hollow cup on a long stalk. Rattle quills, separated by stiff bristles, are found only on the tail. When the tail is vibrated, the bristles act as clappers against the rattle quills, producing a loud, threatening sound. *Hystrix* rattles its tail, stamps its feet, and flares its quills as part of its threat display. It may also chatter its teeth and produce grunting sounds (Smithers 1983, Mohr 1965).

Social Structure   *Hystrix* behavior in captivity shows elements of both sociability and aggression. The animals appear to require a great deal of body contact. They lick each other frequently and rest with their bodies pressed close together. In the wild, such data are less available, but a few species are reported to be monogamous, including *H. brachyura* and *H. africaeaustralis* (Morris and Van Aarde 1985, Gosling 1980). Amicable relationships extend beyond the male-female pair. Mohr (1965) observed four *Hystrix* in a zoo, their quills lightly spread, hopping in a circle "like a group of round-dancing girls in petticoats." The animals were obviously friendly with each other and feeling happy. After some minutes, they lay down next to each other in a corner and rested from their dance.

But according to Mohr, such episodes of friendliness and play can quickly turn into anger. For instance, if one group of dancers has had enough but another group wants to continue, quilling and biting may start, wherein the fearsome incisors can inflict life-threatening wounds. Mohr (1965) recounts one such incident, as told by B. Schneider in 1930.

This morning between 10 a.m. and noon, there was a battle involving the eight porcupines in the pachyderm house. Two individuals are so badly injured we must dispatch them. One animal looks horrible: there is a deep hole in the head, and the left shoulder is peeled off—a palm-sized wound! An equally large wound in the hindquarters. Two quills are embedded in the flesh of the shoulder, as deep as a little finger. The floor is literally buried in quills: long, stiff, short, thick, hairlike; a whole bushelful must lie there. I see a piece of flesh with 8 quills, another with even more, which have been torn out whole with the teeth. Terrible things must have happened here.

Generally the fights start when porcupines who don't know each other are brought together. Under zoo conditions, where animals cannot easily give way or avoid each other, such episodes may be more common than in the wild. But even free-living animals have been found with foreign quills in their muscles. How all those behaviors interrelate to generate a stable social structure remains to be elucidated.

Movements   Like all other Old World porcupines, *Hystrix* are ground-dwelling and nocturnally active. Philip Alkon, who has studied radio-telemetered *H. indica* in the Negev Desert of Israel, reports that animals do not emerge from their dens when a bright moon is shining. Alkon has shown that the activity patterns are exquisitely correlated with moon phase. The porcupines are active every night, but onset and termination of activity are timed to avoid bright moonlight. The animals den in limestone caves of a steeply sloped tributary wadi and travel 1–1.5 km to reach a seasonal food source, the irrigated potato fields of a kibbutz (Alkon and Saltz 1988). In the case of *H. africaeaustralis,* the commuting distance from den to food source may be even longer, since the animals den in rock crevices at higher elevations, and their foods are usually found in the valleys. Mohr (1965) reports that *H. africaeaustralis* may spend almost the whole night traveling.

Distribution   Although *Atherurus* and *Trichys* are associated with dense forests, most *Hystrix* are found in more open countryside. The genus is absent only from areas where plants are also absent, such as the Sahara and the Arabian deserts. But the animals do well in savannah and semidesert habitats, owing their drought tolerance to their nocturnal habits, their excellent water-conserving physiology, and their habit of foraging for bulbs and tubers (Van Jaarsveld and Knight-Eloff 1984). The most extensive species ranges are shown by the crested porcupines: *H. africaeaustralis* (southern Africa), *H. cristata* (northern Africa, Sicily, southern Italy, Albania, northern Greece), and *H. indica* (eastern Mediterranean to India and Sri Lanka).

The disjunct European population of *H. cristata* appears to represent a recent human introduction. Mohr (1965) summarizes the arguments against natural dispersal from North Africa.

- A route east around the Mediterranean would have forced the animals to move through territory occupied by *H. indica*.
- A western route through Gibraltar should have left populations in Spain and southern France, as is true of other animals who have followed that route. But no porcupines are presently found there. Landry (1957) points out, however, that Pleistocene fossils of *Hystrix* are known from all across Europe.
- A Pleistocene land bridge from Tunis to Sicily has no support from geology or zoogeography.

The case for human introduction is supported by the absence of porcupines in Italy and Sicily during Roman times, according to Pliny the Elder (A.D. 23–79). They were still absent at the time of Isidore of Seville (A.D. 560–636), who describes the porcupine of North Africa but makes no mention of its presence in Spain or Italy. At present the *H. cristata* populations of Italy and North Africa are so similar that they do not warrant subspecies status, suggesting a recent common history. Mohr suggests possible economic incentives for the introduction of the porcupine into Italy, including the use in preindustrial times of gilt porcupine quills as hairpins. It is more probable that porcupines were kept for the table, like rabbits and guinea pigs. Porcupines are readily eaten in Italy and are often found in meat markets.

The *H. cristata* of Italy and the northern Mediterranean may not be the only porcupines introduced into Europe by human agency. Recently an unintentional natural experiment played itself out with the Himalayan porcupine, *H. brachyura*. Two Himalayan porcupines escaped from a wildlife collection in Devon, England, in 1969, not only surviving but also reproducing and establishing a population in the wooded valleys of the rivers Oakment and Torridge. The porcupines damaged conifers by eating the bark, a feeding mode they also use in their native range to supplement the normal diet of bulbs and tubers (Gosling 1980). The examples of *H. cristata* and *H. brachyura* suggest that Old World porcupines retain reservoirs of biological adaptability and vigor.

Old World–New World Relationships

Are the Old World (family Hystricidae) and New World (family Erethizontidae) porcupines related, or do they represent parallel evolution of unrelated stock? The issue has been contended for a long time. In terms of skull characteristics, both families are hystricomorphous hystricognath rodents. (For a discussion of those terms, see, for example, Simpson 1980 or Landry 1957.) Hystricomorphy and hystricognathy have to do with patterns of insertion of the masseteris muscle of the jaw; the pattern found in hystricomorphs enhances the anterior-posterior movement of the jaw and should increase the effectiveness of the incisors and cheek teeth. The question then becomes, Do the hystricomorphs have a common evolutionary ancestry?

In the twenties, the great British mammalogist Reginald I. Pocock (1922) pronounced: "There appears to me no good reason for thinking the Erethizontidae especially related to the Hystricidae." For the past 30 years, the leading champion of the theory of parallel evolution has been A. E. Wood, professor emeritus of biology at Amherst College. Wood's (1985) argument has been paleontological: fossil hystricomorphs appear suddenly in the late Miocene of Egypt, Hungary, and India. (Wood refers earlier hystricomorphs from the Old World to other groups.) Fossil caviomorphs (to which the Erethizontidae belong) appear earlier, in the Oligocene of South America. (That chronology is challenged by other workers. See, for example, Woods and Hermanson 1985, who conclude that the oldest hystricomorphs are found from the Eocene of Africa.) In the absence of an obvious dispersal corridor between the two faunas and in the absence of contemporaneous North American hystricomorphs, Wood has argued for separate origins. (During the Oligocene, the North American and South American continents lacked their Panamanian land bridge.) Wood's arguments have been questioned, notably by Stuart Landry (1957), but it is fair to say that for the past 30 years the informed consensus has favored the theory of parallel evolution. For example, such respected texts of mammalogy as those by Anderson and Jones (1967) and Vaughan (1978) supported the position of Wood.

A dramatic reversal came between 1973 and 1985. In 1973, the Zoological Society of London held a symposium on the biology of hystricomorph rodents (Rowlands and Weir 1974). In the words of Stuart Landry (1977), "The acceptance of the term 'hystricomorph rodent' in the title . . . is a quiet signal that a long controversy is over." The research presented at the London symposium showed biological similarities between the Old World and New World hystricomorphs that no reasonable interpretation could picture as parallelism. But the 1973 symposium remained a largely indirect statement.

In 1985, the NATO Conference on Evolutionary Relationships Among Rodents tackled the question head-on (Luckett and Hartenberger 1985). The turnabout came not through new fossil evidence but through the technique of shared-character analysis. Elements of the technique were already implicit in the older discussions of skull characters, but a full analysis evaluates a suite of characters, say 20 or 30, not just 2 or 3. If species A and B share a large number of character states with each other but not with species C, then it is fair to assume that A and B are more closely related to each other than they are to C. To yield useful information, the researcher must choose character states at an appropriate level. A description of the procedure is beyond the scope of this chapter; readers interested in the technical details should consult the proceedings of the conference and the papers of J.-L. Hartenberger, Wilma George, C. A. Woods and J. W. Hermanson, W. P. Luckett, A. E. Wood, as well as the summary statement of W. P. Luckett and J.-L. Hartenberger.

At the NATO conference, no less than five speakers examined the relationship between Old World and New World hystricomorphs, and four concluded that the two groups are more closely related to each other than to any other group of rodents. The fifth speaker, A. E. Wood, found himself in a minority. Yet the biologists at the conference, honoring Wood's long eminence in the field, presented him with a special commendation. In the end it may have been Wood's own intellectual prodding that pushed the question into the forefront of so many attentive minds.

Perhaps the most surprising result of the NATO conference is that the authors of the four concurring studies all examined different aspects of hystricomorph biology, yet all reached a common conclusion. Wilma George based her analysis on 31 reproductive and chromosomal characters. C. A. Woods and J. W. Hermanson based theirs on 26 muscular and skeletal characters. J.-L. Hartenberger considered 24 dental characters. W. P. Luckett analyzed 20 embryonic and dental characters. There is almost no overlap in terms of characters examined, yet all have reached the same conclusion: the hystricomorphs of the world form a natural group, with a common evolutionary origin.

If we accept that conclusion, we are still faced with A. E. Wood's original objection: it is a long trip from Africa to South America, even considering that the two continents were closer during the animal transmigration tens of millions of years ago. Rafting between the two continents is not a likely event; African porcupines have failed to establish themselves on Madagascar. But other mammals of medium size have made surprising ocean journeys. J. H. Prescott (1959) observed a hare (*Lepus californicus*) travel 39–90 miles on a kelp raft. Alfred Russel Wallace described pigs swimming up to 57 miles across ocean straits, and it is generally accepted that the New World primates arrived by a rafting mechanism from the Old World (Landry 1957). E. E. Williams (1969) has warned that "any colonizer making one of the long raft voyages across an ocean will arrive in a very unfavorable physiological condition on an inhospitable shore." But if that animal is a porcupine, it will command instant respect.

It is not at all clear that the hystricomorph rodents that made the journey were porcupines. To say that hystricomorphs are monophyletic (have a common evolutionary origin) is not the same as saying the New and Old World porcupines have a common porcupine ancestor. Quills have evolved several times within the hystricomorphs, not only in the Erethizontids and Hystricids but also in the Echimyids (spiny rats), and among mammals only distantly related to rodents, such as the hedgehogs and tenrecs (insectivores) and the echidnas (monotremes). Therefore, the jury is still out on the narrower question of Erethizontid-Hystricid affinities.

The porcupine families represent in microcosm the great evolutionary adventure of nature. The North American porcupine, evolved to climb trees and survive falls, to digest tree leaves and bark, and to defend itself with barbed quills, is as distinctly American as the buffalo and the wild turkey. Yet it has blood relatives on four continents who have transformed the same basic anatomy to fit physical environments and ecological niches sometimes far from those known by *Erethizon*. Despite the immediate recognizability of many of the porcupines, the animals remain fundamentally mysterious. A study of each of the species remains the best opportunity for illuminating all of them.

References

Alkon, P. U., and D. Saltz 1985. Potatoes and nutritional ecology of crested porcupines in a desert biome. *J. Appl. Ecol.* 22:727–737.

———— 1988. Influence of season and moonlight on temporal activity patterns of Indian crested porcupines (*Hystrix indica*). *J. Mamm.* 69:71–80.

Allison, M. J., H. M. Cook, and D. A. Stahl 1987. Characterization of rumen bacteria that degrade dihydroxypyridine compounds produced from mimosine. Pp 55–56 in: *Herbivore Nutrition Research.* M. Rose, ed. Dept. of Primary Industries, Wool Biology Laboratory, Yeerongpilly, Queensland 4067, Australia.

Anderson, J. F., and L. A. Magnarelli 1980. Vertebrate host relationships and distribution of Ixodid ticks (Acari: Ixodidae) in Connecticut, USA. *J. Med. Entomol.* 17:314–323.

Anderson, J. F., L. A. Magnarelli, R. N. Philip, and W. Burgdorfer 1986. *Rickettsia rickettsii* and *Rickettsia montana* from Ixodid ticks in Connecticut. *Am. J. Trop. Med. and Hygiene* 35:187–191.

Anderson, S., and J. K. Jones, eds. 1967. *Recent Mammals of the World: A Synopsis of Families.* New York: Ronald Press.

Bakuzis, E. V., and V. Kurmis 1978. Provisional list of synecological coordinates and selected ecographs of forest and other plant species in Minnesota. Department of Forest Resources, College of Forestry, University of Minnesota. Staff paper No. 5.

Balows, A., and M. W. Jennison 1949. Thermophilic, cellulose-decomposing bacteria from the porcupine. *J. Bacteriol.* 57:135.

Bartlett, C. M., and R. C. Anderson 1985. The third stage larva of *Molinema arbuta* Highby 1943 (Nematoda) and development of the parasite in the porcupine (*Erethizon dorsatum*). *Ann. Parasitol.* 60:703–708.

Bauchop, T., 1978. Digestion of leaves in vertebrate arboreal folivores. Pp 193–204 in: *The Ecology of Arboreal Folivores.* G. Gene Montgomery, ed. Washington, D.C.: Smithsonian Institution Press.

Belden, G. P., 1872. The White Chief. As quoted in: *Lives of Game Animals,* Vol. 2, by E. T. Seton. 1928. Boston: Chas. Branford Co.

Belovsky, G. E., and P. A. Jordan 1981. Sodium dynamics and adaptations of a moose population. *J. Mamm.* 62:613–621.

225

Besch, D. A., 1987. Animaline. *Animal Kingdom* 90, 3:51.

Betancourt, J., T. Van Devender, and M. Rose 1986. Comparison of plant macrofossils in woodrat (*Neotoma* sp.) and porcupine (*Erethizon dorsatum*) middens from the western United States. *J. Mamm.* 67:266–273.

Bloom, J. C., J. G. Rogers, and O. Maller 1973. Taste responses of the North American porcupine (*Erethizon dorsatum*). *Physiol. Behav.* 11:95–98.

Bradbury, J. W., and L. H. Emmons 1974. Social organization of some Trinidad bats. I. Emballonuridae. *Z. Tierpsych.* 36:137–183.

Bradbury, J. W., and S. L. Vehrencamp 1976. Social organization and foraging in Emballonurid bats. I. Field studies. *Behav. Ecol. Sociobiol.* 1:337–381.

———— 1977. Social organization and foraging in Emballonurid bats. III. Mating systems. *Behav. Ecol. Sociobiol.* 2:1–17.

Brander, R. B., 1973. Life-history notes on the porcupine in a hardwood-hemlock forest in upper Michigan. *Michigan Acad.* 5:425–433.

Bryant, J. P., J. Tuomi, and P. Niemela 1988. Environmental constraint of constitutive and long-term inducible defenses in woody plants. Pp 367–390 in: *Chemical mediation of coevolution*. K. C. Spencer, ed. San Diego: Academic Press.

Bulstrode, C., J. King, and B. Roper 1986. What happens to wild animals with broken bones? *Lancet* 8471 (Jan. 4, 1986):29–31.

Burge, B. L., 1966. Vaginal casts passed by captive porcupine. *J. Mamm.* 47:713–714.

Carey, A. B., W. L. Krinsky, and A. J. Main 1980. *Ixodes dammini* (Acari: Ixodidae) and associated ticks in south-central Connecticut, USA. *J. Med. Entomol.* 17:89–99.

Charles-Dominique, P., M. Atramentowicz, M. Charles-Dominique, H. Gerard, A. Hladik, et al. 1981. Les mammiferes frugivores arboricoles nocturnes d'une foret Guyanaise: Interrelations plantes-animaux. *Rev. Ecol.* 35:341–435.

Clarke, S. H., 1969. Thermoregulatory response of the porcupine, *Erethizon dorsatum,* at low environmental temperatures. Special report, Dept. Forestry and Wildlife Management, University of Massachusetts, Amherst.

Clarke, S. H., and R. B. Brander 1973. Radiometric determination of porcupine surface temperature. *Physiol. Zool.* 46:230–237.

Cogan, M. G., and F. C. Rector 1982. Proximal resorption during metabolic acidosis in the rat. *Am. J. Physiol.* 242:F499.

Conn, E. E., 1979. Cyanide and cyanogenic glycosides. Pp 387–412 in: *Herbivores: Their Interaction with Secondary Plant Metabolites.* G. A. Rosenthal and D. H. Janzen, eds. Orlando: Academic Press.

Conniff, R., 1986. All things considered, a porcupine would rather be left alone. *Audubon* 88(1):88–93.

Coulter, M. W., 1966. Ecology and management of fishers in Maine. Ph.D. thesis, State University College of Forestry, Syracuse University, Syracuse, New York.

Craig, E. H., and B. L. Keller 1986. Movements and home range of porcupines, *Erethizon dorsatum*, in Idaho shrub desert. *Can. Field-Nat.* 100:167–173.

Curtin, S. H., and D. J. Chivers 1978. Leaf-eating primates of peninsular Malaysia: the siamang and the dusky leaf-monkey. Pp 441–464 in: *The Ecology of Arboreal Folivores*. G. Gene Montgomery, ed. Washington, D.C.: Smithsonian Institution Press.

Curtis, J. D., 1941. The silvicultural significance of the porcupine. *J. Forest.* 39:583–594.

——— 1944. Appraisal of porcupine damage. *J. Wildl. Manage.* 8:88–91.

Curtis, J. D., and E. L. Kozicky 1944. Observations on the eastern porcupine. *J. Mamm.* 25:137–146.

Curtis, J. D., and A. K. Wilson 1953. Porcupine feeding on ponderosa pine in central Idaho. *J. Forest.* 51:339–341.

Dathe, H., 1937. Uber den Bau des mannlichen Kopulationsorganes beim Meerschweinschen und anderen hystricomorphen Nagetieren. *Gegebaurs Morph. Jahrbuch* 80:1–65.

——— 1963. Vom Harnspritzen des Ursons (*Erethizon dorsatus*). *Z. Saugetierkunde* 28:369–375.

Denton. D., 1982. *The Hunger for Salt*. New York: Springer Verlag.

Denys, Nicolas, 1908. The description and natural history of the coasts of N.A. (Acadia). Translated and edited by W. F. Ganong. *Publ. Champlain Soc.* 2.

DeReaumur, 1727. Observations sur le porc-epic; Extraites de memoires et de lettres de M. Sarrazin, Medecin du Roy a Quebec et Correspondant de l'Academie. *Memoires de L'Academie Royale des Sciences*, Paris, 1727:383–396.

DeVos, A., 1953. Bobcat preying on porcupine? *J. Mamm.* 34:129–130.

Dodds, D. G., A. M. Martell, and R. E. Yescott 1969. Ecology of the American dog tick, *Dermacentor variabilis* (Say) in Nova Scotia. *Can. J. Zool.* 47:171–181.

Dodge, W. E., 1967. The biology and life history of the porcupine (*Erethizon dorsatum*) in western Massachusetts. Ph.D. thesis, University of Massachusetts, Amherst.

——— 1982. Porcupine. Pp 355–366 in: *Wild Mammals of North America: Biology, Management, and Economics*. J. A. Chapman and G. A. Feldhamer, eds. Baltimore and London: Johns Hopkins University Press.

Dodge, W. E., and V. G. Barnes 1975. Movements, home range and control of porcupines in western Washington. Wildlife leaflet 507, U.S. Dept. Interior, Fish and Wildlife Service, Washington, D.C.

Duthie, A. G., and J. D. Skinner 1986. Osteophagia in the Cape porcupine *Hystrix africaeaustralis*. *South Afr. J. Zool.* 21:316–318.

Earle, R. D., and K. R. Kramm 1980. Techniques for age determination in the Canadian porcupine. *J. Wildl. Manage.* 44:413–419.

———— 1982. Correlation between fisher and porcupine abundance in upper Michigan. *Amer. Midl. Nat.* 107:244–249.

Ebling, F. J., and P. A. Hale 1970. The control of the mammalian molt. Pp 215–238 in: *Hormones and the Environment.* G. K. Benson and J. G. Phillips, eds. Cambridge: Cambridge University Press.

Eisenberg, J. F., 1978. The evolution of arboreal folivores in the Class Mammalia. Pp 135–152 in: *The Ecology of Arboreal Folivores.* G. Gene Montgomery, ed. Washington, D.C.: Smithsonian Institution Press.

———— 1983. Behavioral adaptations of higher vertebrates to tropical forests. Pp 267–278 in: *Tropical Rain Forest Ecosystems.* F. B. Golley, ed. New York: Elsevier.

Emmons, L. H., 1983. A field study of the African brush-tailed porcupine, *Atherurus africanus,* by radiotelemetry. *Mammalia* 47:183–194.

Erdoes, R., and A. Ortiz. 1984. American Indian myths and legends. New York: Pantheon Books.

Estrada, A., and R. Coates-Estrada 1985. A preliminary study of resource overlap between howling monkeys (*Alouatta palliata*) and other arboreal mammals in the tropical rain forest of Los Tuxtlas, Mexico. *Amer. J. Primatology* 9:27–37.

Evans, F. C., 1985. In praise of natural history. *Bull. Ecol. Soc. Amer.* 66:455–460.

Fagerstone, K. A., H. P. Tietjen, and O. Williams 1981. Seasonal variation in the diet of black-tailed prairie dogs. *J. Mamm.* 60:820–824.

Farrell, B. C., and D. P. Christian 1987. Energy and water requirements of lactation in the North American porcupine, *Erethizon dorsatum. Comp. Biochem. Physiol. A.* 88:695–700.

Faulkner, C. E., and W. E. Dodge 1962. Control of the porcupine in New England. *J. Forest.* 60:36–37.

Feeny, P., 1970. Seasonal changes in oak leaf tannins and nutrients as a cause of spring feeding by winter moth caterpillars. *Ecology* 51:565–581.

———— 1976. Plant apparency and chemical defense. In: Biochemical interactions between plants and insects. J. W. Wallace and R. L. Mansell, eds. *Recent Adv. Phytochem.* 10:1–40.

Frame, L. H., and G. W. Frame 1976. Female African wild dogs emigrate. *Nature,* London, 263:227–229.

Frame, L. H., J. R. Malcolm, G. W. Frame, and H. Van Lawick 1979. Social organization of African wild dogs (*Lycaon pictus*) on the Serengeti plains, Tanzania, 1967–1978. *Z. Tierpsych.* 50:225–249.

Frazier, M. K., 1981. A revision of the fossil erethizontidae of North America. *Bull. Fla. State Mus. Biol. Sci.* 27:1–76.

Freeman, R. S., 1949. Notes on the morphology and life cycle of the genus *Monoecocestus* Beddard, 1914 (Cestoda: Anoplocephalidae), from the porcupine. *J. Parasitol.* 35:605–612.

———— 1952. Biology and life history of *Monoecocestus* Beddard, 1914 (Cestoda: Anoplocephalidae), from the porcupine. *J. Parasitol.* 38:111–129.

Gabrielson, I. N., 1928. Notes on the habits and behavior of the porcupine in Oregon. *J. Mamm.* 9:33–38.

Gariepy, Edmond, 1961. Contribution a l'histoire de la medecine Canadienne. These pour le Doctorat en Medecine, Faculte de Medecine de Paris, pp. 20–24.

Gates, C. C., and R. J. Hudson 1979. Weight dynamics of free-ranging elk. *Agric. and Forestry Bull.* 7:80–82.

Gensch, R. H., 1946. Observations on the porcupine in northern Michigan. Unpublished progress report, U.S. Fish and Wildlife Service.

George, W., 1985. Reproductive and chromosomal characters of ctenodactylids as a key to their evolutionary relationships. Pp 453–474 in: *Evolutionary Relationships Among Rodents.* W. P. Luckett and J.-L. Hartenberger, eds. New York: Plenum Press.

Glander, K. E., 1980. Reproduction and population growth in free-ranging mantled howling monkeys. *Am. J. Phys. Anthropol.* 53:25–36.

——— 1984. Group composition in mantled howling monkeys. *Am. J. Phys. Anthropol.* 63:163.

Glassman, H. N., 1948. Surface-active agents and their application in bacteriology. *Bacteriol. Rev.* 12:105–148.

Goodall, J., 1983. Population dynamics during a 15-year period in one community of free-living chimpanzees in Gombe National Park, Tanzania. *Z. Tierpsych.* 61:1–60.

——— 1986. *The Chimpanzees of Gombe: Patterns of Behavior.* Cambridge: Harvard University Press.

Gosling, L. M., 1980. Reproduction of the Himalayan porcupine (*Hystrix hodgsoni*) in captivity. *J. Zool.* (London) 192:546–549.

Greenwood, P. J., 1980. Mating systems, philopatry, and dispersal in birds and mammals. *Anim. Behav.* 28:1140–1162.

Gutterman, Y., 1982. Observations on the feeding habits of the Indian crested porcupine (*Hystrix indica*) and the distribution of some hemicryptophytes and geophytes in the Negev Desert highlands. *J. Arid Envir.* 5:261–268.

Harborne, J. B., 1988. *Introduction to Ecological Biochemistry,* 3rd ed. New York: Academic Press.

Harcourt, A. H., 1978. Strategies of emigration and transfer by primates, with particular reference to gorillas. *Z. Tierpsych.* 48:401–420.

Harder, L. D., 1979. Winter feeding by porcupines in montane forests of southwestern Alberta. *Can. Field-Nat.* 93:405–410.

Hartenberger, J.-L., 1985. The order Rodentia: Major questions on their evolutionary origin, relationships and suprafamilial systematics. Pp 1–33 in: *Evolutionary Relationships Among Rodents.* W. P. Luckett and J.-L. Hartenberger, eds. New York: Plenum Press.

Heaney, L. R., and R. W. Thorington 1978. Ecology of tropical red-tailed squirrels, *Sciurus granatensis,* in the Panama Canal Zone. *J. Mamm.* 59:846–851.

Hebert, D., and I. McT. Cowan. 1971. Natural salt licks as a part of the ecology of the mountain goat. *Can. J. Zool.* 49:605–610.

Highby, P. R., 1943a. *Dipetalonema arbuta* n. sp. (Nematoda) from the porcupine, *Erethizon dorsatum* (L). *J. Parasitol.* 29:239–242.

——— 1943b. Mosquito vectors and larval development of *Dipetalonema arbuta* Highby (Nematoda) from the porcupine, *Erethizon dorsatum. J. Parasitol.* 29:243–252.

Holekamp, K. E., 1986. Proximal causes of natal dispersion in Belding's ground squirrel (*Spermophilus beldingi*). *Ecol. Monogr.* 56:365–391.

Honacki, J. H., K. E. Kinman, and J. W. Koeppl, eds., 1982. *Mammal Species of the World.* Lawrence, Kansas: Allen Press and Assoc. Syst. Coll.

Hoogland, J. L., 1982. Prairie dogs avoid extreme inbreeding. *Science* 215:1639–1641.

Hooper, E. T., 1961. The glans penis in Proechimys and other caviomorph rodents. *Occas. papers, Mus. Zool. University of Michigan* 623:1–18.

Hugot, J.-P., 1982. Sur le genre Wellcomia (Oxyuridae, Nematoda), parasite de rongeurs archaiques. *Bull. Mus. Natn. Hist. Nat.,* Paris, 4:25–48.

Hungate, R. E., 1966. *The Rumen and Its Microbes.* New York: Academic Press.

Irving, L., and J. Krog 1954. The body temperature of arctic and subarctic birds and mammals. *J. Appl. Physiol.* 6:667–680.

Irving, L., H. Krog, and M. Monson 1955. The metabolism of some Alaskan animals in winter and summer. *Physiol. Zool.* 28:173–185.

Janzen, D. H., 1979. New horizons in the biology of plant defenses. Pp 331–351 in: *Herbivores—Their Interaction with Secondary Plant Metabolites.* G. A. Rosenthal and D. H. Janzen, eds. New York: Academic Press.

Jellison, W. L., 1933. Parasites of porcupines of the genus *Erethizon* (Rodentia). *Trans. Amer. Microsc. Soc.* 52:42–47.

Jellison, W. L., and K. A. Neiland 1965. *Parasites of Alaskan Vertebrates.* Norman: University of Oklahoma Research Institution.

Johnson, J. L., and R. H. McBee 1967. The porcupine caecal fermentation. *J. Nutrit.* 91:540–546.

Jones, R. J., and R. G. Megarrity 1986. Successful transfer of DHP-degrading bacteria from Hawaiian goats to Australian ruminants to overcome the toxicity of Leucaena. *Australian Vet. J.* 63:259–262.

Jordan, P. A., D. B. Botkin, A. S. Dominski, H. S. Lowendorf, and G. E. Belovsky 1973. Sodium as a critical nutrient of the moose of Isle Royale. *Proc. North Amer. Moose Conference and Workshop* 9:13–42.

Kano, T., 1984. Observations of physical abnormalities among the wild bonobos (*Pan paniscus*) of Wamba, Zaire. *Am. J. Phys. Anthr.* 63:1–11.

Koenigswald, Wighart von, 1985. Evolutionary trends in the enamel of rodent incisors. Pp 403–422 in: *Evolutionary Relationships Among Rodents.* L. P. Luckett and J.-L. Hartenberger, eds. New York: Plenum Press.

Krefting, L. W., J. H. Stoeckeler, B. J. Bradle, and W. D. Fitzwater 1962. Porcupine-timber relationships in the lake states. *J. Forestry* 60:325–330.

Landry, S. Jr., 1957. The interrelationships of the New and Old World hystricomorph rodents. *University of California Publ. Zool.* 56:1–118.

——— 1977. Book review of *The Biology of Hystricomorph Rodents,* I. W. Rowlands and Barbara J. Weir, Symposia of the Zoological Soc. London, No. 34, Academic Press, in: *J. Mamm.* 58:459–461.

Lindholm, J. S., J. M. McCormick, S. W. Colton, and D. T. Downing 1981. Variation of skin surface lipid composition among mammals. *Comp. Biochem. Physiol.* 69B:75–78.

Luckett, W. P., 1985. Superordinal and infraordinal affinities of rodents: Developmental evidence from the dentition and placentation. Pp 227–276 in: *Evolutionary Relationships Among Rodents.* W. P. Luckett and J.-L. Hartenberger, eds. New York: Plenum Press.

Luckett, W. P., and J.-L. Hartenberger 1985. Comments and conclusions. Pp 685–712 in: *Evolutionary Relationships Among Rodents.* W. P. Luckett and J.-L. Hartenberger, eds. New York: Plenum Press.

Lyford, C. A., 1943. Ojibwa crafts (Chippewa). Indian handicraft pamphlet No. 5. Branch of Education, Bureau of Indian Affairs, U.S. Dept. Interior, Washington, D.C.

Macdonald, D., 1984. *The Encyclopedia of Mammals.* New York: Facts on File.

MacDonald, D. R., 1952. Some observations on porcupine attacks on jack pine. *The Annual Ring* (Faculty of Forestry, University of Toronto), pp. 17–18.

Madison, D. M., 1980. Space use and social structure in the meadow vole, *Microtus pennsylvanicus. Behav. Ecol. Sociobiol.* 7:65–71.

——— 1985. Activity rhythms and spacing. Pp 373–419 in: *Biology of New World* Microtus. R. H. Tamarin, ed. Am. Soc. Mammal. Spec. Publ. No. 8.

Magnarelli, L. A., J. F. Anderson, W. Burgdorfer, R. N. Philip, and W. A. Chappell 1985. Spotted fever group rickettsiae in immature and adult ticks (Acari: Ixodidae) from a focus of Rocky Mountain spotted fever in Connecticut. *Can. J. Microbiol.* 31:1131–1135.

Main, A. J., A. B. Carey, M. G. Carey, R. H. Goodwin 1982. Immature *Ixodes dammini* (Acari: Ixodidae) on small animals in Connecticut, USA. *J. Med. Entomol.* 19:655–664.

Marsh, C. W., 1979. Comparative aspects of social organization in the Tana River red colobus, *Colobus badius rufomitratus. Z. Tierpsych.* 51:337–362.

Marshall, W. H., 1951. Accidental death of a porcupine. *J. Mamm.* 32:221.

Maser, C., and R. S. Rohweder 1983. Winter food habits of cougars from northeastern Oregon. *Great Basin Naturalist* 43:425–428.

Mattson, W. J. Jr., 1980. Herbivory in relation to plant nitrogen content. *Ann. Rev. Ecol. Syst.* 11:119–161.

McDade, H. C., and W. B. Crandell 1958. Perforation of the gastrointestinal tract by an unusual foreign body—a porcupine quill. *New Engl. J. Med.* 258:746–747.

McEvoy, J. S., 1982. Comparative myology of the pectoral and pelvic appendages of the North American porcupine (*Erethizon dorsatum*) and the prehensile-tailed porcupine (*Coendou prehensilis*). *Bull. Amer. Mus. Nat. Hist.* 173:337–421.

Mead-Briggs, A. R., and R. J. C. Page 1975. Records of anoplocephaline cestodes from wild rabbits and hares collected throughout Great Britain. *J. Helminthol.* 49:49–56.

Mech, L. D., 1987. Age, season, distance, direction, and social aspects of wolf dispersal from a Minnesota pack. Pp 55–74 in: *Mammalian Dispersal Patterns.* D. D. Chepko-Sade and Z. T. Halpin, eds. Chicago and London: University of Chicago Press.

Merriam, C. H., 1884. The vertebrates of the Adirondack region, northeastern New York. *Trans. Linnean Soc. New York* 2:5–214.

Milton, K., 1980. *The Foraging Strategy of Howler Monkeys.* New York: Columbia University Press.

Mirand, E. A., and A. R. Shadle 1953. Gross anatomy of the male reproductive system of the porcupine. *J. Mamm.* 34:210–220.

Mohr, Erna, 1965. *Altweltliche Stachelschweine.* Wittenberg Lutherstadt: A. Ziemsen Verlag.

Montgomery, G. G., and Y. D. Lubin 1978. Movements of *Coendou prehensilis* in the Venezuelan llanos. *J. Mamm.* 59:887–888.

Montgomery, G. G., and M. E. Sunquist 1978. Habitat selection and use by two-toed and three-toed sloths. Pp 329–359 in: *The Ecology of Arboreal Folivores.* G. Gene Montgomery, ed. Washington, D.C.: Smithsonian Institution Press.

Morris, D. J., and R. J. Van Aarde 1985. Sexual behavior of the female porcupine *Hystrix africaeaustralis. Hormones and Behavior* 19:400–412.

Morris, P., 1983. *Hedgehogs.* The Oil Mills, Weybridge, Surrey: Whittet Books.

Morse, M., 1903. Synopsis of North American invertebrates 29: The Trichodectidae. *Amer. Nat.* 37:618.

Murie, O. J., 1926. The porcupine in northern Alaska. *J. Mamm.* 7:109–113.

Nicolaides, N., 1974. Skin lipids: Their biochemical uniqueness. *Science* 186:19–26.

Nowak, R. M., and J. L. Paradiso 1983. *Walker's Mammals of the World,* 4th ed. Vol. 2. Baltimore: Johns Hopkins University Press.

Oates, J. J., 1987. Food distribution and foraging behavior. Pp 197–209 in: *Primate Societies.* B. B. Smuts, D. L. Cheney, and R. M. Seyfarth, et al., eds. Chicago and London: University of Chicago Press.

Odle, R., 1971. Porcupine quillwork in the Great Lakes area. *The Explorer* 13:23–28.

Olsen, O. W., and C. D. Tollman 1951. *Wellcomia evaginata* Smitt 1908 (Oxyuridae, Nematoda) of porcupines in mule deer, *Odocoileus hemionus,* in Colorado. *Proc. Helm. Soc., Wash.* 18:120–122.

Orchard, Wm. C., 1971. The technique of porcupine-quill decoration among the North American Indians, 2nd ed. Contributions from the Museum of the American Indian, Heye Foundation, 4, New York.

Payne, D. D., and D. C. O'Meara 1958. *Sarcoptes scabiei* infestation of a porcupine. *J. Wildl. Manage.* 22:321–322.

Po-Chedley, D. S., and A. R. Shadle 1955. Pelage of the porcupine, *Erethizon dorsatum dorsatum*. *J. Mamm.* 36:84–95.

Pocock, R. I., 1922. On the external characteristics of some hystricomorph rodents. *Proc. Zool. Soc. London* 1922:365–427.

Powell, R. A., 1978. A comparison of fisher and weasel hunting behavior. *Carnivore* 1:28–34.

——— 1982. *The Fisher: Life History, Ecology, and Behavior.* Minneapolis: University of Minnesota Press.

Powell, R. A., and R. B. Brander 1977. Adaptations of fishers and porcupines to their predator-prey system. Pp 45–53 in: *Proceedings of 1975 Predator Symposium.* R. L. Phillips and C. Jonkel, eds. Montana Forest Conservation Experiment Station, University of Montana, Missoula.

Prescott, J. H., 1959. Rafting of jack rabbit on kelp. *J. Mamm.* 40:443–444.

Pusey, A. E., 1979. Intercommunity transfer of chimpanzees in Gombe National Park. In: *The Great Apes.* D. A. Hamburg and E. R. McCown. Menlo Park, California: Benjamin/Cummings.

——— 1980. Inbreeding avoidance in chimpanzees. *Anim. Behav.* 28:543–582.

Raeburn, P., 1987. Point of no return? Not so. *Cincinnati Enquirer* Jan. 23.

Rahm, U., 1962. L'elevage et la reproduction en captivite de l'*Atherurus africanus* (Rongeurs: Hystricidae). *Mammalia* 29:1–9.

Reeks, W. A., 1942. Notes on the Canada porcupine in the Maritime provinces. *Forestry Chronicle* 18:182–187.

Reynolds, H. G., 1957. Porcupine behavior in the desert-shrub type of Arizona. *J. Mamm.* 33:418–419.

Richter, C. P., and B. Barelare 1938. Nutritional requirements of pregnant and lactating rats studied by the self-selection method. *Endocrinology* 23:15ff.

Robbins, C. T., 1983. *Wildlife Feeding and Nutrition.* New York: Academic Press.

Roberts, M., S. Brand, and E. Maliniak 1985. The biology of captive prehensile-tailed porcupines, *Coendou prehensilis. J. Mamm.* 66:476–482.

Rose, Burton D., 1984. Clinical physiology of acid-base and electrolyte disorders, 2nd ed. New York: McGraw-Hill.

Rousseau, Jacques, 1957. Michel Sarrazin, Jean-Francois Gaulthier et l'etude Prelinneenne de la Flore Canadienne. Pp 149–155 in: *Les Botanistes Francais en Amerique du Nord Avant 1850.* Paris: Centre National de la Recherche Scientifique.

Rowlands, I. W., and Barbara J. Weir 1974. The biology of hystricomorph rodents. *Symposia of the Zoological Soc. London* No. 34. London: Academic Press.

Roze, U., 1984. Winter foraging by individual porcupines. *Can. J. Zool.* 62: 2425–2428.

——— 1985. How to select, climb, and eat a tree. *Nat. Hist.* 94(5):63–68.

——— 1987. Denning and winter range of the porcupine. *Can. J. Zool.* 65: 981–986.

Roze, U., D. C. Locke, and N. Vatakis 1990. Antibiotic properties of porcupine quills. *J. Chem. Ecology* 16, in press.

Sackett, L. W., 1913. The Canada porcupine: A study of the learning process. *Behavioral Monogr.* 2:1–84.

Sauer, G. C., 1980. *Manual of Skin Diseases,* 4th ed. Philadelphia: J. B. Lippincott.

Schultz, A. H., 1956. The occurrence and frequency of pathological and teratological conditions and of twinning among nonhuman primates. *Primatologia* 1:965–1014.

Seastedt, T. R., and D. A. Crossley, Jr. 1981. Sodium dynamics in forest ecosystems and the animal starvation hypothesis. *Am. Nat.* 117:1029–1034.

Shadle, A. R., 1946. Copulation in the porcupine. *J. Wildl. Manage.* 10:159–162.

——— 1948. Gestation period in the porcupine, *Erethizon dorsatum dorsatum. J. Mamm.* 29:162–164.

——— 1950. The North American porcupine up to date. *Ward's Nat. Sci. Bull.* 24:5–11.

——— 1951. Laboratory copulations and gestations of porcupine, *Erethizon dorsatum. J. Mamm.* 32:219–221.

——— 1952. Sexual maturity and first recorded copulation of a 16-month male porcupine, *Erethizon dorsatum dorsatum. J. Mamm.* 33:239–241.

Shadle, A. R., M. Smelzer, and M. Metz 1946. The sex reactions of porcupines (*Erethizon d. dorsatum*) before and after copulation. *J. Mamm.* 27:116–121.

Shapiro, J., 1949. Ecological and life history notes on the porcupine in the Adirondacks. *J. Mamm.* 30:247–257.

Sherris, J. C., 1984a. Normal microbial flora. Pp 50–58 in: *Medical Microbiology.* J. C. Sherris, ed. New York: Elsevier.

——— 1984b. Skin and wound infections. Pp 555–561 in: *Medical Microbiology.* J. C. Sherris, ed. New York: Elsevier.

Sigg, H., A. Stolba, J. J. Abegglen, and V. Dasser 1982. Life history of Hamadryas baboons: Physical development, infant mortality, reproductive parameters, and family relationships. *Primates* 23:473–487.

Simpson, G. G., 1980. *Splendid Isolation: The Curious History of South American Mammals.* New Haven and London: Yale University Press.

Smith, G. W., 1982. Habitat use by porcupines in a ponderosa pine–Douglas fir forest in northeastern Oregon. *Northwest Science* 56:236–240.

Smithers, R. H. N., 1983. The mammals of the southern African subregion. Pretoria, South Africa: University of Pretoria Press.

Speck, F. G., and R. W. Dexter 1951. Utilization of animals and plants by the Micmac Indians of New Brunswick. *J. Washington Acad. Sci.* 41:250–259.

Speer, R. J., and T. G. Dilworth 1978. Porcupine winter foods and utilization in central New Brunswick. *Can. Field-Nat.* 92:271–274.

Spencer, D. A., 1949. Porcupine problems of the Nicolet National Forest. Unpublished special report, U.S. Fish and Wildlife Service.

———— 1964. Porcupine population fluctuations in past centuries revealed by dendrochronology. *J. Appl. Ecol.* 1:127–149.

Stewart, K. J., and A. H. Harcourt 1986. Gorillas: Variation in female relationships. Pp 155–164 in: *Mammalian Dispersal Patterns.* B. D. Chepko-Sade and Z. T. Halpin, eds. Chicago and London: University of Chicago Press.

Struhsaker, T. T., 1975. *The Red Colobus Monkey.* Chicago and London: University of Chicago Press.

Sutton, J. F., 1972. Notes on skeletal variation, tooth replacement, and cranial suture closure of the porcupine (*Erethizon dorsatum*). *Tulane Stud. Zool. Bot.* 17:56–62.

Taylor, W. P., 1935. Ecology and life history of the porcupine (*Erethizon epixanthum*) as related to the forests of Arizona and the southwestern United States. *Univ. Ariz. Bull.* 6:1–177.

Teale, E. W., 1965. *Wandering Through Winter.* New York: Dodd, Mead and Co.

Tenneson, C., and L. W. Oring 1985. Winter food preferences of porcupines. *J. Wildl. Manage.* 49:28–33.

Terborgh, J., and C. H. Janson 1986. The socioecology of primate groups. *Ann. Rev. Ecol. Syst.* 17:111–135.

Thornton, R. F., P. R. Bird, M. Somers, and R. J. Moir 1970. Urea excretion in ruminants III: The role of the hind-gut (caecum and colon). *Australian J. of Agric. Research* 21:345–352.

Thwaites, R. G., ed. 1907. *Jesuit Relations and Allied Documents: Travels and Explorations of the Jesuit Missionaries in New France 1610–1791.* Cleveland: Burrows Bros.

Tindal, J. S., and G. S. Knaggs 1970. Environmental stimuli and the mammary gland. Pp 239–258 in: *Hormones and the Environment.* G. K. Benson and J. G. Phillips, eds. Cambridge: Cambridge University Press.

Tohme, H., and G. Tohme 1981. Quelques donnees anatomiques sur le porc-epic *Hystrix indica* Kerr 1792 (Rodentia). *Mammalia* 45:363–371.

Tryon, C. A. Jr., 1947. Behavior and postnatal development of a porcupine. *J. Wildl. Manage.* 11:282–283.

Van Aarde, R. J., 1985. Reproduction in captive female Cape porcupines (*Hystrix africaeaustralis*) *J. Reprod. Fert.* 75:577–582.

Van Aarde, R. J., and J. D. Skinner 1986. Reproductive biology of the male Cape porcupine, *Hystrix africaeaustralis. J. Reprod. Fert.* 76:545–552.

Van Jaarsveld, A. S., and Annette Knight-Eloff 1984. Digestion in the porcupine *Hystrix africaeaustralis. South Afr. J. Zool.* 19:109–112.

Vaughan, Terry A., 1978. *Mammalogy,* 2nd ed. Philadelphia: Saunders College.

Voss, R., 1979. Male accessory glands and the evolution of copulatory plugs in rodents. *Occas. papers Mus. Zool. Univ. of Michigan* 689:1–26.

Waser, P. M., and W. T. Jones 1983. Natal philopatry among solitary mammals. *Quart. Rev. Biol.* 58:355–390.

Weeks, H. P. Jr., and C. M. Kirkpatrick 1976. Adaptations of white-tailed deer to naturally occurring sodium deficiencies. *J. Wild. Manage.* 40:610–625.

——— 1978. Salt preferences and sodium drive phenology in fox squirrels and woodchucks. *J. Mamm.* 59:531–542.

Weir, B. J., 1974. Reproductive characteristics of hystricomorph rodents. *Symp. Zool. Soc. London* 34:265–301.

White, J. A., 1970. Late Cenozoic porcupines (Mammalia, Erethizontidae) of North America. *Amer. Mus. Novit.* 2421:1–15.

Wiles, G. J., and H. P. Weeks, Jr. 1986. Movements and use patterns of white-tailed deer visiting natural licks. *J. Wildl. Manage.* 50:487–496.

Williams, E. E., 1969. The ecology of colonization as seen in the zoogeography of anoline lizards on small islands. *Quart. Rev. Biol.* 44:345–389.

Wood, A. E., 1985. The relationships, origin and dispersal of the hystricognathous rodents. Pp 475–513 in: *Evolutionary Relationships Among Rodents*. W. P. Luckett and J.-L. Hartenberger, eds. New York: Plenum Press.

Wood, J. W., P. E. Smouse, and J. C. Long 1985. Sex-specific dispersal patterns in two human populations of highland New Guinea. *Amer. Nat.* 125:747–768.

Woods, C. A., 1972. Comparative myology of jaw, hyoid, and pectoral appendicular regions of New World and Old World hystricomorph rodents. *Bull. Amer. Mus. Nat. Hist.* 147:117–198.

——— 1973. *Erethizon dorsatum. Mammalian Species* 29:1–6.

Woods, C. A., and J. W. Hermanson 1985. Myology of hystricognath rodents: An analysis of form, function, and phylogeny. Pp 515–548 in: *Evolutionary Relationships Among Rodents*. W. P. Luckett and J.-L. Hartenberger, eds. New York: Plenum Press.

Wrangham, R. W., 1986. Ecology and social relationships in two species of chimpanzee. Pp 352–378 in: *Ecological Aspects of Social Evolution*. D. I. Rubenstein and R. W. Wrangham, eds. Princeton, New Jersey: Princeton University Press.

Wyss, O., B. J. Ludwig, and R. B. Joiner 1945. The fungistatic and fungicidal action of fatty acids and related compounds. *Arch. Biochem.* 7:415–425.

Tables

Table 1. Ojibwa quill dyes and mordants (based on Lyford 1943).

Plant	Part used	Color
Alder (*Alnus incana*)	inner bark, used with bloodroot, wild plum, red osier dogwood	red, yellow
Bloodroot (*Sanguinaria canadensis*)	root	red
Bur oak (*Quercus macrocarpa*)	inner bark with hazel burrs, butternut inner bark, earth	black
Red osier dogwood (*Cornus stolonifera*)	inner bark with ashes of birch, oak, cedar bark	red
Goldthread (*Coptis groenlandica*)	root	yellow
Lichens (*Usnea barbata*)	whole plant	yellow
Maple (*Acer* spp.)	rotted wood	purple
Puccoon (*Lithospermum carolinense*)	dried root with ocher	red
Sumac (*Rhus glabra*)	inner bark, pulp of stalk	yellow
White birch (*Betula papyrifera*)	inner bark with ashes of dogwood, oak, and cedar bark	red
American plum (*Prunus americana*)	inner bark, with bloodroot root, red osier dogwood bark, alder bark	bright red

Table 2. Porcupine population density in Ottawa National Forest.*

Year	Porcupines/ 100 km²
1962	1180
1970	510
1971	400
1972	440
1973	610
1974	320
1975	400
1976	280
1979	80

*Data from Powell 1982.

Table 3. Weights of major porcupine organ systems.

Organ	% porcupine body weight
skeleton	13
digestive system	26
muscles	26
skin, quills and fur	27
heart and lungs	3
miscellaneous	5

Table 4. Weight changes in female porcupine, 1983.

Date	Weight
April 30	5.0 kg (11 lbs)
June 10	6.3 kg
July 10	5.6 kg
August 21	6.22 kg

Table 5. Salt use as a function of concentration.
Two-by-two pine lumber (5 cm $\times$ 5 cm $\times$ 39.5 cm) was soaked in NaCl solutions for 48 hours at room temperature. After drying, the sticks were mounted along the sides of the house, interspersed randomly among 141 untreated sticks and 31 sticks impregnated with other salts. Sticks were removed at monthly intervals between April 4 and September 7, 1986, for drying to constant weight (48 hrs, 110°C), weighing, and reimpregnating. To keep the walls covered at all times, two identically treated sets of sticks were alternated along the walls. Sticks showing excessive wood removal were replaced. Thirteen different porcupines were captured at or near the salthouse in 1986.

Two-way ANOVA. NaCl concentration: F = 20.1, P = 0.0001. Month: F = 10.04, P = 0.0001. Interaction: F = 1.11, P = 0.386.

NaCl concentration	grams of wood removed per peg per month					
	April	May	June	July	August	Average
0.15 N	38.4	40.0	12.9	9.8	14.4	21.1
	33.8	41.9	16.0	11.2	6.0	
	35.8	25.3	13.5	14.7	3.2	
0.30 N	71.8	90.7	26.0	52.0	52.8	51.7
	50.2	34.9	40.3	28.8	13.2	
	66.9	122.9	45.7	56.6	22.5	
0.45 N	87.6	85.3	13.4	55.0	35.5	55.9
	84.6	47.0	54.8	64.7	24.9	
	87.7	52.3	35.5	61.2	49.5	
Average	61.9	60.0	28.7	39.3	24.7	

Table 6. Salt consumption as a function of potassium-sodium ratio of source.
The same protocol was followed as in Table 5, except that nitrate salts were used to impregnate the wood. Sticks were randomly interspersed among 141 untreated sticks and 30 sticks impregnated with other sodium salts. Weight losses were determined at monthly intervals between May 5 and September 7, 1986.

Two-way ANOVA. Na/K ratio: $F = 64.67$, $P = 0.0001$. Month: $F = 14.16$, $P = 0.0003$. Interaction: $F = 9.98$, $P = 0.0004$.

impregnating solution Na concentration	K concentration	K/Na	amount removed, in grams May	June	July	August	Average
0.075 N + 0.75 N		10	0	0	0	0	0.3
			2.6	0	0	0	
	0.75 N		0	0	0	0	0
			0	0	0	0	
0.075 N + 0.075 N		1	1.4	5.0	3.0	0	3.4
			5.3	6.5	6.2	0	
	0.075 N		0	0	0	0	0
			0	0	0	0	
0.075 N		0	35.6	10.0	16.8	7.3	15.6
			25.6	12.1	17.0	0	
Average amount removed from sodium-impregnated sticks			11.8	5.6	7.2	1.2	

Table 7. Fecal sodium and potassium loss in porcupines, 1986.
Dried feces were extracted with a 10-fold excess of distilled water, and the extract analyzed by atomic absorption. Sodium loss did not vary significantly by month (ANOVA). Potassium losses differed significantly between months (ANOVA: $F_{11, 24} = 6.279$, $P < 0.001$).

Month	Sodium, mM	Potassium, mM
January	5.0 ± 0	8.0 ± 0
February	4.5 ± 1.3	10.0 ± 2.2
March	4.5 ± 0.6	7.5 ± 1.7
April	5.0 ± 1.0	8.3 ± 6.6
May	4.7 ± 0.6	29.0 ± 1.0
June	4.3 ± 0.6	14.7 ± 11.0
July	3.9 ± 1.0	18.0 ± 2.6
August	2.5 ± 1.1	9.0 ± 0
September	2.5 ± 1.1	17.5 ± 3.5
October	3.9 ± 1.0	12.0 ± 3.5
November	3.9 ± 1.0	6.3 ± 0.6
December	3.3 ± 1.3	8.5 ± 5.0

Table 8. Correlation between mast feeding, apple feeding, and salt use.

Year	Heavy mast crop	End of apple feeding	Secondary peak in sodium drive
1985	+	August	narrow
1986	−	October	broad
1987	+	August	narrow
1988	−	October	broad

Table 9. Urinary sodium output as a function of the diet.

Day	Diet	Urinary Na output, mμM/hr
0	wild	2.0
1	Red Delicious apples	3.0
2	"	17.0
3	linden leaves	38.0
4	"	50.0
5	"	0.4
6	"	0.8
7	"	0.8
8	"	0.4

Table 10. Relative densities of porcupine summer food trees.
Relative density = (number of stems of species i/total number of stems) × 100

Tree species	% use	Relative density in forest
Linden (*Tilia americana*) leaves	34	0.9%
Apple (*Pyrus malus*) fruit*	30	0.0%
Aspen leaves* (*Populus grandidentata, P. tremuloides*)	26	0.1%
Yellow birch (*Betula lutea*) leaves	1.9	2.0%
Shadbush (*Amelanchier canadensis*) leaves	4.1	0.6%
American elm (*Ulmus americana*) leaves*	1.0	0.0%
Raspberry (*Rubus* spp.) canes	2.7	N.A.

*Species found mostly on the forest edge.

Table 11. Intraspecific selection of lindens, 1984 and 1985.
Trees within 100 feet of each other are identified by a common letter. Total number of niptwigs counted in 1984 was 234; niptwigs per tree, 18. Total number of niptwigs in 1985 was 625; niptwigs per tree, 36.8.

	% of total niptwigs	
Tree	1984	1985
A	4	4
A'	65	10
B	0	0
B'	1	1
C	0	0
C'	0	0
D	0	7
D'	5	10
E	0	1
E'	0	2
F	—	2
G	—	8
H	—	5
J	0	0
K	0	2
766	—	19
853	25	30

Table 12. Dates of permanent den entry (in calendar days) for den-using animals, 1982–1987.
ANOVA. Between years: df = 5, SS = 1611.9, MS = 322.4, Fs = 10.5, P = 0.0001. Within years: df = 22, SS = 675.3, MS = 30.7.

	1982	1983	1984	1985	1986	1987
	310	302	314	286	298	297
	302	295	315	286	315	284
		302	314	292	298	297
		303	314		298	304
			314		306	305
			314		297	304
						297
mean	306	301	314	288	302	298

grand mean: 302 (October 29)

Table 13. Major winter food choices of porcupines at two sites in Minnesota.*

	French Creek		Green Lake	
	% of forest	% in diet	% of forest	% in diet
White pine	6.7	50	1.1	19
American elm	5.8	20	0.8	0
American linden	12.3	20	8.5	4
Quaking aspen	0	0	11.4	14
Red oak	0	0	3.0	41

*Data from Tenneson and Oring 1985.

Table 14. Major winter foods of porcupines in North America.

Food species	Location	Author
Spruces, white cedar	New Brunswick	Speer and Dilworth 1978
White cedar, hemlock, beech	Maine	Curtis 1944
Hemlock, beech, sugar maple	Massachusetts	Dodge 1967
Hemlock, red spruce	New York (Adirondacks)	Shapiro 1949
Beech, sugar maple	New York (Catskills)	Roze 1984
Jack pine	Ontario	MacDonald 1952
Hemlock, sugar maple	Michigan	Brander 1973
Sugar maple, yellow birch	Wisconsin	Krefting et al. 1962
Yellow pine, Douglas fir, piñon	Arizona	Taylor 1935
Ocotillo	Arizona desert	Reynolds 1957
Ponderosa pine	Idaho	Curtis and Wilson 1953
Douglas fir, limber pine	Alberta	Harder 1979
Yellow pine	Oregon	Gabrielson 1928
Spruces	Alaska	Murie 1926

Table 15. Tree distribution in feeding and control areas of two porcupines.

	Porcupine 1	
	Number in feeding area	Number in control area
beech*	87 (55%)	31 (31%)
other	79	69

$\chi^2 = 14.29$, df $= 1$, $P < 0.001$

	Porcupine 2	
sugar maple*	16 (57%)	33 (33%)
other	12	67

$\chi^2 = 5.40$, df $= 1$, $P < 0.025$

*primary feeding choice

Table 16. Observed mating success (guarding episodes) of six males in 1987.
Average success rate for males: 1.17, standard deviation 1.47. Correlation of success with weight (excluding Finder): $r = 0.94$, df $= 3$, $P < 0.05$. Correlation of success with home range (excluding Finder): $r = 0.99$, df $= 1$, $P > 0.05$.

Male	Guard episodes	Weight, kilograms	Nonwinter home range, hectares
Killer	3	7.8	147.3
Jasper	3	7.9	*
Taylor	1	6.8	58.5
Finder	0	8.4	36.7
Ram	0	4.5	36.6
Goff	0	4.1	*

*Home range unavailable because animals were collared in midseason.

Table 17. Reproductive success of three females, 1983–1988.
Average success rate for females: 0.89, standard deviation 0.32.

	Babies produced					
	1983	1984	1985	1986	1987	1988
Squirrel	+	?	+	+	+	+
Rebecca	?+	+	+	+	–	+
Moth	+	+	+	+	+	+

Table 18. Mating phenology in Catskills porcupines.

	Interactions observed	Rate (interactions per month)
First half of September	3	6
Mid-September to mid-October	22	22
Second half of October	2	4
November	4	4
December	2	2

Table 19. Weight changes in mother and offspring.

Date	Rebecca's weight, in kilograms	Baby's weight, in kilograms
Feb. 23	5.6	—
May 5	—	0.45
May 20	5.5	0.85
July 6	5.65	1.85
July 26	5.95	—
Aug. 3	—	2.15

Table 20. Observed and estimated periods of lactation in four females.

Mother	Birth of baby or first observed lactation	Baby's weight, kg	Last observed lactation	Observed lactation in days	Estimated lactation in days
Rebecca	May 5, 1986	0.45	July 26, 1986	82	110
Squirrel	May 9, 1987	0.60	Sept. 3, 1987	116	146
Squirrel	June 7, 1986	0.85	Aug. 26, 1986	81	112
Acidie	June 22, 1985	1.00	Sept. 22, 1985	92	113
Moth	May 15, 1988	0.60	Oct. 8, 1988	146	153
			Average	103	127

Table 21. Male and female nonwinter home ranges, in hectares, 1983–1988 (calculated by the minimum convex polygon method).

None of the male-female differences are significant until 1987 (t-test). In 1988, when both males under observation were dominants, male-female territories were significantly different ($t = 1.1$, $df = 3$, $P < 0.01$). Female territory sizes differ significantly between years: $F_{5, 12} = 13.62$, $P < 0.001$ (ANOVA). Male territory sizes do not differ significantly between years (ANOVA).

Females	1983	1984	1985	1986	1987	1988
Moth	78.4	63.9	32.9	40.0	35.9	19.0
Rebecca	67.0	60.6	21.4	21.6	17.9	21.6
Squirrel	50.1	71.3	12.6	21.6	30.8	29.1
Average	65.2	65.3	22.3	27.7	28.2	23.2
Males						
Imp	77.5					
Homer		109.5	30.3			
Topmost		60.0*				
Finder	65.6*	70.1	31.9	70.2	36.7	
Killer				86.2	147.3	84.4
Taylor				107.1	58.5	
Ram				28.0*	36.6	
Jasper						75.6
Average	71.6	79.8	31.1	72.9	69.8	80.0

*Subadult.

Table 22. Population density and female nonwinter territory size, 1983–1988.
Correlation between population density and female territory size: r = −0.905,
df = 4, $P < 0.05$.

Year	Captures per year	Captures per 100 days	Female territory, in hectares
1983	14	12.1	65.2
1984	18	16.4	65.3
1985	26	25.7	22.3
1986	27	30.7	27.8
1987	26	30.6	28.2
1988	39	37.1	23.2

Table 23. Sex ratios in porcupine populations.

Source	Number of animals	Female/male ratio
Spencer 1949	54	1.7
	124	1.53
Gensch 1946	124	1.14
Dodge 1967	214	1.08
Brander 1973	70	1.59
This study	96	1.91
	Total 682	
		Weighted average 1.39

Table 24. Scabies infections in porcupines.

Year	Number of infected animals	Fate of animal
1979	1	Den encounter; animal not treated.
1980	1	Treated with hexachlorobenzene; died.
1981	1	Scapo. Treated with hexachlorobenzene; died.
1982	1	Advanced disease; untreated. Fate unknown.
1983	1	Treated by dip in 1% malathion; recovered.

Table 25. Scabies and porcupine population density.
Population density estimated from the number of individuals captured per year, corrected for a constant capture effort (unique animals captured per 100 days in the field).

Year	Captures per year	Days in field	Corrected captures per year	Scabies
1983	14	116	12.1	+
1984	18	110	16.4	−
1985	26	101	25.7	−
1986	27	88	30.7	−
1987	26	85	30.6	−
1988	39	105	37.1	−

Table 26. Tick species recovered from porcupines.

Total	*I. cookei*	*I. dammini*	*I. texanus*	Identified by
33	31	2		M. Nathanson
37	36		1	R. Dowler and D. Fish

Table 27. Old World porcupines.

Genus *Trichys* ("with hair," referring to the hairy bristles of the tail)
  T. fasciculata, long-tailed porcupine. The single species is found on the Malay Peninsula, and on Borneo and Sumatra.

Genus *Atherurus,* the brushtail porcupines
  A. macrourus, Asiatic brushtail porcupine. Found in Assam (India), South China, Hainan, Burma, Thailand, Indochina, Malay Peninsula, and Sumatra.
  A. africanus, African brushtail porcupine. Found in west and central Africa.

Genus *Thecurus*
  T. pumilis, dwarf porcupine. Philippines (Palawan and Busuanga islands).
  T. sumatrae, Sumatra.
  T. crassispinis, Borneo.

Genus *Hystrix* ("porcupine" in Greek)
  Subgenus *Acanthion*
    H. brachyura, short-tailed porcupine (Himalayan porcupine). Nepal to eastern China, Malay Peninsula, Hainan, Sumatra, Borneo.
    H. javanica, Java to Flores.
  Subgenus *Hystrix,* crested porcupines
    H. indica, Indian crested porcupine. Eastern Mediterranean to Central Asia, India and Sri Lanka.
    H. cristata, crested porcupine. Northern Africa, Sicily, southern Italy, Albania, northern Greece.
    H. africaeaustralis, Cape porcupine. Southern Africa.

Common and Scientific Names

agouti: *Dasyprocta* spp.
alfalfa: *Medicago sativa*
anemone, Canada: *Anemone canadensis*
apple: *Pyrus malus*
armadillo: family Dasypodidae (Edentata)
arrowhead: *Sagittaria* spp.
ash, white: *Fraxinus americana*
aspen, bigtooth: *Populus grandidentata*
aspen, quaking: *P. tremuloides*
baboon, hamadryas: *Papio hamadryas*
bat, white-lined: *Saccopteryx bilineata*
bear, black: *Ursus americanus*
beaver: *Castor canadensis*
bee, honey: *Apis mellifera*
beech: *Fagus grandifolia*
beetle, rove: family Staphylinidae
belladonna: *Atropa belladonna*
bindweed: *Convolvulus* spp.
birch, yellow: *Betula lutea*
blackfly: family Simuliidae
bladderwort: *Utricularia* spp.
bobcat: *Lynx rufus*
box elder: *Acer negundo*
buffalo: *Bison bison*
butterfly, monarch: *Danaus plexippus*
capybara: *Hydrochaeris hydrochaeris*
caribou, woodland: *Rangifer caribou*
carrion beetle: *Nicrophorus* spp.
cats: family Felidae (Carnivora)
cattle: *Bos taurus*
cedar, northern white: *Thuja occidentalis*
cherry, black: *Prunus serotina*
cherry, choke: *P. virginiana*
chimpanzee, common: *Pan troglodytes*
chimpanzee, pigmy: *P. paniscus*
chinchillas: *Chinchilla* spp.
chipmunk, eastern: *Tamias striatus*
clover: *Trifolium* spp.
cohosh, blue: *Caulophyllum thalictroides*

colobus monkey, red: *Colobus badius*
columbine: *Aquilegia canadensis*
cottontail, eastern: *Sylvilagus floridanus*
coyote: *Canis latrans*
cricket, field: subfamily Grillinae
daggerwing moth, American: *Acronicta americana*
dandelion: *Taraxacum officinale*
deer, white-tailed: *Odocoileus virginianus*
deer mouse: *Peromyscus maniculatus*
dog, African wild: *Lycaon pictus*
Douglas fir: *Pseudotsuga menziesii*
echidna: family Tachyglossidae (Monotremata)
eft, red: *Notophthalmus viridescens*
elephant, African: *Loxodonta africana*
elk: *Cervus canadensis*
elm, American: *Ulmus americana*
fall cankerworm: *Alsophila pometaria*
fall webworm: *Hyphantria cunea*
fern, Christmas: *Polystichum acrostichoides*
fisher: *Martes pennanti*
fox, red: *Vulpes vulpes*
garlic, wild: *Allium canadense*
gibbon: *Hylobates* spp.
goat, domestic: *Capra hircus*
goat, mountain: *Oreamnos americanus*
goosefoot: *Chenopodium* spp.
gorilla: *Gorilla gorilla*
ground squirrel, Belding's: *Spermophilus beldingi*
grouse, ruffed: *Bonasa umbellus*
grouse, sharptailed: *Tympanuchus phasianellus*
guinea pig: *Cavia* spp.
gundi: family Ctenodactylidae (Rodentia)
hare, snowshoe: *Lepus americanus*
hare, black-tailed: *L. californicus*
hedgehog: family Erinaceidae (Insectivora)

hedgehog, European: *Erinaceus europaeus*
hemlock: *Tsuga canadensis*
hemlock, western: *Tsuga heterophylla*
hop hornbeam: *Ostrya virginiana*
horse: *Equus caballus*
howler monkey, mantled: *Alouatta palliata*
Indian hemp: *Apocynum cannabinum*
indri: *Indri indri*
Jack-in-the-pulpit: *Arisaema atrorubens*
koala: *Phasolarctos cinereus*
lemur, sportive: *Lepilemur mustelinus*
linden: *Tilia americana*
linden looper: *Erannis tiliaria*
liverwort: class Hepaticae (Bryophyta)
louse, porcupine: *Trichodectes setosus*
lynx: *Lynx canadensis*
maple, mountain: *Acer spicatum*
maple, red: *A. rubrum*
maple, striped: *A. pensylvanicum*
maple, sugar: *A. saccharum*
milkweed: *Asclepias syriaca*
mistletoe, dwarf: *Arceuthobium pusillum*
mite, scabies: *Sarcoptes scabiei*
moose: *Alces alces*
mountain lion: *Felis concolor*
mouse, deer: *Peromyscus maniculatus*
  white-footed: *P. leucopus*
nematodes of North American porcupine
  Dipetalonema arbuta
  Dirofilaria spinosa
  Molinema diacantha
  Wellcomia evoluta
nutria: *Myocastor coypus*
oak, red: *Quercus rubra*
ocotillo: *Fouqueria splendens*
opossum: *Didelphis virginiana*
owl, barred: *Strix varia*
owl, great horned: *Bubo virginianus*
paca: *Agouti* spp.
phalangerids: family Phalangeridae
  (Marsupialia)
pine, jack: *Pinus banksiana*
pine, limber: *P. flexilis*
pine, ponderosa: *P. ponderosa*
pine, western yellow: *P. ponderosa*
pine, white: *P. strobus*
piñon: *Pinus edulis*
pitcher plant: *Sarracenia* spp.
poplar: *Populus* spp.

porcupines, New World
  North American: *Erethizon dorsatum*
  thin-spined: *Chaetomys subspinosus*
  upper Amazonian: *Echinoprocta rufescens*
  prehensile-tailed: *Coendou bicolor*
  C. mexicanus
  C. pallidus
  C. prehensilis
  C. rothschildi
  Sphiggurus insidiosus
  S. spinosus
  S. vestitus
  S. villosus
porcupines, Old World
  long-tailed: *Trichys fasciculata*
  brush-tailed: *Atherurus africanus*
  A. macrourus
  dwarf: *Thecurus pumilis*
  Sumatra: *T. sumatrae*
  Borneo: *T. crassispinis*
  short-tailed: *Hystrix brachyura*
  Java: *H. javanica*
  Cape: *H. africaeaustralis*
  crested: *H. cristata*
  Indian crested: *H. indica*
prairie dog, black-tailed: *Cynomys ludovicianus*
raccoon: *Procyon lotor*
raspberry: *Rubus* spp.
rat, mole: *Myospalax* spp.
rat, spiny: family Echimyidae (Rodentia)
rat, wood, *Neotoma* spp.
shadbush: *Amelanchier canadensis*
sheep, domestic: *Ovis aries*
skunk, striped: *Mephitis mephitis*
sloth, three-toed: *Bradypus variegatus*
snake, coral: *Micrurus fulvius*
spring beauty, Carolina: *Claytonia caroliniana*
springtail: order Collembola
spruce, red: *Picea rubens*
spruce, white: *P. glauca*
squirrel, fox: *Sciurus niger*
squirrel, gray: *Sciurus carolinensis*
squirrel, red: *Tamiascurus hudsonicus*
squirrel, red-tailed: *Sciurus granatensis*
tamarack: *Larix laricina*
tapeworms of porcupines
  Cittotaenia pectinata

Monoecocestus americanus
M. variabilis
tenrec: Tenrecidae (Insectivora)
thistle: *Cirsium* spp.
thrush, wood: *Hylocichla mustelina*
ticks of porcupines
   dog, *Dermacentor variabilis*
   Ixodes cookei
   deer: *I. dammini*
   I. texanus
tobacco: *Nicotiana tabacum*
toothwort: *Dentaria diphylla*
toothwort, cutleaf: *Dentaria laciniata*
turkey, wild: *Meleagris gallopavo*
violet, round-leaf yellow: *Viola rotundifolia*

vireo, red-eyed: *Vireo olivaceus*
vole, meadow: *Microtus pennsylvanicus*
vole, tree: *Phenacomys longicaudus*
warbler, mourning: *Oporornis philadelphia*
water lily, yellow: *Nuphar* spp.
weasel: *Mustela* spp.
weevils, acorn: family Curculioninae
willow: *Salix* spp.
winter moth: *Operophtera brumata*
wolf: *Canis lupus*
wolverine: *Gulo luscus*
woodchuck: *Marmota monax*
wood rat: *Neotoma* spp.
yellowthroat: *Geothlypis trichas*

Index

DATE DUE

FEB 17 1992			
NOV 10 1992			
1CC			
12/3/94			
11/29/94			
APR 4 1997			
OCT - 8 1997			
DEC 21 2011			
GAYLORD			PRINTED IN U.S.A.